HEADLINES THAT MATTER

HEADLINES THAT MATTER

HOW NEWS MOVES MARKETS

KAVITA CHANDRAN AND SALDENE LYTE

FOREWORD BY STEVE SOSNICK

GEORGETOWN UNIVERSITY PRESS / WASHINGTON, DC

Cataloging-in-Publication Data is on file with the Library of Congress.

ISBN 9781647125929 (hardcover)
ISBN 9781647125936 (paperback)
ISBN 9781647125943 (ebook)

♾ This paper meets the requirements of ANSI/NISO Z39.48-1992 (Permanence of Paper).

EU GPSR Authorised Representative
LOGOS EUROPE, 9 rue Nicolas Poussin,
17000, LA ROCHELLE, France
E-mail: Contact@logoseurope.eu

26 25 9 8 7 6 5 4 3 2 First printing

Printed in the United States of America

Cover design by Jeremy John Parker
Interior design by BookComp, Inc.

We dedicate this book to:

curious minds,
knowledge seekers,
corporate investors,
business journalists,
stock market players,
and financial traders around the world.

CONTENTS

FOREWORD

Financial news is ubiquitous. But even though market professionals recognize that news is the catalyst for a significant portion of intraday and day-to-day price movements, few have given much thought to how that news is collected and compiled. The authors of this book have done just that. They have utilized their extensive experience as journalists and educators to create a definitive analysis of how the vast financial media ecosystem turns fact-finding into investable data. And to the best of my knowledge, no one has compiled this type of analysis in this magnitude before this book. For this reason, among others, this is a consequential undertaking.

Like so many traders, I am an unabashed news junkie. From the first day of my career through the present, I've been planted in front of a terminal displaying scrolling news headlines. Although I have stepped back from full-time trading in favor of market punditry, I remain transfixed by the parade of news items that cross my vision throughout the workday.

Despite my immersion in an ever flowing stream of financial news, the vast majority of items are of little consequence to me. Frankly, I can't imagine that some of the headlines are of consequence to anyone, until of course I find myself succumbing to obvious clickbait anyway. But the ones that matter *really* matter. Just as old miners unearth tons of ore to find an ounce of precious metal, traders and investors sift through a constant stream of news to find the item that might allow them to profit mightily or avoid a material loss.

The efficient market hypothesis (EMH) asserts that asset prices reflect all available information. Therefore, by implication, new information—news—should be the only influence on price movement. Like any reductive hypothesis, this one has its limitations. We all know that asset prices move constantly, even in the absence of market-moving news. That can be attributed to changes in perception, interpretation, or even mood. But while we might quibble with the real-world accuracy of EMH, we can't dispute the role that news plays in moving prices, often quite significantly.

There has always been a fierce race to gain a first-mover advantage from breaking news. The Rothschilds used carrier pigeons to become the first to learn of and act on Napoleon's defeat at Waterloo. Before electric telegraphy, a visual telegraph connecting New York and Philadelphia terminated at the latter city's Merchant Exchange. The difficulty and expense of developing and maintaining such systems to deliver news spoke to the financial advantage that could arise from learning news first.

We now exist in a market environment where tiny fractions of a second make the difference between executing or missing a trade. Thus, there is an increased emphasis on being able to receive and process news and create executable trades as quickly as possible. Recently, algorithmic trading firms have made tremendous strides in utilizing news to their immediate advantage.

A few years ago, when I was an options market maker, we found ourselves increasingly victimized by aggressive trades that were responding to significant news items before we could. Remember, a market maker is obligated to post continuous two-sided quotes in their designated securities; in the case of options, that can mean simultaneously posting hundreds of prices for individual puts and calls on a given stock. We realized that someone—we never learned who—was using natural language processing to determine the content of a news story and immediately executing trades based on the content. It could be particularly profitable—or painful, depending on your point of view—if, say, a takeover announcement hit the wires and they were able to buy large amounts of call options before anyone else could react.

We knew that we had to adapt quickly, especially when we learned that our market-making counterparts were facing similar difficulties. By definition, market makers are naturally on the defensive. They post prices continuously and tend to trade when others choose to cross the bid–ask spread to establish a position. That results in negative selection. Most of the time, a nimble market maker can utilize that spread and navigate the risks. But that doesn't work when someone clearly has better information than the dealer.

Recognizing that it would be impossible for a natural goalkeeper to play offense as skillfully as a dedicated striker, we opted for a speedy, defensive strategy. We made sure that we were acquiring the fastest possible news feeds, machine reading the metadata; when it yielded the symbol of a name that we traded, we immediately adjusted our quotes to the maximum allowable width and the smallest permissible size. That minimized our exposure if the news item was meaningful; if a trader then determined that the news was unlikely to have a meaningful impact, we resumed quoting normally. One could assert that our reaction to headlines momentarily reduced liquidity, even for routine items—but if we had not reacted, our ability to provide any liquidity would have been permanently affected. This is how the ability to process news can cause markets to evolve.

While speed is of the utmost importance regarding news, it is useless if one lacks the ability to interpret the items at their disposal. It is not at all uncommon to see stocks react to earnings reports in one direction, only to reverse course a few minutes later. Machines that read headlines must be told not only what to look for but also how to react. Thus, one might program an algorithm to buy a stock if its earnings exceed the prevailing estimate by a certain amount, only to discover that investors are more concerned that the company has reduced its guidance for the coming quarter or year. The first mover might push the stock higher, only to see the stock sink shortly thereafter.

Judgment also comes into play when a widely anticipated news item is released. There is an old market adage: "Buy the rumor, sell the news." If investors seem to have fully priced in an event, then the formal announcement of its occurrence may prove unlikely to shift outlooks, and thus prices. This is quite consistent with EMH. If the market has already digested the potential outcome of a news item, then it is also already reflected in the stock's current price.

For example, let's say a central bank is widely expected to cut interest rates by a given amount. When it then announces the cut at its scheduled meeting, is that announcement something that is likely to move the market or to simply confirm what the market already expects? Often it is the latter, unless it is accompanied by some other nuance that offers greater insight into the central bank's mindset. My colleagues surely got tired of my constant reminder that "the first move is often the wrong move" in the aftermath of an expected Federal Reserve announcement, but it often proved correct.

With so much emphasis on alacrity, it would seem there is no place for longer-form financial journalism or more analytical news. Nothing could be further from the truth. Remember, judgment and interpretation are key elements for how a trader or investor utilizes news for their decision-making. Skilled decision-makers understand the need for a wide range of inputs, and they also realize that sometimes the best ideas can arise from seemingly minor details.

Perhaps the best trade of my career was based on recognizing the broader consequences of an important news item. In early 2007, I happened to board our building's elevator one floor before Thomas Peterffy, our firm's founder. I had the morning newspapers under my arm, and he asked if I had read anything interesting. I mentioned that I was fascinated by an article reporting that some Bear Stearns hedge funds might be facing losses of up to $20 billion. The ensuing dialogue went like this:

> TP: How big is Bear Stearns?
> SS: I think their market cap[italization] is about $20 billion or so.
> TP: Are you telling me that you think Bear could be broke?
> SS: Not in so many words, but yes, I guess so.
> TP: Oh #*@! Let's talk about this.

I followed Thomas to his office and we hashed out a plan. I was responsible for our market-making activities in US financial stocks, and I was told in no uncertain terms that we should not have downside risk in that sector—especially in Bear Stearns. That became increasingly difficult as the global financial crisis unraveled, but that conversation—based on a single newspaper article—saved us millions of dollars.

Lately, there is a new class of market-moving items that can have an impact similar to major news—more so, perhaps. As the world was recovering from COVID-19, hordes of new investors entered the market. Many were empowered by a potent combination of stimulus checks, boredom, and lax work-from-home policies, and they utilized social media for both companionship and education. That led eventually to the meme stock craze, when key influencers were able to move their favorite names by dint of personality and a malleable following.

Traders and market reporters at major outlets alike now needed to follow X and forums like Reddit's r/WSB (Wall Street Bets) to understand what was moving certain stocks. In early 2024, the craze reignited, when the previously dormant "Roaring Kitty" account posted a cryptic meme that was interpreted by his followers as a signal to buy GameStop shares once again. That became genuine news, however, when the stock and its options soared, and it was later revealed through SEC filings that Keith Gill, aka Roaring Kitty, had indeed purchased a major stake in the company. Like it or not, journalists needed to report about the real-world goings-on that were inspired by social media.

Because news can and does move markets, there has always been a temptation for nefarious players to attempt to game the system. The temptation to "talk one's book" always exists, and there are indeed some programs on financial networks that give a forum for their repeat guests to do just that. Vague takeover rumors appear in news items from time to time, and there were sometimes suspicions that those items were planted by traders who had already established long positions in the affected shares, intending to sell them into an ensuing run-up. Once in a while, even truly false stories sneak into legitimate news sources. One occurred in 2016, when France's Vinci momentarily plunged 19 percent after a fake press release said that its finance director was leaving because the company's books needed restatement.[1] The stock recovered quickly when the truth emerged, but the person who planted the story might have made a substantial profit if they had been able to short the stock before the fraudulent release hit the newswires.

The bottom line: financial news is crucial to anyone who trades, invests, or simply follows market movements. Teams of journalists at myriad organizations toil constantly to bring an edge—large or small—to their readers or viewers. When I subscribe to a newspaper or wire service, or watch ad-supported financial networks, I am hoping to glean some valuable information that can guide my decision processes. I formerly used news to guide my trading and risk management activities, and now I use it to attempt to explain market activities to my own readers. I'd like to think that my interpretation of financial current events can help their own decision processes.

I've often wondered, how "meta" is it when I not only utilize financial journalism but also become part of the reporting itself? I'm frequently quoted by reporters and make numerous media appearances. The question makes my head spin. This is one of the reasons that I am proud to offer an entrée into the book that follows. While I have offered a few anecdotes in the paragraphs above to illustrate some key moments when news spurred key trading decisions during my career, they fall short of truly explaining the crucial role that financial news plays in modern markets. But this book does just that—it not only explains why so many are engaged in market-related journalism but also shows how journalists compile their reporting into something actionable and illuminates the many ways in which financial journalism has been incorporated into the investment process.

Steve Sosnick
New Canaan, Connecticut
October 2024

ACKNOWLEDGMENTS

At the outset, we want to thank Hilary Claggett at Georgetown University Press for her willingness and excitement to publish this book from the time she read the proposal. We are grateful for her support and guidance throughout this journey.

We, the authors, have had the opportunity to work at three of the most prominent news agencies—Bloomberg, Dow Jones, and Reuters—and we are grateful to our editors for the training, knowledge, and adrenalin rushes we experienced and enjoyed as business journalists. We want to give a shoutout especially to Kevin Reynolds—our former manager at Bloomberg News, who ran the Headlines team—for respecting our news judgment and giving both of us the task to call out breaking news to other Headliners. We are very grateful to our former colleagues Susan Abbotts, Bethany Harshaw Bantle, Karen Mielcarek, and Bruce Rule for sharing their anecdotes and experiences; and to Allison Saunders, for her feedback.

Many thanks to the former Reuters journalists Emily Kaiser, Ajay Kamalakaran, Ana Nicolaci, Christina Pantin, Abi Sekimitsu, and Catherine Trevethan for their support, and to many other colleagues whose work inspired us to write this book.

FROM KAVITA

I embarked on this journey while teaching business journalism in Singapore, and I want to thank my students for asking the right questions, which sowed the seeds for this book. I could not have written this book without my coauthor Saldene, whose composed demeanor and practical thinking helped us reach the finish line. I will dearly miss our weekly Zoom calls from opposite time zones, me starting my day and her ending it (this works very well if you are a morning person and your coauthor is a night owl). I am grateful for the time spent on the New York Stock Exchange as a news associate for CNBC way back in 1998—where I rubbed shoulders with screaming traders in the "pit" of the exchange—and understood the power of news and how it could move markets. I am grateful to Raghav Bahl, for teaching me the basics of business journalism during my first job in New Delhi; to my colleagues at Bloomberg News in New Jersey, for helping me hone my skills as a breaking news journalist; and to senior editors at Reuters, for supporting me throughout my stint in Asia. Finally, I give so much gratitude to my husband and daughters for their love and encouragement, and for always embracing my many varied passions.

FROM SALDENE

Unending thanks to my friend, former colleague, and coauthor Kavita, for inviting me to write this book with her. In doing so, she made me accomplish a lifelong dream and likely the first thing on my bucket list. A very robust and satisfying career as a journalist enabled me to do this. So hats off to all the daring and intrepid colleagues with whom I worked, especially during my foray into the field at the former *Home News* newspaper in East Brunswick, New Jersey. (Local news is important and is needed.) To my husband, I deeply appreciate your tremendous patience, love, and support. And to my dear, wonderful daughter—everything I do is for you. I hope you find your passion(s) to bring you joy and happiness for all times.

A NOTE ON SOURCES

We have interviewed several journalists for this book. Where we have quoted from these interviews without citing a source in a note, the interviews were conducted as follows (listed in order of dates of interviews and/or information exchange via email):

1. Kevin Reynolds, written document of his experience sent to the authors, July 13, 2022.
2. Christina Pantin, Zoom interview with Kavita Chandran, June 17, 2024.
3. Bethany Harshaw Bantle, email to the authors, June 28, 2024.
4. Karen Mielcarek, email to Kavita Chandran, June 4, 2024.
5. Susan Abbotts, email to the authors, July 5, 2024.
6. Bruce Rule, email to Saldene Lyte, June 26, 2024.
7. Catherine Trevethan, email to Kavita Chandran, July 24, 2024.
8. Ajay Kamalakaran, WhatsApp message to Kavita Chandran, July 24, 2024.
9. Several other journalists contacted during the process of writing this book requested not to be named.

INTRODUCTION

News is information. And investors need this information to make financial decisions.

But who are the news providers, and how do investors get their news? Who are the people who connect the two, and how do they do it?

The purpose of this book is to provide a detailed look at what news headliners and beat reporters look for when they speak to their sources, or attend conferences, or dig into press releases and statements from corporations and government organizations around the world. Most of the headlines they flash are generated within nanoseconds of receiving information, often causing noticeable movement of securities in financial markets. From information about corporate earnings to tsunami warnings, the newsroom is always awake and alert, even after stock exchanges close.

The book connects the two sides—information and interpretation—and divulges the "why" and the "how" of news that affects investor sentiments, leading to movements in share prices.

Not every news announcement grabs a stock trader's attention, but those that do prompt an immediate action to buy or sell securities. Traders in financial markets around the globe are almost always alerted to Breaking News because they subscribe to newswires or news feeds from media outlets—such as Bloomberg, Reuters, Dow Jones, and the Associated Press, as well as regional wire services such as Agence France-Presse, the Press Trust of India, the Algemeen Nederlands Persbureau, and many others. Every few seconds, important information scrolls by on their screens—information that helps them become better informed and thus make better decisions for their clients or firms.

These decisions are triggered by what stock traders see, hear, watch, and interpret that will have an impact on their client's investment portfolio. Breaking News or alerts are always released on computer terminals as a "flash" or a short headline—often highlighted in red, or all caps, or both—to attract the attention of a subscriber so they can immediately act on that information. What is it that these journalists look for in company announcements? Why do they select certain information to headline—and ignore the rest? What types of specific numbers, data points, or information do reporters search for in regulatory filings and press releases, or monitor on social media? What is the impact, and why are markets frequently so reactive to scrolling headlines? This book aims to address these questions, and more.

While financial journalism and business are taught in journalism schools and business schools separately, there is not a single source of information that links the world of business to the pace in a newsroom, highlighting how each move can affect the everyday lives of financial traders, investors, and, therefore, financial markets.

The idea for this book came to fruition when one coauthor, Kavita Chandran, set out to teach business journalism online to undergraduates in 2021, a period when COVID-19 was still wreaking havoc around the world. As a former headliner, trainer, and mentor in newsrooms, she asked students to make a list of news events on a Zoom whiteboard. She then guided them through each point on the list to explain which types of positive news released by a company could potentially prompt someone to buy its shares, how the reverse could possibly trigger a sale, and the "why" behind such market movements.

While researching material for students to read, Kavita realized that no specific book or study material existed that investigated the link between the work of a business news journalist and a stock market trader, despite both focusing on identical information. There was barely anything out there that talked about the role of a Headlines Department, or simply the importance of news flashes and how much they are monitored by investors in the financial markets. This is what spurred the idea to write this book. Saldene Lyte, a former colleague of Kavita and fellow Headliner at Bloomberg, agreed to be Kavita's coauthor, and they both generated a systematic approach to introducing various topics and subtopics, and explaining why they matter.

This book breaks down just about every major business situation—as well as situations outside those businesses—that can directly affect investments in markets around the world as well as the role journalists play in sifting through information and disseminating what they understand and know to be important. Traders rely heavily on such journalists—those who can swiftly interpret information with expertise—as trusted purveyors of news on whom they can reliably depend to make crucial decisions that can result in gains or losses within financial markets.

Competition is fierce between Headliners at top news agencies. It is a game of speed and accuracy to get the latest news out fastest. As part of its journalism hallmarks, the *Reuters Handbook of Journalism* pointedly advises its reporters that accuracy always takes precedence over speed: "It is our job to get it first, but it is above all our job to get it right."[1]

Kevin Reynolds, the former head of Breaking News at Bloomberg's Headlines desk, recalled, "To keep track of how competitive we were doing on headlines versus the other news services, at Bloomberg we would do a daily "autopsy" that compared our headlines times versus the competition, measured down to the hundredth of a second."

A business journalist working for a news agency who spoke to one of the authors and requested anonymity shared how the need to beat the competition "by a millisecond" can lead to comic situations: "I have sat on the curb of a ministry door-stepping a talkative finance minister for days; I have raced across conference halls to get news alerts out; and once, I had to snatch documents off a press officer who handed budget releases to one news outlet at a time (and to the competition first)."

A lot has changed since 2002, when the authors worked as colleagues on Bloomberg's Headlines team: this was a time when financial traders would rub shoulders with each other on the floors of stock exchanges and yell out information to investors by screaming on phones or making hand gestures that signaled a buy, hold, or sell. Now, savvy teenagers and young adults make split-second decisions with their pocket money from their laptop screens. In 2022, a study done by *Magnify Money*, a personal finance website, found that younger generations feel confident in pursuing riskier investment strategies themselves while older investors rely on financial advisers.[2]

In 2017, at the age of twenty-three, Lauren Simmons became the youngest full-time, female trader on the New York Stock Exchange (NYSE); remarkably, she made $1 million in 2022 in a stock market that is 85 percent male dominated.[3] At twenty-seven, she was hosting a show on TV called *Going Public*.[4]

Anyone over eighteen years old can trade in the financial markets. So let us get the basics out of the way before you start flipping through these pages.

HOW STOCK MARKETS WORK

Every publicly traded company—companies that allow the public to invest in them by offering their shares for sale—is listed on a stock exchange and assigned a unique ticker symbol (also known as a stock symbol). The company's leadership team hires an underwriter or investment bank that guides them through their initial public offering and advises at what price the shares should be listed. They look at many factors, including market demand, performance of peers in the sector, growth potential, and the number of interested investors.

In the United States, companies can list their shares on the world's largest exchange, the NYSE, which is owned by Intercontinental Exchange, Inc. Located on Wall Street in New York City, it has a floor where traders once screamed and shouted out news and numbers for placing orders for stock trades. But technology has quieted this mayhem because orders and trading are now computerized. There is also Nasdaq, an electronic exchange in New York City that is a favorite of tech companies. The NYSE American or NYSE MKT largely trades small-cap companies. Other significant world exchanges include the London Stock Exchange, the Hong Kong Stock Exchange, the Shanghai Stock Exchange, and twelve more around the globe.

While a stock exchange is a marketplace that facilitates equity trading, various stocks are selected to make an index, such as the Dow Jones

Industrial Average, which is composed of thirty major American companies listed on the NYSE and Nasdaq. Often referred to as "the Dow," this index is one of the most-watched indicators of market performance globally. The companies in the Dow are also called blue chip stocks because they have a reliable reputation, most pay dividends, and they represent different sectors.

Unlike the Dow, which through its thirty stocks has a narrower representation of different sectors, the Standard & Poor's (S&P) 500 Index is made up of 500 large public companies. While the Dow is a price-weighted index (meaning it takes into account the sum of the share prices of its thirty component stocks), the S&P 500 Index is a market-cap-weighted index and is broader in scope.

Then there are other US indices—such as the Nasdaq Composite, NYSE Composite, and Russell 2000—as well as other global indices: among others, the FTSE 100, with stocks listed on the London Stock Exchange; the Hang Seng Index of the Hong Kong Stock Exchange; the DAX 40, which consists of forty big German companies trading on the Frankfurt Stock Exchange; the CAC 40, which is a French stock market index; EURO STOXX, which comprises fifty stocks in the euro zone; the Nikkei 225, for the Tokyo Stock Exchange; and NIFTY 50, from the National Stock Exchange of India.

Grouped together, many indices can be referred to as "the stock market"; for example, while the Dow and S&P 500 are different indices, together they can be referred to as "the stock market." Other financial assets have their own markets: commodities markets, which consist of crops, oil, copper, gold, and the like; currency markets or foreign exchanges (Forex); bond markets; and cryptocurrencies, such as Bitcoin and others that trade on crypto exchanges.

When a person decides which company or companies to invest in, they open an account with a brokerage firm and make a deposit that is used to buy shares. They can invest in stocks, mutual funds, or exchange-traded funds that contain a mix of securities. Investing can also be done by buying mutual funds through an account with a mutual fund company or partner banks.

So, why does news move markets? One word: money.

People who invest in the stock market hope for gains—although selling stocks does not guarantee a profit. A disclosure required by regulators from companies that engage in investment activities is that their past performance is not an indicator of their future results.

The stock market is where money is made or lost at a rapid pace every day, so it is imperative for traders to watch share price moves on a regular basis. When news about a company comes out, it flashes across screens on trading floors. Positive news usually sparks an interest among investors to buy more shares, so traders get busy acquiring more for that shareholder. As more buyers invest in the same stock, the share price goes up, which means more value and profit for their investments.

Bad news does the opposite. Traders will frantically sell shares, resulting in a fall of share prices. The more people sell or offload a stock, the cheaper the stock's valuation becomes, resulting in a loss for most investors—but not for those who engage in a strategy in which they profit when a stock declines. Basically, in the end, it all comes down to return on investment—that is, profits.

FROM ANALOG TO ALGORITHMS

As with everything else, innovation has seeped into stock markets. Artificial intelligence and algorithms—a set of computer-programmed codes to solve problems built on high complexity and trading instructions—are now being used to interpret data and guide market-savvy investors.[5] Many decisions made in stock trading are based on historical data and patterns, and this is where algorithms are playing a major role. Millions of trades are now happening via machines that exclude human emotions and action and are faster and more data-centric, leading to higher profit margins for financial firms on Wall Street and elsewhere. Machines can make timely decisions on buying and selling shares, eliminating human errors and a trader's possible wrong judgment call. Historical data can be compared with current data in milliseconds to highlight risk factors, something traders can physically overlook during high-pressure moments.

The speed of sending news flashes has increased as preprogrammed software disseminates the main headline of a press release as soon as it hits a newswire service. Not just that, artificial intelligence capabilities have enabled algorithms that sweep through press releases and push out what may appear like "market-moving news" to subscribers. Yet you still need humans with news judgment—or reporters with beats who know the background of companies and can add context—to read the same releases and headline urgent information that a set of programmed algorithms may have overlooked.

In the chapters that follow, we begin by explaining the role of news agencies and what it means to be at the forefront when a gush of news flows onto a Headliner's screen, how they work with speed and accuracy, and how they try their best to maintain a calm composure. At press conferences and closed-door meetings (central banks often lock journalists in a room with information and an embargoed time for dissemination), journalists compete against each other to be the first to get the news out.

"The lock-up is a heightened version of the intense news agency experience," a news agency business journalist shared. "First come the heart palpitations as you dig through a pile of documents to find the news, then the fear of a correction as you send alerts that could affect market trade, followed by a tremendous sense of relief that you made it out unscathed, and finally the brain fog from hours of exam-like conditions."

This book seeks to help readers understand the value of news flashes reported by journalists who could be working at the Headlines desk inside a newsroom, or those getting tips and information from sources outside, or via conferences and conventions, or while risking their lives in hostile environments. Their motive is the same—to get accurate news to their consumers as fast as they can. For financial market traders, this news can result in immense monetary gain or loss.

We break down different business topics in the book into materials that matter to markets, thereby making an impact on investment decisions. In chapter 2, on Newsmakers, we tell you how markets react to some people more than others, how quotations from individuals or their social media posts can change people's perceptions (think Donald Trump, Elon Musk, or any influential person who regales their followers with wordplay). We explain how updates about a company's financials, from revenues to earnings to cash flow to outlook, can move markets. We reveal how internal turmoil and changes in business operations, be it mergers or acquisitions or restructuring, can make investors change their minds and divest their stock portfolio. We also list Key Performance Indicators for business sectors. In all this, we tell you about the role of sentiments—investors are humans, after all, and their feelings can play a huge part in their investments—and how sometimes influential shareholders can turn into activists and hold a board for ransom. We also zoom out and explore macroeconomics, so you can understand how data on economic indicators can move markets: from decisions by central banks on interest rates and inflation; how jobs data are a big factor to consider while investing; and why big economic events, such as Group of Twenty meetings and World Economic Forum meetings, are keenly watched by market players. How do journalists cover policy changes, legislation, and court decisions, and what impact can such news have on financial traders? We also look at how technological updates by companies are covered by reporters, from idea to invention to innovations, and why new products and technology matter to markets. We consider how government relations and international trade can build or break momentum in a stock market, and why diplomacy is necessary for economic and monetary stability. And finally, we touch on nonfinancial topics that are under no one's control—and how they have a huge impact on financial markets: climate change, war, assassinations, diseases, and disasters. Unexpected events cause disruptions and knee-jerk reactions because of uncertainties, creating milestones in history and financial markets.

Please note that the examples of headlines throughout the book have been written by the authors for demonstration purposes. We have also tried to insert interesting anecdotes of news stories at the end of each chapter—news that moved markets in some way—to explain the connection between Breaking News and market reactions, hoping this will improve your understanding of the subject. If that does not, the short assignments surely will.

Remember, not every sentence spoken or written by information providers is newsworthy. It is the job of journalists to weed out the noise and find information that can be told to the world, be it in the form of flashing headlines, scrolling banners, or news articles. What is crucial is to read enough to connect the dots, so you can comprehend why people reacted in a certain manner to a scrolling headline that went by.

1

FASTEST FINGERS FIRST

As a news consumer, you have surely seen a running scroll of headlines at the bottom of your screen, whether on the TV or your laptop. Such news alerts also pop up on the screens of financial traders, albeit a tad earlier, because they monitor real-time financial news and data alerts to help make quick decisions—causing the market to move up, down, or stay relatively unchanged on any given day. These news flashes, or Headlines, that they receive from news agencies are put out by journalists with great news judgment and working at warp speed. The members of the general public are likely to get the same news a few minutes later, once they are picked up by the news organizations they follow. Journalists in news agencies are usually the first to get company press releases, which they interpret quickly and send out as headlines within seconds to their subscribers.

"What I enjoyed most about working for a news agency was being an insider," said Christina Pantin, who joined Reuters in 1987 after a summer internship at its Washington bureau and stayed with it for twenty-five years. "It was knowing that you possessed information that the rest of the world did not know about yet, or may have been waiting for, or may not even have been waiting for because they didn't know what was going to happen. And it was then the ability to put that out and to see the after-effects, . . . basically how the market moved, how the stock moved, what that triggered, how the analysts reacted, just to see it catalyze a whole set of actions and reactions. . . . I think it was just that, it just gave you a thrill."

The source of this news could be a press release from a company, a press conference, a phone call, an interview, a social media post, or a regulatory filing. The job of a news agency journalist is to alert subscribers by writing a headline as succinctly as possible, divulging the most pertinent information. Therefore, news judgment is key for any journalist who wants to work at a news agency.

"It's important to note that generally it's the flash headlines, and not the [press] releases themselves, that traders react to, placing bets as to whether the shares of the releasing companies will rise or fall," said Kevin Reynolds, former head of the Headlines Desk at Bloomberg, New York, who spent more than two decades creating, spearheading, and managing a "speed team" that did him proud.

"We weren't looking for people who viewed themselves as 'writers' who'd be looking to get off the desk in six months; we were looking for those who wanted to do the job that clients cared about most. We were looking for quick fingers, quick minds, and fiercely competitive spirits."

"With millions of dollars on the line at all times, getting those headlines out fast and accurately is everything," said Reynolds, an award-winning news professional who later built and led the newsroom at CoinDesk, a news and data company that focuses on cryptocurrencies.

Why are traders the first to get critical financial news? Because they are paid subscribers of global news agencies, such as Bloomberg, Reuters, the Associated Press, Dow Jones, and Agence France-Presse, to name a few that were also mentioned in the earlier chapter, which sell news and other real-time financial data. News companies—such as CNN, CNBC, BBC, and the like—have staff in their newsrooms who monitor the terminals or service of financial news providers and alert editors to breaking news. The editors then holler to reporters to follow up and get cracking on writing a story that gives fuller or more detailed information. Other subscribers of news agency work include government departments, stock exchanges, investment banks, law firms, and individuals who can afford subscriptions worth thousands of dollars per month—anyone who wants immediate access to the latest financial information, as well as breaking news on general and political news, insights, and data.

News agencies were created because not every news organization could have a presence in every part of the world. Global news agencies have "stringers"—local reporters, photographers, and videographers in places where news bureaus have not or cannot set up operations for various reasons—and "fixers," or intermediaries who assist reporters with access to local people and inaccessible regions, enabling them to get information to share as quickly as possible with the rest of the world.

The oldest news agency, Agence France-Presse, was established in 1835 in Paris, and one of its earliest employees was Paul Julius Reuter, the founder of Reuters—one of the largest international news agencies, which is now part of Thomson Reuters. Legend has it that Paul Julius Reuter started his news service with the help of forty-eight carrier pigeons. Their job was to deliver news and stock prices between Brussels and Berlin within 2 hours instead of the 6 hours a train ride would take.[1] He then opened an office near the London Stock Exchange, which used telegraphic cables to transmit stock market quotations and news across Europe, including a speech by Napoleon III. On its website, Reuters boasts of its news speed by citing examples of being the first to have reported news of the sinking of the *Titanic*, the assassination of Mahatma Gandhi, and the dismantling of the Berlin Wall, among other headlines.[2]

FROM PHONES AND FAXES TO "RUSHES" AND AUTOMATION

News veterans who spent significant time headlining breaking news during their careers reminisced about the days when most of the work was done manually and journalists sometimes depended on unreliable machines for the source of news headlines. "In those old days, there was this one phone which was a hotline to the New York Stock Exchange. Literally, if that phone rang, you better pick up right away because the Exchange was calling. It could be about some kind of block trade, or a stock was halted for news pending, which meant there was unexpected news that wasn't prescheduled. And yes, it came over a printer; . . . and there would be someone standing by the printer to read off the headline to someone who was sitting at the desk and typing furiously away to formulate that 80-character alert and send that off. And yes, you definitely moved stocks, sometimes the whole market, depending on what the news was about," said Pantin.

The same nostalgia resonated with Reynolds as he recollected that when he joined Bloomberg in August 1992, more than 90 percent of all corporate press releases were delivered via fax, and it was the job of two gentlemen to sort through and send headlines on them to alert the market to the news. "With faxes, getting headlines out fast was problematic. Distribution was at the mercy of paper jams, ink supply, and how many press releases were coming in at one time. And as fax machine speeds increased, we were frequently upgrading our machines in a sort of fax machine arms race. It could be the most important news in the world, but if a machine ran out of paper, another release was ahead of it, or if you had old machines, the market would have to wait," recalled Reynolds.

Faxes gradually faded away as companies started sending press releases through electronic distribution systems. In the United States, newsrooms started relying on PR Newswire and Business Wire, which would transmit corporate press releases in a systematic manner during specified time slots. But soon that created its own set of problems. PR Newswire was acquired by Cision in 2015 and, according to its website, has a presence in 440,000 newsrooms around the world. Business Wire was acquired by Berkshire Hathaway in 2006. Similar press release distributors are EIN Presswire, GlobalNewswire, and eReleases, among others.

"Companies could specify a specific time for their news to go out, and as human nature would have it, almost all companies chose round numbers—the tops and bottoms of the hours before the markets open and after the close to release their news. This meant literally hundreds of releases were now hitting the news services in huge rushes," said Reynolds. "These 'rushes' were particularly brutal during what finance people call 'earnings season,' the four-week period every quarter when 90 percent of all companies released their quarterly results."

The heaviest flood of press releases at the time of the writing of this book still occurred from 0600 hours to 0830 hours, before US stock markets open, and from 1600 hours to 1700 hours, when markets close. Reynolds created a highly flexible work schedule with adjustable shifts in which some team members worked a few hours from very early morning to mid-morning, and then returned for the "rushes" just before the market closed.

"To make sure we had the best talent and fit, I required day-long try-outs in which a candidate's degree of interest could be measured, along with their quickness up the learning curve, how quickly they could spot news buried deep in releases, how fast they could type and how well they played with others," said Reynolds, an ex-marine who also devised a strategy he called an "attack plan" to quickly find important information in press releases as soon as they appeared on screens. Different team members had designated roles to quickly enter, browse for market-moving news, and exit in a coordinated fashion.

In a competitive news environment, news agencies have also evolved and embraced advanced technology to ensure that their own dissemination services are tech-savvy. At some time about 2010, automation was introduced, so software programs could read press releases and push out multiple headlines within nanoseconds. Until then, according to Reynolds, "human headliners were arguably the most important people in the financial newsroom."

In 2004, Reuters became the first news agency to offshore some of its editorial work to Bangalore, at a time when the *New York Times* journalist Thomas Friedman wrote *The World Is Flat, 3.0*, a book that explored a level playing field for businesses around the world because of technological innovation and globalization.[3] This meant that press releases from US and UK companies could be handled and headlined by young journalists in India working night shifts to compensate for the opposite time zones.[4]

"I was terrified at the hours," said Pantin, who was sent to Bangalore to kick off the pilot project. "When we set up the snapping [headline] operation, there were all these conversations about where the server had to be, we had to determine what the latency was, and how many seconds delay was tolerable. It was just the level of competitiveness where we had to make sure that the pipes were actually fast enough." More newsroom duties were moved to the Bangalore Bureau from overseas; and at the time of the writing of this book, it was the third-largest Reuters newsroom after New York and London.

"Working for a news agency helped me quickly identify hidden and important news from wordy press releases. I learned the art of managing speed and accuracy to ensure the most important news was out in the fastest possible time," said Ajay Kamalakaran, a freelance writer and author who worked with Reuters in Bangalore. "These skills have helped me become a better long-form and feature writer."

SPEED AND ACCURACY

To understand the mechanics of how information moves—from a company press release to a financial trader's screen—it is important to appreciate the speed and accuracy of journalists who transfer information. The journey of a corporate news headline begins inside a well-crafted press release, drafted by a company official, with its own headline.

Let us suppose it is a press statement with this headline: "Company XYZ Sees Cost Savings of $1 Billion Over Next Two Years." As this press release hits the screens of the Headlines team in a news agency via a wire service such as PR Newswire or Business Wire, the headline on the press release is automatically pushed out by a set of algorithms or programmed software. A Headliner knows, however, that the real news about a company saving costs could also include details about the "how"—how is it achieving this cost savings?—maybe by closing stores, cutting jobs, and so on?—and that is the pertinent information they need to manually find and send out as a news flash—that is, if it was not picked up automatically by the software. Within seconds, Headliners find it—very often hidden toward the bottom of the press release—and send out such headlines as

> COMPANY XYZ TO CLOSE 20 STORES IN US, 30 WORLDWIDE
> COMPANY XYZ TO CUT 8,000 JOBS
> COMPANY XYZ SEES $900 MLN IN ONE-TIME CHARGES

These headlines land on a trader's screen, flashing in all caps, revealing that Company XYZ will be incurring a loss in the near term to achieve savings after two years. A financial trader could be inclined to sell the shares of Company XYZ or decide to hold them, or even buy more, depending on how they perceive the action to be—good or bad for the company's future. If many traders think alike and decide to dump the stock (sell), the share price of Company XYZ's stock may fall, with a red arrow pointed downward against its ticker symbol. Conversely, if they decide to buy more shares, the share price will rise, indicated by a green arrow against its ticker. The decision a financial trader makes based on such headlines is what affects the fate of a company's stock that day.

What happens next to this piece of news that has started to move markets? As soon as the headlines start moving, the beat reporter who covers the stock (who usually has one of the display monitors showing the headlines) gets to urgently write a quick two paragraphs about the news—basically, a very short story that uses information from the headlines along with some context for the reader. Typically, this should go out within 5 to 10 minutes of the first headline that moved on that story. After that initial short story, the reporter does an Update 1, which is a slightly longer piece that provides more context, background, interviews, and stock movement, if it is worth mentioning. Updates after updates can follow, wrapping up with a complete and comprehensive market story if the stock reacted significantly to the news.

Amid all the adrenaline rush, a Headliner has to maintain calm and ensure the information sent out is accurate. Clearly, this game is not for the faint-hearted.

What happens if a Headliner makes a mistake? There is immediate concern if a trader may have initiated a trade based on this headline. A correction of the headline needs to be done right away, as soon as the error is realized. Another headline is sent out immediately to alert all subscribers, and the incorrect one is pulled or removed from the wire/terminal so there is no confusion:

> CORRECT: COMPANY XYZ TO INCUR $90 MLN, NOT $900 MLN, CHARGES

Reynolds had an interesting tale to tell on "corrections" related to a press release he handled in 2000 by a company called Emulex. What

Reynolds did not know was that he was typing headlines off a fraudulent and damaging press release that had been crafted and disseminated by a disgruntled market player who had lost heavily by betting incorrectly in the markets.[5]

"Emulex went on to lose $2.2 billion in market capitalization before the shares recovered. At the end of the day, shareholders wound up with almost $100 million in losses," recalled Reynolds, who almost lost his job that day.

To err is human but to fess up and correct mistakes immediately is a sign of integrity and credibility. That is what journalists should strive for.

"We aren't brain surgeons, and no one would die on our table if we made a mistake [because] we could correct it and the stock would recover," said Karen Mielcarek, a former Bloomberg Headliner who has worked in the financial news industry for more than twenty years. "But it would tarnish our collective reputation for a while."

A fun fact on corrections was shared by another former Headliner, Bethany Harshaw Bantle, when she recalled how one has to be extra vigilant on April Fool's Day. "I will never forget the horror of sending out the resignation of a governor once, only to learn that it was a joke release," remembered Bantle. "Once the reporter started on the story, we got the call and the full weight of embarrassment hit me. There was simply no room for error, and the higher-ups were not pleased."

In a nutshell, news agency journalists have no deadline. This "very moment" is the deadline. Unlike the 2 a.m. publishing time for newspapers, or the weekly and monthly luxury of publishing for magazine writers, when you work for a news agency, you are running against time. For Headliners, the job requires one to not only be well aware of global affairs and financial news but also to have great news judgment and a demeanor that thrives on thinking fast and valuing accuracy. It is no wonder the corporate desk or Headlining area is sometimes called the "pit," given that it is akin to the frenzy on the floor of the New York Stock Exchange before automation took over. In the chapters that follow, we break down various information from companies and countries that get headlined by news agency reporters and the key information and figures they push out, and why, and how such news flashes end up moving stock markets.

SUGGESTED ACTIVITIES

1. What was the hoax news that was disseminated by Emulex in 2000? How were the shares affected? (Online research.)
2. Name three important qualities to be a good Headliner at a news agency.

2

NEWSMAKERS

Stock prices change when many trades, or one or more large blocks of trades, are made by individuals or institutions. News that can cause trades and stock price changes—up or down, positive or negative—is, as mentioned above, what this book is about. Some individuals, and the words they speak, have the power to cause trades that can send stock prices soaring or into a significant decline. Their words, with implicit or implied thoughts and actions, can have a remarkable impact. It is why some people and what they say matter more than others. Who are these individuals, what is it about them, and why is it that what they say can affect stock trading, is the focus of this chapter.

Individuals who have the ability to move markets include political leaders, certain executives and/or businesspersons (with both of the latter two likely to be billionaires). Consequently, when they speak—whether verbally or through written communication, and for political leaders even about legislation they are considering, their words are parsed by journalists, traders, and financiers for insight or possible policy action, and are taken into consideration when making trading and investment decisions.

POLITICIANS AND GOVERNMENT OFFICIALS

Because of their powerful positions, political leaders, presidents, prime ministers, and heads of financial entities—such as the Federal Reserve, the European Central Bank, and the Chancellor of the Exchequer—can affect markets by simply giving their opinions or viewpoints. A speech and/or statement that states an opinion on policy or is filled with a certain degree of nuance, will be reported and talked about by everyone in the financial world.

On July 16, 2024, chip stocks posted significant declines in trading on reports that President Joseph Biden's administration was considering further measures to curtail the exporting of chip manufacturing equipment to China. On the same day, former president Donald Trump, who was seeking to be elected again, said in an interview that Taiwan should pay the United States for defense support. The hit to chipmakers revenue from any further trade restrictions under President Biden, and former president Trump's statement implying that the United States might not totally commit to defending Taiwan if he is president, both exacerbated the sell-off of chip stocks.[1]

One of the most famous examples of market influence is a speech given by Alan Greenspan, who was at the time chairman of the US Federal Reserve Board, on December 5, 1996, at the annual dinner of the American Enterprise Institute for Public Policy Research. "But how do we know when irrational exuberance has unduly escalated asset values, which then become subject to unexpected and prolonged contractions as they have in Japan over the past decade?" he asked in his speech on "The Challenge of Central Banking in a Democratic Society."[2]

"Irrational exuberance" was interpreted as Greenspan indicating that stocks and the market at the time were overvalued. Widespread reporting of the phrase led to declines of stock markets worldwide. Major European stock markets fell steeply the next day—with an intraday loss of $150 billion, before recovering by the close to a decline of more than 4 percent.[3] The Dow Jones Industrial Average fell more than 2 percent within an hour after opening, as did the Standard & Poor's 500 Index and the Nasdaq.[4] Irrational exuberance has now become a term that is immediately understood when used. The attention that was given to Chairman Greenspan's speeches and subsequent analysis has continued with other officials and has given rise to the term "Fedspeak," which refers to speeches and interviews by past and present chairmen and governors of the Federal Reserve Board. In 2023, amid continued high inflation in the United States and the Federal Reserve stating its target of a 2 percent inflation rate, Federal Reserve Chairman Jerome

Powell made news whenever he said anything. In mid-December, all three indices—the Dow, Nasdaq, and Standard & Poor's 500—rose 1.4 percent, with the Dow closing at a record high, from reports on the December Federal Reserve policy meeting indicating that there would be at least three rate cuts in 2024, and comments by Powell at the press conference after the meeting.

Political leaders can have a similar effect on the market if their administration proposes policy that is not market friendly, or if they make comments or statements that hint at conflict, disruption of trade, trade policy, restrictive laws and/or regulation of financial activities, or a relaxation or rollback of restrictions to lessen or change regulation or oversight. Liz Truss, on becoming prime minister of the United Kingdom, promised to usher in economic policies that would set the country and its people on a better course. Those policies included enacting significant tax cuts for businesses and those who were wealthy. Those tax cuts would have been the largest to be enacted in fifty years. The policies also included billions of pounds of spending and would be funded by borrowing. The plan was presented by Chancellor of the Exchequer Kwasi Kwarteng in a "minibudget" to the House of Commons in late September 2022. It was viewed by markets as too radical. It triggered a fall in the pound to the lowest level in four decades to near parity with the dollar, from previous average trading lows of £1 to about $1.25 to highs of $1.70 in the past decade.[5] It also sent bond rates higher, signaling there would be a significant jump in interest rates. In mid-October, Truss resigned as prime minister because her policies were seen as disastrous and untenable, causing immense turmoil in markets.

COMPANY LEADERS

Executives in the C-suite—the chief executive officer (CEO), chief operations officer (COO), and chief financial officer (CFO)— chart the strategy and success of their companies. Some C-suite executives at the biggest or best-known companies are larger than life because they are in charge of the creation of products and services we use. Their comments and analysis make business news broadcasts and can move markets.

Because of their personality, charisma, business acumen, and the weight their companies carry, these executives can be newsmakers who affect trading. Their words matter separately from any comments related to earnings or company news that are part of the standard requirements of all publicly traded companies. They are often sought after to give speeches at events, and such speeches often become the topics and subjects of news stories.

These newsmakers often have influence beyond their industry or sector, and they are respected for qualities such as their knowledge, expertise, and entrepreneurship, as well as their success running their respective companies. Their viewpoints matter, and the insights and analysis they offer are credible, so traders and investors make decisions based on what these executives say. Only a few of them have such influence and are viewed as market movers because of their sustained success. Their pronouncements about the state of a company, an industry, or an investing strategy may indicate a cautious outlook and influence stock selling, cause a pause in selling or buying, or generate excitement and optimism and trigger more buying. This was what happened during the week of January 25, 2021, when Tesla CEO Elon Musk posted on the platform X, then called Twitter, about GameStop Corp. (GME) and Etsy, Inc. (ETSY). (See the anecdote at the end of the chapter.)

Reporters and editors must keep abreast of when and where government and industry leaders are giving speeches and cover other methods of communication that may provide valuable information by newsmakers. Journalists also need to be aware of the tendencies of newsmakers to dispense newsworthy information in nontraditional media—such as knowing if they have ever given opinions about current topics and issues through posts on social media, in blogs, or in podcasts. (In July 2024, when President Joe Biden decided not to seek reelection and endorsed his vice president, Kamala Harris, to seek the presidential nomination, he made the announcement by posting two statements on the platform X.) Broad monitoring of various communication channels that can be used by newsmakers, especially ones that are not a part of traditional media, can become sources to "break a story" and beat the competition to market-moving news.

SUGGESTED ACTIVITIES

1. Examine recent speeches by the chairman or any governor of the Federal Reserve. Write two or three headlines about any newsworthy information.
2. Find one or more speeches and/or interviews by prominent executives about economic issues. Identify the differences in the messaging of executives compared with the Fed officials. (The Federal Reserve website where speeches are posted is www.federalreserve.gov/newsevents/speeches.htm)

A Social Media Post, a Meme Stock, a Stratospheric Rise

GameStop ended 2020 valued at $4.71 per share but started having double-digit percentage gains in January—over 10 percent—and in a couple of days, it went over 50 percent. The stock was performing poorly because the company's business model was not doing well due to changes in the gaming sector and the rise of competitors. It was, however, one of the stocks that were performing poorly that suddenly started a spectacular rise, due mostly to members in a group forum on the social media platform Reddit who started heavy trading of the stock, buying and touting the shares daily. Other poorly performing stocks that were being bought in similar actions were AMC Entertainment Holdings and Bed, Bath & Beyond (which filed for bankruptcy on July 23, 2023). These stocks became known as "meme stocks"—a phenomenon that gained momentum in January 2021. The rise of meme stocks is believed to have been fueled by trading during the COVID-19 pandemic, along with increased use of the Robinhood app, which offered digital trading without paying commissions. The app was also marketed to appeal to the average person, so it gained a foothold among younger, individual investors. Stocks such as GameStop became popular with individual and small investors, and went viral with huge increases in their share price from social media hype in postings about buying activity, share gains, and profits.

On January 26, 2021, just after the market closed, Musk's one-word posting was "GAMESTONK!!" "Stonk" is internet slang for stocks, so Gamestonk is short for gaming stocks.[6] The next day, GameStop soared over 150 percent intraday, and it closed with a gain of about 135 percent, although the company's business was seen as struggling. Short-sellers were heavily invested in the stock, expecting its decline to new lows. The collective buying action of individuals on the social media platform was also aimed at thwarting and hurting GameStop's short-sellers who lose money if the shares of stocks that are shorted rise, trading completely opposite to what is expected. Another Musk tweet, on Tuesday, January 26, 2021—"I kinda love Etsy"—about three hours before the market opened, sent ETSY stock rising to open over 8 percent above its previous close. That positive activity was not sustained, however, as it closed about 2 percent lower than the day before.[7] Share movements of both GameStop and Etsy showed the reaction that Musk could generate by just commenting or sharing his view on a stock.

Also on January 26, about an hour after the market opened, billionaire investor and venture capitalist Chamath Palihapitiya posted a screenshot of his purchase on X, saying he bought 50 call options in GME. "Lots of $GME talk soooooo. . . . We bought February $115 calls on $GME this morning. Let's gooooooo!!!!!!!!." The post continued, "Tell me what to buy tomorrow and if you convince me I'll throw a few 100ks at it to start. Ride or die."[8] The trades of prominent, successful investors who have garnered billions in wealth will make news and influence others, particularly average investors who are hoping to buy a winning stock.

But rapid stock movements without any good, underlying reason can exacerbate volatility and cause disruption in markets. Meme stock activity led the Securities and Exchange Commission to approve a change that shortened the settlement of trades to one business day after the transaction, from two, starting in May 2024. The commission's chair said that the "adoption addresses one of the four areas the staff recommended the Commission address in response to the meme stock events of 2021. Taken together, these amendments will make our market plumbing more resilient, timely, orderly, and efficient."[9]

Social media is now a source of news, as shown by Musk's and Palihapitiya's posts. Reporters of news organizations now cover social media as a beat and have software to scour sites for information or to pay for services from other providers and companies that mine social media posts for current news and information, often in real time as it is unfolding.

3

COMPANY FINANCIALS

Just as there are four seasons in a year—well, in most parts of the globe, anyway—the corporate world also relies on four quarterly earnings seasons. These are the times when publicly listed companies are required to declare their assets, liabilities, profits, losses, cash, and other developments to regulatory authorities. While most companies in North America and Asia report their financial accounts four times a year, the United Kingdom allows for two half-yearly disclosures.

In this chapter, we look at how markets and newsrooms react to company financial statements, and what these mean for stock markets, investors, and countries where the entity operates. Sometimes, reporting financials in one country can affect results in another because of the factories and employees in different locations of the same company. For example, Apple hires many people in China to manufacture its gadgets. Any concerns or issues that can affect production delays of these gadgets will reflect on Apple's quarterly earnings, and therefore can make an impact on how the market reacts to the news.

This is what happened to Apple's stock in November 2022—it fell almost 3 percent on the back of production concerns in China at a time when COVID-19–related restrictions forced workers to be absent from Apple's Foxconn factory in Zhengzhou, which was under lockdown because China was aiming for a zero-COVID policy, a hard measure that they reversed in December 2022.[1] Foxconn employed more than 200,000 workers and because many were absent, production was delayed, and even halted. Some workers also took the opportunity to demand overdue payments amid the lockdown. Bloomberg reported on November 28 that there was likely to be a production shortfall of almost 6 million iPhone Pro units, citing sources familiar with Apple's assembly line.[2] This news affected the shares of Apple on the day of the Bloomberg report, as investors took this news to indicate that future earnings would decline for the world's largest smartphone maker.

While "earnings" are largely what the markets focus on when a company's quarterly report is released, there is a lot more that journalists dig into in those financial statements. When we say "company financials," we are referring to three core account statements that companies are required to make public: balance sheet, account statement, and cash flow statement. Once all statements are out—usually in one large document that is submitted to regulatory authorities and an abridged version given to the press—reporters and traders alike scrutinize the numbers to understand the financial health of a company.

BALANCE SHEET

What you own and what you owe makes up the items in a balance sheet. It includes a company's assets, liabilities, and shareholder equity, which is the money invested by shareholders in the company.

A balance sheet is an essential document that a company must keep updated at any given time, as it reflects the financial state of a company. It is easy to tell from the balance sheet whether the company has borrowed too much, whether it has enough liquidity or cash to weather a difficult period, and whether its debt-laden structure could make it a target for acquisition.

There are three columns in a balance sheet: assets, liabilities, and shareholders' equity. The assets typically should equal the sum of liabilities and shareholders' equity, but in most cases they do not. The formula simply is Assets = Liabilities + Shareholders' Equity.

Assets

The assets column includes everything that helps the company run—from the liquid cash it has to the short-term or long-term securities it has invested in, such as stocks and bonds, as well as money yet to be received from clients and partners, that is, accounts receivable. Assets also include the company's inventories, plants, and equipment; these are nonliquid assets. There may also be prepaid expenses, such as deposits for rents, insurance premiums, and contracts with other companies.

When a company has more assets and less liabilities, investors view the company as financially healthy and stable. Conversely, if liabilities outweigh assets and the company goes around scouting for financial support, it is unlikely anyone would bet on a firm laden with debt or liabilities. A case in point is FTX Trading Company, the cryptocurrency exchange operator that went bankrupt in 2022. FTX was desperate to get funding with a balance sheet that showed $16 billion in liabilities and an equal amount in assets—mostly consisting of bitcoins, which some may have found ironic, considering the company's failing business was linked to trading in invisible digital tokens.[3]

Liabilities

The money that has not yet been paid falls under liabilities. It could be in the form of a bank loan, property tax, and interest that needs to be paid on any borrowing or dividend obligations that need to be fulfilled. Accounts payable are amounts that the company still must pay to clients depending on the time left on an invoice, which can range from one month to three months or longer. Long-term liabilities are payments the company must distribute over a long period of time, such as retirement funds to its employees, pension or provident funds, and interest on fixed income.

Shareholders' Equity

Shareholders' equity is the financial obligation the company has to a shareholder or investor, who could even be the founder of the company. Part of this equity is "retained earnings," which basically is the money the company made through its lifetime as a profit, but was not paid to shareholders as dividends.

A business reporter often becomes quite intrigued by negative "retained earnings" as a line item in the shareholders' equity section and might end up headlining or writing a short story about it. Why is this figure important for the markets? For dividend givers, negative retained earnings indicate that the company has a deficit and has "retained" some of the earnings instead of giving them all out as dividends to shareholders. A reporter might want to know what the company plans to do with the money it has retained; perhaps it plans to buy a plant or launch a new product?

A report in the *Harvard Business Review* called retained earnings "deferred dividends" after doing a study of fifty companies whose profits did not end up going to shareholders and were probably reinvested by management. The list in the *Harvard Business Review* study of publicly traded companies for the period 1970–84 included Coca-Cola and American Express.[4]

EARNINGS/INCOME STATEMENTS

Ask any reporter who covers business, and they will tell you the most important and often stressful time in the newsroom is when companies report earnings, often also called the "earnings season." For newswire services, the members of the Headlines team are responsible for flushing out important figures and developments that are often hidden in the content of press releases or regulatory filings, such as those filed with the Securities and Exchange Commission (SEC) in the United States.

Traders who subscribe to newswire services know when to expect earnings announcements, and they eagerly wait for the headlines to show up on their screens. Often, these headlines flash in red and all-caps to get their attention. The news media gets press releases from news dissemination services such as PR Newswire and Business Wire. Sometimes, beat reporters get press releases ahead of time marked "embargo," meaning they need to wait for the date and time stipulated by the company to release the news. So yes, journalists are sometimes privy to information before the markets, but ethics are part of the job, and breaking an embargo or trading off such information can ruin journalism careers.

So what are definite numbers that Headliners and traders look for when earnings reports show up on their screens? The next subsections outline several line items.

Earnings per Share

Earnings per share (EPS) are the profits of the company that quarter for each share outstanding. A basic EPS is calculated by dividing the earnings by the outstanding shares in the market. A diluted EPS is calculated by dividing the earnings by the total shares outstanding, including those that could be converted under employee stock options or warrants. It is, therefore, a more correct figure.

EPS, Excluding Items

Any business reporter will tell you that EPS, excluding items, is the magic number. A trader will concur. Why? Because every quarter is compared with the same quarter of the past year, and if there were unexpected or exceptional costs or gains incurred this quarter—one-time items that were not present in the past year-ago quarter, then it makes sense to remove them from the current earnings. The number that excludes those items is an apple-to-apple comparison with the similar quarter of the previous year. This figure may be referred to as adjusted EPS; non-GAAP EPS; EPS ex-items; excluding extraordinary items; and excluding special items.

Earnings or Loss

The net profit or loss the company incurred in the reporting period is another important number that journalists and traders are interested in. It removes the operating expenses from gross profit and gives a clearer picture versus the year-ago period. This is also called a company's "bottom line," as it is found at the bottom of the financial statement. Earnings that exclude one-time gains or charges are matched against figures that analysts at brokerage firms had estimated.

Analysts' Estimates

The figures mentioned above need to be put into context, and that is the job of brokerage firms that have researchers and analysts to provide recommendations to investors regarding a company's stock—whether to buy, hold, or sell the shares. Analysts not only estimate where the share price of the stock could be within a certain period based on their research; they also provide a range of earnings and EPS estimates for each quarter. When the earnings, EPS, or revenue in the financial statement of a company misses or beats those estimates, or sometimes is in line with the estimates, that is an indicator of how well or badly the company is performing. Therefore, a reporter usually has estimates handy before a company's earnings are released.

In 2006, Google missed analysts' estimates for the first time since its initial public offering (IPO) in 2004. Analysts had expected the new tech company to report adjusted EPS of $1.76, but it reported $1.54 per share, excluding costs related to one-time research and development and stock options. Headliners at Bloomberg, Reuters, and Dow Jones flashed the news as soon as the press release came out. The market did not take it well—the news sent the shares down more than 12 percent.[5]

Revenue/Sales

Revenue/sales is the top line—the first line item in a financial statement, from which certain items are removed, such as the cost of goods and expenses related to operations—which gives rise to the net income or loss. Companies can refer to their top line as either sales or revenue, and reporters typically stick to the term used by the company. While revenue is the total amount of money a company makes in that financial period, sales is often used by companies that sell goods or services to customers.

As more and more companies sign subscription contracts with their customers, another interesting figure that market pundits look for in software-as-a-service companies is annual recurring revenue. This is the annual expected revenue that a software-as-a-service company might earn from its subscription-based services.

Outlook/Forecast

While the numbers reflected in the quarterly or half-yearly statements are from the past few months, the market is also looking for guidance or an indication of what to expect from the company for the next reporting period(s). This outlook can make a big difference to a stock price despite the revenue, earnings, and EPS reported. If the company does so much as hint that it sees something in the future that could result in a material loss or gain, this news can lead to a big change in how the market reacts to the earnings announcement. Remember, investors are holding on to the shares only until they have reason to sell. Any negative statement about future results by a company—in the press release or during a conference call—can signal a "sell" to market players. A positive or upbeat outlook will do the reverse, leading to an increase in the share price.

Conference Calls

Most US and UK companies tend to have a conference call after the earnings announcement, in which senior managers review the earnings report and answer questions from analysts. This is an opportunity for managers to clarify any doubts and do damage control in case the market reacted adversely to any news pertaining to the company. While the conference calls are strictly for analysts, journalists are allowed to listen in. Often, the company's outlook or forecast and other details (or story ideas) come from conference calls. Business reporters have a joke that it is always the one conference call they decide to skip that will generate a lot of attention because of something the CEO or a C-suite executive said or indicated that caused the share price to move. So, even though these can be dreary and long, beat reporters will sit through conference calls hoping not to miss anything, even if they are distracted for a minute to grab a snack or get coffee. Fortunately, there is always a recording.

CASH FLOW STATEMENTS

The cash flow statement tends to be treated like an unloved cousin and barely given attention by journalists, when in fact, story ideas rest in this column. Cash flow indicates the amount of money flowing in and out of the company. So a negative cash flow is a story to pounce upon. This basically means the company is spending more than it is bringing in during a particular period, or more is flowing out of the company than is incoming. A journalist who quickly runs through all the negatives in a cash flow statement and understands why has done justice to this statement. But not everything negative is a red flag. For example, companies need to use their cash for growth—and that can be understood by looking at how funds are being allocated. But if cash flow stays negative too long, it could mean that payments are not being made on time, and this could put a strain on client and/or supplier relationships.

Twitter, now called X, was expecting a negative cash flow of $3 billion in 2023, according to Elon Musk, because of all the outflows from acquisition-related activities. But he quickly reversed this stance a few weeks later to say the company was on track to be "roughly cash flow break-even."[6]

"Firms' income statement, balance sheet, and cash flow statement contain numbers that are stories to be had for the taking. And any journalism student would be wise to take a class to learn how to decipher them because that skill is likely to come in handy on any beat, not just business," writes the journalist and professor Chris Roush in his book *Show Me the Money: Writing Business and Economics Stories for Mass Communication*.[7]

REGULATORY FILINGS

A lot of news can be buried inside documents that companies are required to file with regulatory authorities to remain in compliance with corporate laws in their countries, and many newsrooms have reporters whose job is to sift through such documents to flesh out news that could potentially affect stocks. Companies in the United States submit their documents to the SEC via the Electronic Data Gathering Analysis and Retrieval (EDGAR) system.[8] Journalists are trained to check these filings thoroughly and know precisely where to look for what. For example, an 8-K form is likely to be a replica of a press release that is sent out by a company, but an amended 8-K form might just have information that was not mentioned in a press release.

There are many other filings, which to an unknowing person would seem to have strange numbers and alphabets or EDGAR codes, that alert journalists and traders to company announcements and developments. They include quarterly reports (10-Qs), annual reports (10-Ks), Form 4s (change in shareholdings), 20-Fs (annual reports of non-US companies), and others. Journalists can peruse these documents using keywords and then write headlines with unexpected news that can get the markets to notice and react.

The one form that can make almost any regulatory reporter jump from their seat is the S-1 filing. This is the form a company files when it plans to go public, or in other words, notify the SEC that it plans an IPO. Here, the reporter will deftly search for key information, such as the number of shares the company plans to offer to the public, the range at which the shares are expected to be priced, who are the underwriters, the proposed ticker symbol, and the exchange it is likely to trade on. Reporters will also quickly calculate the estimated market capitalization of a new publicly traded company based on information given to the SEC via the S-1 filing.

In the IPO filing, investors will look for business sustainability, strategies, and profits. One of the most controversial and talked-about IPO filings was by the shared workspace provider WeWork in 2019, in which the company declared huge losses, expensive lease agreements, and cash burn in the millions.[9] Investors were not happy, especially with disclosures such as the company having an all-male board, a confusing corporate structure, and a conflict of interest with founder and CEO Adam Neumann.[10] Valued at $47 billion at that point, WeWork struggled for two years before dismissing Neumann, being acquired by Softbank, and refiling for an IPO in 2021. Shares of the company rose 9 percent when it finally got listed on the New York Stock Exchange on October 22, 2021.[11] The early concerns of investors proved to be a harbinger, because, unable to pay its debt, WeWork declared bankruptcy in November 2023, a year after COVID-19 significantly lowered demand for office space and large numbers of employees opted to work from home.[12]

Another example of a scoop from an 8-K SEC filing was in August 2023.[13] The filing revealed that Clorox, the cleaning supplies company, had identified unauthorized activity—someone had hacked into the information technology systems at some of its business operations.[14] Therefore, the company had to switch to processing orders manually until the issue was resolved. This meant Clorox cleaning supplies would soon be in short supply. The firm's shares fell about 2 percent in the early hours of trading as soon as this news was announced.[15]

At about the same time Clorox slipped its online glitching news into an SEC filing, there were reports of cyberattacks at hospitals and meat processing units of certain food companies. MGM Resorts, too, reported via an SEC filing that it had a cybersecurity issue that caused disruptions in its online booking system.[16] To uncover news, journalists in other countries also browse filings found in their respective regulatory agencies' systems, such as SEDAR in Canada, Companies House in the UK, and EDINET in Japan.

Not every news organization has the luxury of a dedicated resource to dig into regulatory filings. In some companies, reporters themselves monitor regulatory filings of companies on their beats, very often getting to a 10-K (annual report) after they are done publishing their news story for the day. Some even ignore filings because of a lack of time and inclination. But getting to filings quickly—and patiently—is very important because you never know if a company decided to bury market-moving information deep inside a document that can sometimes be 100 pages or more. That is another reason this is tasked upon the Headlines team of a newswire service.

"Be patient and dig harder; you'll find gold," an editor was once heard yelling after a reporter missed information buried in an SEC filing. The anecdotal example at the end of this chapter happened during the COVID crisis at a company that the world was banking its hopes on. There was probably nothing wrong with how the senior management, including the CEO, updated their employee share plan while creating a vaccine that was to save the world, but it reveals how subtly that news was buried inside an SEC filing. Kudos to the journalist who dug it out and wrote about the millions that were pocketed by Moderna executives.

Here is a partial list of specific SEC forms mentioned above that tend to attract the attention of beat reporters because they may include newsworthy updates (usually, the document runs several pages and requires a fair amount of time from a journalist, which is a challenge in itself):

8-K: typically a replica of a press release, but sometimes could have additional updates;

10-Q: Quarterly reports with financial statement and other details;

10-K: Annual report with details of all financials for the past year;

S1: IPO filing details;

F1: IPO filing details for foreign companies seeking to be listed in the United States;

13-D: Mandatory filing for the SEC if a person or an organization acquires 5 percent or more of a company's voting shares, meaning they can vote on company policies;

Form 4: Indicates any transaction that has resulted in a change in ownership of company securities.

SUGGESTED ACTIVITIES

NVIDIA Fiscal 2025 First Quarter Earnings

Fast fingers, speed reading, and an agile mind are "must have" attributes for journalists who cover breaking news. Earnings season is highly anticipated and meticulously planned for by Headliners, reporters, and editors because it includes several weeks of a daily onslaught of breaking news. Very often, newsrooms are aware of the time when some of the biggest companies will report their results. It could be before the market opens—usually between 7 a.m. and 8:30 a.m. Eastern time—or after the market closes at 4 p.m.

That is when NVIDIA (Nasdaq: NVDA) reported its fiscal 2025 first quarter earnings.[17] The stock exchange and symbol are usually mentioned in parenthesis by all companies. (You can find the press release in note 17 here.) As soon as news agencies received this press release, these headlines would have likely been flashed on screens of financial traders, thanks to an algorithm of a software program (please note that these headlines were written by the authors for demonstration purposes):

NVIDIA Q1 REV $26B, UP 18% VS Q4 AND UP 262% VS YR AGO

NVIDIA Q1 DATA CENTER REV $22.6B, UP 23% VS Q4

NVIDIA 10-FOR-1 STOCK SPLIT EFFECTIVE JUNE 7

NVIDIA CASH DIV RAISED 150% TO 1C/SHR POST-SPLIT

NVIDIA Q1 GAAP EPS $5.98, UP 21% VS Q4 AND 629% VS YR AGO

NVIDIA Q1 NON-GAAP EPS $6.12, UP 19% VS Q4 AND 461% VS YR AGO

NVIDIA SEES Q2 REV $2B PLUS OR MINUS 2%

NVIDIA SEES 2Q GAAP, NON-GAAP GROSS MARGINS 74.8% AND 75.5%

NVIDIA SEES YR GROSS MARGINS IN MID-70% RANGE

NVIDIA SEES Q2 GAAP, NON-GAAP OPER COSTS ABOUT $4B AND $2.8B

NVIDIA SEES YR OPER COSTS GROWTH IN LOW-40% RANGE

NVIDIA 2Q GROSS MARGINS OUTLOOK PLUS OR MINUS 50BPS

1. Why is the second headline important for financial markets?
2. What is the key word in the last headline that may have prompted it to be disseminated?

These headlines would be generated automatically based on the layout of subheads and content in the NVIDIA press release. Because the headlines are autogenerated, not all of them are very important. The ones that matter most are for overall revenue, data center revenue (you would know "why" if you were a beat reporter who knows the importance of artificial intelligence chips), non-GAAP EPS, the quarterly dividend increase, and the second quarter forecast or outlook for these same key performance indicators. Simultaneously, headlines with the current quarter results compared with analyst estimates would also be sent to show how the company's performance matched up against expectations:

NVIDIA Q1 REV $26B vs $X EST
NVIDIA Q1 NON-GAAP EPS $6.12 vs $XY EST

3. Why would a Headliner compare a non-GAAP EPS with a market analyst's estimates?

Additional headlines would also be sent that directly compare the company's current results with those for the same period a year ago, or to the previous quarter. The period comparison depends on the knowledge a beat reporter has about their companies, and believes is relevant:

NVIDIA Q1 REV $26B vs $7.19B YR AGO
or NVIDIA Q1 REV $26B vs Q4 $22.1B
NVIDIA Q1 NON-GAAP EPS $6.12 vs $1.09 YR AGO
or NVIDIA Q1 NON-GAAP EPS $6.12 vs Q4 $5.16

4. What is the difference between the two stacked headlines for Revenue and EPS?

In the age of autogenerated headlines, headliners still have the role, however, of speed reading the press release to find other newsworthy and relevant information. In NVIDIA'S case it would be news about its Data Center and the next AI chip.

These headlines would likely move markets as they are forward-looking:

NVIDIA: DATA CENTER GROWTH FROM STRONG DEMAND FOR GEN AI TRAINING

NVIDIA DATA CTR GROWTH ALSO FROM "INFERENCE ON HOPPER PLATFORM"

NVIDIA SAYS BLACKWELL PLATFORM IN FULL PRODUCTION

NVIDIA: BLACKWELL FOUNDATION FOR TRILLION-PARAMETER-SCALE GEN AI

NVIDIA: SPECTRUM-X OPENS NEW MKT FOR LARGE-SCALE AI TO DATA CTRS

NVIDIA CITES SPECTRUM-X FOR AI TO ETHERNET-ONLY DATA CENTERS

Based on the first set of headlines, the beat reporter would have written a quick, two or three paragraph story about the results beating market expectations, the company boosting its dividend and also declaring a stock split.

How do you think the markets reacted to all of the above? Here is how. In after-hours trading, after Nvidia announced its results on May 22, 2024, its stock rose 7 percent and traded above $1,000 for the first time. It closed trading at $949.50 on volume of 548.6 million shares traded. The next day, the stock rose as high as $1,063.20 intraday. It closed below the intraday level but at a record high of $1,037.99—9.3 percent above the previous close—on volume of over 835 million shares.[18]

"It's Nvidia's market and we're all just trading in it," said Steve Sosnick, chief strategist, interactive broker, and head trader at Timber Hill, to CNBC on that day, explaining how Nvidia is spearheading the tech sector's growth, adding context to the story.[19]

5. How did the Nvidia story end on May 22? What did the story headline say?

A few things to note about writing headlines. Whether they are automated or manual, there is a character limit. It is also important to note that certain abbreviations are used as a speedier way to put out the information. At all times, a Headliner is constantly aware of what is significant news and the fastest way to write it. For example, if the news of Nvidia's dividend was in the body of the text and not picked up by the software, a Headliner would write "NVIDIA BOOSTS DIV" or "NVIDIA RAISES DIV" because that is faster and sends the information out faster than including an additional word, such as, "NVIDIA RAISES QUARTERLY DIV," or even one that adds words and numbers, such as, "NVIDIA RAISES CASH DIV BY 150%." Headliners can also set up keyboard shortcuts for words and phrases to enable faster writing of headlines.

When an earnings period ends, headliners and reporters will continue their roles, but with different trajectories. Reporters may have gotten one or more ideas to investigate for a longer story, which they will work on while also writing any story, as needed from time to time, based on other significant news that is released. Although the number of press releases doubles or triples during earnings season, there is still a deluge of press releases every day before the markets open, after they close, and more sporadically throughout the day.

Top Execs Rake in Millions While Promising to Save the World from a Pandemic

An SEC filing broke controversial news, created chatter, and became a market-moving story about financial gains made by the leadership team of a healthcare company on the back of vaccine data. It was information inside a Form 4 SEC filing by Moderna that showed its CEO Stephane Bancel had updated his executive stock plan soon after the pharmaceutical company announced positive results from its coronavirus vaccine trials.[20]

Bancel owned three times more shares because of his updated share plan. When the vaccine trial news came out, a fearful world and a jittery market rejoiced. Shares of Moderna went up 30 percent. Two months later, Bancel sold 72,000 shares and walked away with $4.8 million. Other SEC forms revealed similarly updated stock plans for a board director named Elizabeth Nabel and the president of the company, Stephen Hoge.[21]

Reporters started investigating whether the company's revised stock plan was illegal and could be deemed "insider trading"—when company executives can make money from information that is not yet made public. In this case, the officials had sold their shares 'after' the announcement but had discreetly updated a prearranged stock plan internally.

An investigation by NPR into the entire executive stock sale and disclosures found that despite concerns raised by the media and market players, Moderna executives continued to sell their shares although the revised stock plan was questionable.[22] And some senior executives had sold all their shares even though corporate best practices recommend that ideally officials should not do so.

An anticorruption organization, too, requested that the SEC investigate the internally modified stock plan and the millions made by company officials. But no one was charged and the question of whether this tactic could be punishable as a crime remained just that—a question. As of late 2024, Stephane Bancel continued to serve as CEO of Moderna.

4

BUSINESS OPERATIONS AND INTERNAL TURMOIL

Profits, it can be said, are certainly the most important thing for companies and their operations. So anything that disrupts or negatively affects revenue and profits can potentially cause significant trading in the company's stock. Various events and activities—or any sort of internal turmoil—can cause an unwelcome focus on companies, affect their operations and the outlook of investors, and lead to repercussions in the market.

MANAGEMENT CHANGES

Why would a prominent CEO step down from that role on a Sunday? That is the question reporters, traders, and investors were asking on Monday, August 8, 2022, after the private equity company the Carlyle Group had unexpectedly put out a press release the day before to announce that CEO Kewsong Lee "will step down today as CEO and a member of the Board of Directors."[1] As unexpected as the news would be, it was one of those press releases with very straightforward subheads from which these headlines would most likely have been flashed either by a Headliner or by automation:

> CARLYLE ANNOUNCES SENIOR LEADERSHIP CHANGES
> KEWSONG LEE STEPS DOWN AS CEO, CARLYLE SAYS
> BILL CONWAY TO SERVE AS INTERIM CEO, CARLYLE SAYS
> CARLYLE NAMES NEW OFFICE OF CEO TO SUPPORT TRANSITION

The release of such significant news on a Sunday did not deter reporters from immediately trying to reach out to sources, and the company's spokesperson, to get more information so that by the time the markets opened on Monday, updated news was already disseminated. Carlyle's stock fell as much as 7 percent intraday on Monday and closed down almost 4 percent, with more than twice the average volume of shares traded compared with past sessions.[2]

Carlyle's press release stated that "a newly formed Search Committee of the Board will drive the search for a permanent successor." This was a clear statement that a succession or transition plan was not in place and that the resignation was a surprise. This was the point that dominated news of the resignation. The announcement and effective resignation on a Sunday were unusual, causing reporters to question what could be the real reason, beyond what the company cited in the release—the end of the CEO's five-year employment agreement was approaching, and it was the right time to begin the search for a successor. This is an example of a case in which reporters would be on the phone nonstop, making calls and conducting interviews to glean reasons for the sudden resignation. A few weeks later, at the end of the month, the *New York Times* cited "a generational struggle" and internal disagreements about running the firm.[3]

A company would not disclose such reasons because of the obvious negative attention that would result. It takes extensive reporting, contacting sources, engaging in research, and knowledge of the company and the industry to ferret out what may really be going on when there is an unexpected resignation of a top company executive.

"When a CEO change is announced, there are a lot of immediate questions," said Bruce Rule, who has been an editor and writer at news agencies and currently operates his own company, Rule Communications: "Is it a planned transition with a target date in the future? If it is immediate, the big news stops being the CEO has left and immediately shifts to who is taking [the former CEO's] place." Rule added that "what analysts and investors are saying about who should succeed the outgoing CEO" is also very important.

Because of the pivotal role of C-suite executives—chief executive officer, chief financial officer, chief operations officer, chief legal officer, and the chairman of the board—individuals in these prominent roles are known to the media, institutional investors, and analysts. The strategy and execution required for a company to consistently deliver good financial results and growth in its operations depends on the performance of these individuals. That is why abrupt management and leadership changes can cause a significant downside in the market. Investors will want to know what is known about the new CEO and how that individual may change things at the company.

The situation can exist, however, in which an executive is not viewed positively and has been getting criticisms about the company's operations. In that case, an unexpected departure can be positive news for the stock. But companies that are being optimally managed are expected to have a succession plan to facilitate smooth transitions of key management roles, especially for the CEO, CFO, COO, and chairman. The markets will therefore react strongly when a management change does not follow this script, as was the case with Carlyle.

On August 14, 2023, Discover Financial Services also did not have a succession plan in place when it announced the departure of the company's CEO without citing a reason. He had been with the company for a total of twenty-five years. The company's stock fell 4.5 percent in the hours after the close of trading when this news was announced.[4]

In contrast to Discover Financial Services, PayPal Holdings issued a press release on the same day after hours naming a new CEO—its stock rose almost 3 percent. PayPal's CEO had announced in February 2023 that he planned to leave his position at the end of the year, making shareholders aware and giving the company adequate time to conduct a search. The positive reaction of the stock also indicated that shareholders were pleased with the individual who was named as the new CEO, an experienced executive with a leadership position at Intuit.[5]

When Netflix's chief content officer, Ted Sarandos, was named co-CEO and a member of the board in July 2020, the news was largely expected given his success in bringing significantly more original content and programming to the streaming company, which greatly increased revenue and subscribers. The company included the information in its shareholder letter, which included the company's second quarter earnings report. When shares fell as much as 12 percent after the news of the management change and earnings report, reporters attributed it to the company's results not meeting analyst expectations for earnings per share, and its forecast of low subscriber growth in the third quarter.[6] To the news media, and particularly to business journalists who follow the company, as well as those trading Netflix's stock, the management change was "non-news." It was the company's disappointing earnings performance that mattered, resulting in heavy selling of the shares, causing the stock's value to plummet.

As the person at the helm, and very often the public face, of the company, the CEO is the most important executive. But it is not the only important managerial role that helps to determine the performance of the company or the results it produces. As mentioned, others in the C-suite are all part of senior management who can trigger trading in the stock if there is any unexpected change, such as a sudden departure, scandal, or even illness, because there will be concern about who will be the replacement and whether the company's strategy and initiatives may change.

In some companies, there is an "Office of the CEO" with a few executives who are part of a core management team. And in other companies, because of industry-specific operations, different managerial positions are important, such as chief content officer in streaming companies. Whatever the structure, it is meant to ensure stability and uninterrupted business performance, which is why reporters and investors keep tabs on management changes and succession planning at companies.

The questions about, and reaction to, especially a CEO or other C-suite executive change will depend on whether it was a planned transition with a future target date or was an immediate resignation, a firing, or due to illness. The reaction will be different if a company said the CEO plans to leave in several months or a year compared with an announcement that the CEO has left the company immediately. An unanticipated resignation is likely to cause a significant move in the stock—likely negative—unless the individual was highly unpopular. Along with news of the departure, the other significant announcement will be who is the replacement, or who will be taking over, is the new person named to the role permanently or for an interim period, and what is known about the individual. All such information would be sent out in headlines from news agencies, followed by short- and longer-form follow-up stories. If a successor is not named, it is of interest to include in subsequent stories the views of analysts and investors about who could be a possible successor, and what changes, if any, they would like to see from that successor.

PRODUCT RECALLS

In running the company, CEOs and other executives seek to have all operations go according to plan to produce revenue and profits—the ultimate positive outcome. But inevitably, something may not go as planned. Manufacturing a product that is later determined to have flaws and needs to be withdrawn or recalled is a problem that casts a negative light on the company and will consume a lot of attention from company executives.

Quite simply, product recalls are when any type of product that has already been sold directly to consumers or to distributors for shipment to various marketplaces or sites is identified as having a defect and must no longer be sold or used in its current form. The defect may be a flaw in the design, labeling, dosage, or manufacturing of a product, deeming it to be unsafe by quality control authorities and regulators.

When any type of defect is confirmed in a product by a regulatory authority or other government body, an order is issued for (1) consumers to immediately stop using or to discard the product, or to have it fixed for continued use; and (2) for the company to recall the affected products that have been sold or are currently with retailers. For products such as food and medicine, contaminated batches are usually destroyed. For mechanical products, a fix is required, if possible. But a product that has a severe design flaw that makes it highly unsafe will be pulled off the market from being offered for sale.

Product recalls that require the total removal of a product definitely reflect negatively on a company. This is when its reputation may take a hit. And if consumers lose faith and trust in a company's products, that will certainly hurt future sales and profits.

On September 30, 2004, Merck issued a worldwide recall of its painkiller Vioxx, which was the source of billions of dollars in revenue, based on new data from a trial that showed a higher risk for serious cardiovascular events, such as heart attacks and strokes, after months of treatment with Vioxx compared with the placebo.[7] The action caused Merck's shares to plunge 27 percent on extremely high trading volume of over 152 million shares compared with a typical volume of 5 to 8 million. In the next week, Merck's shares continued to trade in higher-than-average volume, and its stock continued to fall, from $42 before the recall to just under $30 a month later. Research that was published in the *Lancet*, the renowned medical journal, estimated that 88,000 individuals in the US who had taken Vioxx had suffered heart attacks, of which 38,000 had died.[8] In an agreement with the US Department of Justice, Merck pleaded guilty to a misdemeanor and agreed to pay $950 million for illegal marketing.[9]

Unlike recalls in the pharmaceutical industry, automobile recalls are different. Vehicle recalls in many cases do not have a significant effect on the stock performance of auto companies. It could be because such recalls do not usually require a complete cessation of sales of the vehicle or any alerts or warnings for drivers to no longer operate them. Consumers are made aware of the flaw by news reports, and/or from information disseminated by the US National Highway Transportation Safety Authority. Individual notices are then sent to all buyers from the auto companies with advice about how the flaw or defect can be fixed—usually at no cost, by taking the affected vehicle to an auto dealer.

LAWSUITS

Similar to product recalls, when a company is engaged in serious litigation, it takes time away from the core focus on its operations. Resources need to be spent on legal preparation, and company officials may need to do more than the usual media interviews to offset any negative impact and put their own spin on the situation.

Companies can be engaged in litigation from class-action lawsuits by consumers claiming that they were harmed by its product. Examples of these are lawsuits against cigarette companies in the early 2000s, after it was scientifically proven that nicotine in cigarettes directly caused or contributed to individuals who smoked or were exposed to smoke (secondhand smoke) developing lung cancer. And in 2022, a class-action suit was brought by almost 20,000 women against Johnson & Johnson with claims that using its signature Baby Powder for many years led to cases of ovarian cancer.

Lawsuits can also arise from breaches over proprietary information when one company believes that ideas and products that it developed or is in the process of developing, and which are unique and core to its operations and competitive advantage, have been obtained in an unfair or illegal manner. The allegedly wronged party will seek to publicize this and begin or threaten litigation. Based on early perceptions of the strength of each party's case, traders may buy or sell the stocks of the companies, which can significantly affect share prices.

A lawsuit presents the risk of significant monetary liabilities because legal costs can be hefty, whether for a settlement out of court or payment if the case is lost. Companies account for such expenses as "one-time, nonrecurring" charges that are excluded from other usual business expenses (see the section on earnings in chapter 3). Still, as soon as the amount of any payment is publicized—in the millions or even billions—it becomes news that will hurt the company's finances, which could potentially cause a sell-off in the stock. Johnson & Johnson's stock fell over 3 percent on January 30, 2023, when an appeals court dismissed the bankruptcy filing of a unit the company had formed solely to bear the burden of thousands of lawsuits.[10] A product recall, lawsuits, and numerous problems piling up that cause a company to seemingly always be trying to defend or negate an issue, are some reasons they may consider pursuing a different path and strategy.

CORPORATE REBRANDING AND REPUTATION

Though a company's reputation is not measured in dollars and cents, it is equally important as profits. Product recalls and lawsuits can potentially have a significant negative effect on the revenue of companies, as well as their reputation. The public's perception about a company can be formed in a few ways. The most direct way is from using its products. Sales, therefore, go a long way to send a message to individual consumers about the quality of a company's products, what they think of them, and how they regard the company. Then there is also general awareness and knowledge. Advertising is a powerful tool that companies use to communicate, build their brands, and generate mass appeal.

When the sale of a product is affected by a recall or a lawsuit, it can be a double whammy hit to the company's profit and reputation. For example, Johnson & Johnson's iconic Baby Powder with talc was a top product that defined the company for decades and cemented its identity as a trusted baby products company, alongside being a pharmaceutical conglomerate. But when hundreds of consumers filed lawsuits claiming that they had used Johnson & Johnson talc-based Baby Powder over decades and had developed cancer and other health problems, the negative news about this flagship product caused the company to make several decisions to repair and protect its reputation.

In August 2020, the company discontinued sales of its talc-based Baby Powder in the United States and Canada, and globally in 2023. It also decided to change the composition of its Baby Powder to use cornstarch instead of talc.[11]

In January 2024, the company reached a tentative settlement with several states that started investigations into the marketing of its talc-based Baby Powder. Johnson & Johnson agreed to pay $700 million under the terms of the tentative agreement. However, that settlement did not include or resolve the numerous lawsuits brought by consumers.[12]

As mentioned above, in light of the ongoing lawsuits, Johnson & Johnson sought to separate liabilities for the lawsuit costs by forming a company just for the litigation. Johnson & Johnson did, however, undertake a rebranding of sorts when it decided to split its operations. The pharmaceutical operations, which include prescription drugs and medical devices, were retained under the Johnson & Johnson brand, while the consumer health division was spun off into a new and publicly traded company named Kenvue. The company said, however, that the business separation was not a result of the lawsuits. Johnson & Johnson's shares rose 3 percent on news of the planned company split.[13]

Johnson and Johnson's split illustrates the primary reasons companies undertake rebranding and why it is market-moving news—to change how they operate, to maximize the potential of one or more business units that can operate independently as a stand-alone company, and to change public perceptions of the company, especially after negative news. A new and independent company can also create value for shareholders if it is publicly traded.

More than two decades ago, in 2001, another conglomerate, Philip Morris USA, decided to change its name to Altria Group, Inc., after negative effects from the harmful nature of tobacco and smoking became widely known, and the company entered a settlement with several states for health care costs arising from tobacco use. Philip Morris, at the time, though known for cigarettes, was also the owner of well-known consumer brands—Kraft Foods and Miller Brewing. News reports said the reason for the name change was for the food and beer businesses to steer clear of negative publicity from the tobacco units.

In 2021, one of the biggest technology companies also changed its name after negative publicity. Facebook had come under fire particularly after a whistleblower provided documents to government officials as proof that the social media giant's primary focus was on maximizing use of its platform to generate profits, without much concern for, and to the detriment of, billions of users of its platform. The company deflected that reason by stating that its new name, Meta Platforms, Inc., signaled a change in strategy to focus on a virtual reality metaverse, which it believed would be the next iteration and future of the internet. Meta became an umbrella company for all its brands—Facebook, WhatsApp, Instagram, and its Oculus virtual reality gadget.

Similarly, tech giant Google also changed its name in 2015 to Alphabet Inc. to reflect other businesses and not just its Google search engine. And when the billionaire entrepreneur and Tesla CEO Elon Musk bought Twitter, he renamed it X, in part citing his vision to expand the social media platform into a multimedia entity.

Changing a company's course because of a recurring problem or issue is all part of the goal to keep operations going and to be profitable—to keep the company as a "going concern," meaning there is the expectation that it will continue to exist into the future. The accounting term is most often used with companies, however, that are experiencing serious financial difficulties. It is therefore important news whenever it is mentioned for any company.

A GOING CONCERN

When the term "going concern" appears in any statement or report from a company, it usually means that there are "doubts about ABC company's ability to continue as a going concern." But what does "going concern" mean? Most companies are going concerns because they are operating normally each day to generate revenue, and meet obligations such as paying vendors, suppliers, and employees, and making loan and debt payments. However, it is the ability to satisfy such financial obligations that matters. When a company expresses "doubts" about continuing as a "going concern," it means it could be low on cash, already has or will have difficulties repaying loans or making debt payments, and perhaps is not able to fulfill payroll requirements.

The inability to meet obligations will make the cash situation worse because it will be more difficult for the company to borrow or otherwise raise money to fund its operations. The lack of cash and lack of options to get cash creates a crisis that is likely to lead the company to declare bankruptcy. For these reasons, a "going concern" statement from a publicly traded company will command attention in the newsroom. The news will also be sure to cause some sell-off in the stock because the immediate perception will be that of looming bankruptcy. On January 5, 2023, when the well-known retailer of household products Bed, Bath & Beyond issued a "going concern" statement, its stock fell 30 percent at the end of the trading day.[14] (Also see the anecdote at the end of the chapter.)

There are times, however, when, after issuing a going concern statement, a company manages to get a cash infusion from bankers or even an individual investor. In most situations, however, a "going concern" statement is sure to attract market attention and cause significant selling, leading to a decline in the stock's price because it is a red flag that signals the next step could be a bankruptcy filing.

BANKRUPTCY PROTECTION

A company that files for bankruptcy is unable to make payments as required, in a timely manner, on its debts. Bankruptcy serves the purpose of discharging at least some of the company's debts with the potential to reach an agreement on other debt payment terms. When the market first learns that a company has filed for bankruptcy, its stock will undoubtedly fall because of heavy selling from the negative sentiment associated with bankruptcy.

Before filing, two other actions that may generate headlines and are market-moving are (1) as mentioned above, a going concern statement; and (2) a default. If a company is unable to make a debt payment on the due date, that is considered a default on that payment. After making a "going concern" statement, markets pay attention to the period when debt payments are due and monitor whether the company meets those obligations or negotiates an extended time to make the payment. If not, it receives a default notice. This happened to Bed, Bath & Beyond, which, after receiving a notice of default, said it would consider "strategic alternatives," including restructuring its debt in bankruptcy.

Although a bankruptcy filing is negative and is not good news, it does not necessarily mean the end of the road or the death knell for the company. A company may use a bankruptcy filing to put its operations on a different and better footing. That is because the process gives the company some time, or a reprieve, from making payments, and may provide possibly better terms for the repayment of debt. The bankruptcy process enables payment on some debt, discharges some obligations, and provides an opportunity for the company to operate unencumbered by previous debt. That is why when companies file for bankruptcy, they are often described as undergoing a reorganization.

A company in bankruptcy may seek to restructure its debt by reaching agreements with creditors and bondholders to make it less onerous and more manageable to make payments. It may also seek financing, referred to as debtor-in-possession, to be able to pay lawyers working on the case, salaries, suppliers, and others to keep its operations running normally. It could also seek to restructure or change its operations, for example, by selling some units or part of its business. A worst-case scenario is when it decides to wind down and cease operating. In the United States, depending on the strategy or objective of the company, on whether it is solvent or not, it could file a specific chapter or type of bankruptcy.

Chapter 7 Bankruptcy

A Chapter 7 type of bankruptcy is filed by US companies that plan to cease operating. In this bankruptcy process, the court administers liquidation of all assets, excluding any that may be "secured," or are "exempt," and subject to liens. Any money collected from the sale of assets is used to pay unsecured creditors based on the class of their claim as established by the court. When all assets are sold, the company ceases operations and gets a discharge of debt from the courts.

Because Chapter 7 bankruptcy means going out of business, most publicly traded companies do not usually use this filing method. Having said that, some listed companies have filed Chapter 7: Bon-Ton Stores in 2018; Borders Group first filed Chapter 11 bankruptcy (in February 2011) but later converted to Chapter 7 (in July 2011) after it was unable to find a buyer for its operations; Movie Gallery in April 2010; Monaco Coach Company also first filed Chapter 11 in March 2009, then converted to Chapter 7 in June 2009.

Chapter 11 Bankruptcy

A Chapter 11 type of bankruptcy is filed when a US company is unable to meet its debt payments and seeks an alternative means to survive. Sometimes, when a company gets a large judgment in a lawsuit against it, it may file for Chapter 11 bankruptcy. It may be voluntary if the decision was made solely by the company, or involuntary if creditors forced the company into filing. It is the most used type of bankruptcy filing, and it may also be called a "reorganization" as the company uses the bankruptcy process to get more favorable terms for debt payments. Because the company plans to continue its operations, it may also seek financing, which is called debtor-in-possession (DIP) financing during the process. Seeking and getting DIP financing is newsworthy and could cause positive movement in the stock.

For the reorganization to happen, the company's creditors need to agree on a proposed reorganization plan. That plan includes payments to creditors over time, but details of the debt agreements may be different. A reorganization therefore gives the company time and some flexibility to meet its obligations. If no relief results from reorganization efforts, the company could liquidate and wind down its business, or another company—likely a competitor—could purchase all or most of the bankrupt company's assets.

Some of the biggest Chapter 11 bankruptcies in the United States have been General Motors, in June 2009, with assets valued at $82.29 billion and debt of $172.88 billion—the company restructured by selling off car brands and assets and emerged from bankruptcy within a month, much faster than expected; Lehman Brothers, at the peak of the financial crisis in September 2008, with assets of $639 billion and liabilities of $613 billion—its liquidation process would end fourteen years later; Washington Mutual, with assets of $307 billion and $188 billion in deposits, was closed by the Office of Thrift Supervision and the Federal Deposit Insurance Corporation was named receiver in September 2008, a few days before the fate of Lehman Brothers, after depositors withdrew more than $16 billion over nine days. At the time, it was "the largest failure of an insured depository institution in the history of the Federal Deposit Insurance Corporation." Video rental chain Blockbuster's physical store business declined with the rise of streaming services along with DVD rental by mail and through kiosks, led it to file bankruptcy in September 2010 with assets of $1.02 billion and liabilities of $1.46 billion. The supermarket chain Great Atlantic & Pacific Tea Company, known as A&P, filed for bankruptcy twice—once in July 2015, with assets of $2.5 billion and liabilities of $3.2 billion; and then in November 2009—citing competition from discount stores offering groceries and also new retail chains.

Other prominent Chapter 11 filings include the pharmacy chain Rite Aid, which until its filing in October 2023 seemed to compete with CVS Health and Walgreens Boots Alliance to establish retail stores at prominent locations on main streets and at multiple sites in larger towns and cities. Rite Aid cited weak sales and costs from settling opioid lawsuits; the company received $3.45 billion in financing to restructure its business. Similarly, the trucking company Yellow Corp. cited depleting cash flow issues as a result of business slowdown, debt load, and disagreements with the Teamsters Union, and it filed for bankruptcy on August 6, 2023.

Operating at a profit to keep a business going is the ultimate aim of all companies. But it takes balancing multipronged responsibilities that involve key personnel and product management. While it is important to pay much attention to news distributed by the company—especially financial reports and the Key Performance Indicators and metrics detailed in the next chapter—from time to time, reporters also need to look beyond the obvious to assess if all is drumming along fairly fine or if there are issues that could be of concern to shareholders and the general public. For example, finding and reporting news about disagreements in the executive suite, underperformance of a unit, or problems with a product will be sure to attract attention in financial markets.

SUGGESTED ACTIVITIES

1. Find three public companies that had a change of CEO, CFO, or COO in recent months. Were the changes planned or unexpected? What was the stock reaction on the announcement?
2. Identify a public company's product or service that has been the subject of news reports, complaints from a consumer group, a class-action lawsuit, or government action. Examine recent press releases from the company for any comment about the matter.

How a Dependable Everything-for-the-Home Store Went Kaput

Bed, Bath & Beyond filed for bankruptcy on April 23, 2023, after being unable to pay its debt, citing continuing poor sales after the lockdown effects of the COVID-19 pandemic. The home store received a loan of $240 million during bankruptcy proceedings to operate as needed.

Causes for Bed, Bath & Beyond's demise could be reduced to two words—strategy and reinvention. As its performance weakened, the company changed strategy, deciding to end sales of its store brand items and instead focus on known, branded products. In the absence of reinvention, it lost significant foot traffic from shoppers who once relied on the store to make their homes, apartments, and living spaces look and feel very homey.

In its heyday, when shopping meant leaving your home, walking into a store, browsing, and touching and comparing items, Bed, Bath & Beyond was the ultimate store for essential and stylish products for the home. That meant it was filled with a variety of items and maintained a robust inventory. But at least two big things happened in the retail landscape that undercut the company's business and its particular model—the rise and overwhelming use of online shopping, and better product lineup and pricing from other brick and mortar companies that also sold home goods and whose marketing campaigns were more successful at attracting shoppers—think Target and Walmart.

Trends play an important role in the success of any business. That is why journalists and the media will often report on what may seem like a fad. They call attention to something that may ultimately bring change to a way of life, an industry, or a business, and has become a standard new norm. Bed, Bath & Beyond became a statistic for not being successful in finding a new strategy to enable a reinvention for changing trends and shopping habits.

The company raised red flags when it cited doubt about continuing as a "going concern," restructuring its operations, and mentioning the possibility of bankruptcy in a pre–earnings statement on January 5, 2023. Its stock fell 30 percent by the end of that day, to its lowest level in decades. But problems could be seen even earlier, in August 2022, when the company said it started a series of actions to cut 20 percent of its workforce, close 150 stores, and reduce capital spending—all aimed at cutting overall costs. In the same press release, the company also said it had strengthened its liquidity by getting more than $500 million in new financing commitments, which included an expanded $1.13 billion asset-backed, revolving credit facility and a new $375 million "first-in-last-out" facility. Personnel changes and the shift away from its "owned brands" were also reported in the August 2022 press release.[15]

Despite those actions, by year end, when all retailers put maximum effort into bolstering sales for the holiday season and expect results to put their finances into the "black" (thus the Black Friday sales phenomenon), Bed, Bath & Beyond's sales were disappointing, which caused the warnings in early January 2023 about lower-than-expected upcoming quarterly results. In late April, on a Sunday, the company issued a press release that said it had "filed voluntary petitions for relief under

Chapter 11 . . . Bankruptcy . . . to implement an orderly wind down of its businesses." It also received a commitment of about $240 million in DIP financing. While it planned a wind down of its operations, the company said it was also "strategically managing inventory to preserve value," in case a buyer emerged.[16]

Bed, Bath & Beyond eventually had close-out sales and shut all its physical retail stores. Online retailer Overstock bought its remaining inventory. But as proof of the value of the name, brand, and store, Overstock changed its name to—Bed, Bath & Beyond, retaining even the company's stylized name in blue. So, in August 2023, a year after that first but initially failed strategic initiative to boost results, Bed, Bath & Beyond was reinvented to reside online at bedbathbeyond.com, continuing to sell "all your favorite furniture, rugs and home goods."

On October 24, 2023, it announced more changes, issuing a statement in which it announced a new corporate name—Beyond Inc., with the stock symbol BYON, a new logo, and news that its listing would move from Nasdaq to the New York Stock Exchange. Bed, Bath & Beyond would remain one of the company's brands. And almost two weeks later, the newly named Beyond Inc. announced leadership changes, saying its CEO had stepped down from that position and the board immediately, and that the president and the CFO would assume expanded roles—the former being named interim CEO while remaining president, and the latter adding oversight responsibilities for legal and human resources functions.[17]

5

KEY PERFORMANCE INDICATORS

Every company has a list of performance metrics that indicate its progress and health. These Key Performance Indicators (KPIs) help keep the company on track to achieve its goals for revenues and profits and to be able to distribute the same to shareholders.

These KPIs are also metrics that are well understood by journalists who cover specific beats or sectors, such as retail, autos, pharmaceuticals, real estate, and airlines. These metrics are what news Headliners look for in press releases and what beat reporters write stories about, often comparing KPIs of different companies to get a better grasp of how a particular sector is performing. These figures also enable financial traders to react and respond to clients regarding the implications of such financial news.

The KPIs that matter most to news reporters and traders in determining how a business is doing are described in the next sections. Reporting these metrics helps to keep the news focused and not get lost in a sea of press information and filings provided by companies.

AIRLINES

To the average person, it may seem straightforward that an airline company's business performance probably depends on the number of passengers each flight carries, the cost of tickets, and the expenses incurred to operate the planes. These aspects are certainly important, but they are measured and described in terms that may appear as gibberish, except to those in the media who cover airlines and those who invest in them. Apart from the obvious earnings statements, metrics important to the airline industry are as follows.

Load Factor

The closer the load factor is to 100 percent, the better. This is a measure of how many passenger seats or capacity was used or, simply put, how much of the plane was filled with paying passengers. Load factor became a concern with the onset of the COVID-19 pandemic. The number of flights declined drastically as lockdowns stopped people from traveling, but as vaccinations reduced incidences of COVID-19, the number of flights resumed. Airlines did not sell middle seats for a while to ensure safe distancing and reduce the probability of COVID spreading between passengers. But as vaccinations greatly reduced incidences of severe COVID cases and eased restrictions, travel resumed, along with normal seating, which included middle seats.

Available Seat Miles

Stated in millions, available seat miles (ASM) indicate the capacity of the airplane from the passenger seats available and the miles the airplane will fly on a route.

Revenue Passenger Miles

Revenue passenger miles (RPM) are also given in millions and measures how many ASMs are actually used or sold; it is an indication of revenue level because it is calculated from each paying passenger flying the miles on a route.

Passenger Revenue per ASM

Given in cents, passenger revenue per ASM (PRASM) is a measurement of passenger unit revenue. It indicates the passenger revenue per seat (empty or occupied) flown 1 mile.

Total Revenue per ASM

Total revenue per ASM (RASM) is a "unit revenue" measurement for the total operating revenue per seat (empty or occupied) flown 1 mile. Like all companies, airlines report quarterly results that will include metrics specific to the sector. The metrics specific to the sector are also reported monthly, giving journalists, analysts, and investors closer insight into their performance.

AUTOMOBILES

Despite the availability of rideshare apps that now provide transportation on request, many people still prefer to own a car for their convenience, especially given that in some areas outside city limits, reliable public transportation may not be available. But buying a car is a major expense. Car sales therefore provide key data that can give indications about the state of an economy and the economic health of consumers.

All major car companies report their sales, monthly and/or quarterly, providing insight into the overall performance of the company for investors and the public to be aware of the performance of key brands, preferences, and trends among buyers. Journalists and markets watch these monthly and/or quarterly sales figures: selling days, passenger car sales, sport utility vehicles (SUVs) and truck sales, electric vehicles (EVs), hybrids, and total vehicle/unit sales, as well as light and new vehicle production numbers.

Sales figures are provided on a seasonally adjusted annual rate basis, a daily selling rate, or a volume basis. The increase or decrease in sales percentages compared with the same period a year ago—monthly or quarterly—as well as comparisons with estimates provided by analysts at brokerage firms and industry entities, indicate whether sales have met, exceeded, or fallen below expectations.

Also important are events or situations that may have affected sales: production and/or labor problems, supply chain issues, and broader economic conditions, such as inflation or rising interest rates. Consumer preferences and trends, as mentioned above, can also affect overall sales, as evidenced when US consumers bought more SUVs than cars or sedans for the first time in 2015.[1] And with growing concerns about climate change and the environment, there is now a push toward fully electric and hybrid vehicles instead of those that run on fossil fuels. In early 2023, *Automotive News* noted that Tesla, which makes only electric vehicles, had replaced BMW as the top luxury brand in the United States in 2022.[2]

In August 2022, California regulators voted to ban the sales of gasoline-powered cars in the state by 2035 and set quotas for small pickups or light trucks sold in the state to be zero-emission, plug-in hybrid, or powered by hydrogen. Other states are expected to adopt similar rules, further quickening the pace of EV sales. In November 2023, New Jersey announced a requirement for all new car sales to be electric by 2035, with the transition to start in 2026, when some requirements will need to be adopted by automakers.

The stock of an automaker may move on sales reports if results are disappointing, or there has been lackluster performance of a key brand(s), or if market share is being lost to a rival. With just about all car makers now offering one or more EVs, growth and performance in that category will be key data to watch in the foreseeable future.

BANKING

Contagion and liquidity, at one time, would more likely be associated with the fields of medicine and science. Both terms are now, however, firmly associated with, and very important to, the banking sector and financial markets. Contagion and liquidity were both immense concerns during the global financial crisis in 2008. It was precipitated by the subprime mortgage crisis, which started in the United States with the collapse of investment banking giants Bear Stearns and Lehman Brothers and spread to the rest of the world. The first bank that showed signs of problems from panic and massive withdrawals—also called a bank run—was Northern Rock in England.[3] A recap of the 2008 financial crisis is useful to provide context and a broad understanding of contagion, liquidity, and bank metrics that matter.

Bear Stearns was a well-known powerhouse investment banking firm on Wall Street. In 2008, it was the fifth-largest investment bank. Its demise was the start of what would become a large-scale crisis that caused economic distress in many banks and financial institutions worldwide, along with a severe downturn in the economies of many countries.

The problems at Bear Stearns started with a liquidity issue, when the value of assets at two of its hedge funds declined severely. That was because their investments in certain mortgage-backed securities started to lose value as house prices fell. A worsening economy had also caused many borrowers with high-interest (subprime) mortgage loans to fall behind or fail to make payments on those mortgages. It was very early in what would become the "subprime mortgage crisis" that brought about the 2008 economic meltdown. Simply put, US banks had given loans to people with impaired credit records, and when interest rates rose and property bubbles burst, borrowers started defaulting on their loan payments—and the banks that had signed up for this risky lending practice did not see this coming. The decline of the two hedge funds was exacerbated when traders started to redeem, or request redemptions, of their investments and the funds were unable to meet those obligations—a classic problem of a lack of funds or liquidity. The two funds eventually declared bankruptcy, and Bear Stearns received additional cash through a partnership deal.

Bear Stearns's problems ballooned when it reported its first ever loss in the fourth quarter of 2007 and wrote down its subprime mortgage portfolio by $2 billion. The credit rating agency Moody's cut its rating to junk in January 2008. That severely affected the bank's ability to raise enough capital, leading to the resignation of CEO James Cayne, who was succeeded by Alan Schwartz, then president and chief operations officer.

By March 2008, other credit rating agencies also cut Bear Stearns into junk territory. As a result, many trading partners stopped trading activity with the bank, worsening its cash crunch. The credit cuts and losses from reduced trading activities caused a "bank run," as clients withdrew or moved their deposits and investments. The Federal Reserve intervened at this point and lent $30 billion to JPMorgan to save Bear Stearns, backed by the caveat that the loan would not need to be repaid if Bear Stearns was unable to repay it.

The Federal Reserve ended up prodding JPMorgan to eventually buy Bear Stearns for a paltry $2 per share, tragically below the $170 per share it was trading at only a year earlier. The collapse of Bear Stearns caused great consternation because it cast light on murky investments in the portfolios of investment banks.

Banks suddenly pulled back and withdrew from the robust activity of lending to each other—a contagion that caused a liquidity crisis. The stories written by journalists analyzed and explained the news to consumers as market traders and analysts provided research on mortgage lending and foreclosures.

Lehman Brothers was another global financial services firm that also experienced a credit crunch because of portfolios heavy in subprime mortgage loans. Its difficulties further highlighted the problem of subprime lending and related investments, which would precipitate the 2008 financial crisis. Lehman Brothers was eventually sold off in parts.

With the failure of these two big financial entities and the resulting global repercussions, central banks worldwide intervened to inject and provide loans to financial institutions with very generous terms, and they also implemented other monetary measures.[4] Such actions were deemed necessary to preserve the integrity of economies and correct the functioning of the intertwined international financial system. This situation revived and popularized the term "too big to fail"—which was first used by a congressman in 1984 during hearings on a bank bailout—to capture the absolute importance of the biggest financial firms to their individual countries and internationally.[5] The crisis and cooperation of central banks resulted in new regulations on capital reserve limits and other standards for all banks, but especially the largest financial entities, which were deemed to be "systemically important" or were considered too big to fail.

In March 2023, yet a different problem led to the failure of two significant banks, Silicon Valley Bank and Signature Bank. The latter, which was in New York City, focused on cryptocurrency and digital assets, and it became the third-biggest bank to fail, just two days after the failure of Silicon Valley Bank in California. Signature Bank was taken over by the New York Department of Financial Service after concerned depositors withdrew their assets after a 25 percent decline in the bank's stock price.

Silicon Valley Bank had invested a large portion of its assets in long-term bonds. With interest rates rising, the value or price of those bonds fell because they had lower rates. When customers heard that Silicon

Valley Bank might be experiencing cash problems, they started withdrawing their money, causing a classic bank run. The bank was forced to sell its bonds at lower prices, or at a discount, but the proceeds were insufficient to cover the billions of dollars of withdrawals. The Federal Reserve assumed control of the bank and agreed to cover all its deposits, even those above the $250,000 limit on insurance by the Federal Deposit Insurance Corporation (FDIC).

The fate of Silicon Valley Bank once again threatened contagion and a liquidity problem, this time among regional banks in the United States, many of which are integral lenders to small businesses. Analysts, pundits, and government representatives have questioned why regulators did not uncover the situation with Silicon Valley Bank, which caused concern about the possibility for additional (regional and small) bank failures, or banks under duress, and consequently had implications for the economy. One point noted is that the bank did not have a chief risk officer for most of 2022, which is when its problems started before becoming a full-blown crisis in 2023.

BANK METRICS

Although banks run the gamut from being small or midsize enterprises that are primarily depositories of money and lenders to vast, cross-border operational entities, attention to certain metrics can indicate how sound and stable their operations are.

Net Interest Margin

The basic function of a bank is to be a depository of customers' money and a lender of money. These two activities account for the important bank metric of net interest margin (NIM). The NIM is the difference between the interest banks pay on deposits and its loans (interest expense) and the interest received from payments by borrowers on loans, divided by average earning assets—which are assets that are earning income. The FDIC describes NIM, which is expressed as a percentage, as "a key profitability ratio."[6]

A positive NIM means the bank is receiving more interest than it is paying out. A negative NIM would therefore be cause for concern because the bank's interest expense would be higher than its interest income.

Net Interest Income

Net interest income is also called net interest revenue. Stated in dollars, it is the difference between money received from interest on assets, such as various loans and investments, minus the cost of interest paid on customer deposits. This metric, like NIM, can indicate a bank's ability to balance liabilities relative to generating income from its assets. An imbalance between generating income and being able to meet its liabilities or obligations, is what caused problems for Silicon Valley Bank in California and led to its failure—the second-biggest bank failure in US history.

Common Equity Tier 1 Ratio and Tier 1 Capital Ratio

The Common Equity Tier 1 (CET1) and the Tier 1 Capital Ratio are risk-based capital requirements. They have minimum levels that banks, especially large ones or globally systemically important financial institutions, must meet. The requirements are set by the Basel Committee on Banking Supervision, which has representatives from several countries who set international regulatory requirements. CET1 must be at least 4.5 percent of risk-weighted assets, and the Tier 1 Capital ratio should be at least 6 percent of risk-weighted assets. But many financial firms, especially the "too big to fail" ones, will have a much higher ratio.[7] Tier 1 Capital is a measure of the strength of a financial institution.

The 6 percent requirement means that at least 6 percent of risk-weighted assets must be in Tier 1 Capital—such as common stock and reserves—that are easily accessible to maintain operations, if needed in the event of a severe loss. The Basel framework is subject to added proposals, which means that requirements for banks will likely undergo changes.

Nonperforming Loans

Stated as a dollar amount and also as a ratio, nonperforming loans refer to the amount of loans in default. These are classified as loans in default because payment has not been made for at least 90 days. If the ratio is high, it is a signal of more risk and losses. Nonperforming loans are important to note because they are assets that are not generating revenue.

Book Value/Share

The book value/share is a KPI that is used to measure the worth or value of the company or entity. Book value/share is compared with the stock price to indicate if the stock price, and the company, is overpriced or underpriced. Analysis and tracking of book value are used to indicate the health of the bank.

Other KPIs equally important to banks, brokerages, and other financial companies are assets under management; inflows and outflows; provision for loan/credit losses, which are funds set aside to account for loans that may be in default due to payments not collected; net charge-offs, which are the gross amounts of loans not recovered; and the net charge-off ratio, which is the debt a bank believes it may never recover.

COMMODITIES

Raw materials used in the production of any goods or services are called commodities. Usually, a company's supply chain begins at the point where a raw material is sourced, further developed, packaged, and turned into a finished product that is ready for sale—wholesale or retail. When a disruption happens at any point in the supply chain, it affects productivity and sales, and therefore also affects the company's stock, its particular industry, or financial markets as a whole.

Consider the example of Apple again. The company manufactures its iPhones in factories in China, where raw materials—such as copper, glass, plastics, rare earth elements, gold, steel tin, and zinc—are brought in to create the gadgets. During the COVID-19 pandemic, manufacturing activities at the Foxconn factories that produce Apple products were disrupted, as China went into lockdown and workers were not allowed to assemble the products. Raw materials were also not reaching the factories on time. The result was a shortfall of iPhone production that could not meet demand in the United States. Consequently, the share price of Apple dropped.

HEALTH CARE

In the pharmaceutical industry, billions get invested in research and development (R&D) with the hope of producing blockbuster drugs, but those efforts sometimes fail. The response of the US Food and Drug Administration (FDA) to the research results and data for a company's prospective drug can result in market-moving news. The market is always looking for hints and direction on the demand and viability of a new product, along with the continued prospects for an existing one.

Those companies that manage to produce even one blockbuster drug, or multiple marketable products that serve patients, are the ones likely to luck out and see gains in their share price over time because they are considered stable stocks with strong R&D. Sometimes very small companies also achieve scientific breakthroughs that can lead to big returns for shareholders.

Pharmaceutical companies are always faced with the threat of other new, more effective drugs and patents that could replace their existing products, or the expiration of their own exclusivity in the marketplace. They also have to balance developing good partnerships with suppliers and buyers amid competitive rivalry in the industry. Any of these scenarios can make headlines and move shares. It is especially important for health sector reporters to keep tabs on when the patent on a blockbuster drug is likely to expire, because once a drug loses its patent, smaller rivals and generic drug companies can start selling duplicate products at lower prices. Intellectual property rights to a drug that has a monopoly in the market is a big asset for any company. Any news that endangers that position, such as FDA concerns or consumer complaints, can have a massive impact on a company's share price.

Clinical Trials

It is a long journey for a drug from preclinical trial to final FDA approval and availability in the market. And all along this journey, a health reporter needs to be aware of the various stages of the drug during the development and approval processes. Any setback or a positive result can lead to market-moving news because it may eventually mean expediting or delaying the drug launch, affecting revenue for the company. Clinical trials are conducted in phases based on certain milestones or targets.

Preclinical Trials

Preclinical trials are the first stage, where companies announce how the drug or the medical formulation was received in the laboratory, typically by testing on animals. There is always a scientific metric that shows statistical significance—a term that endorses whether the drug has the potential to continue development for possible use in humans.

Phase 1

Phase 1 is designed to evaluate the "safety" of the treatment in humans.

Phase 2

Phase 2 is designed to evaluate the "efficacy" of the treatment and the dosage that works for a small and carefully selected sample of patients, some of whom get a placebo instead of the actual drug.

Phase 3

Phase 3 is designed to compare both "safety and effectiveness" in a larger group of people and the results with existing treatments. This phase is the most costly for companies, and its outcome defines whether the drug has the possibility to be commercially available for patients. The results are based on a scientific ratio that indicates whether it is "statistically significant" or not. Typically, companies file for FDA approval if this phase has been successful, but testing could also go to Phase 4 trial if the company is required to evaluate long-term side effects more carefully.

Data from all the stages are very closely watched by health reporters, who need to be able to comprehend medical writing and jargon. A journalist who covers health is adept and possesses the knowledge to understand if the outcome of a trial was significant. For example, any news about a drug trial "not meeting statistical significance" can send shares into a nosedive. Negative findings from any of the trials raise questions about the survival of the drug, so any abnormal results are scrutinized by financial traders and those who have invested in the company.

Primary Endpoint

When the results of the drug study appear promising to treat a specific disease or ailment, the company will put out a press release saying data collected showed its primary endpoint was met. Hurrah for the markets!

But it can be the opposite if the reverse were to happen, as it did in late 2022 for a small biotechnology company called Tricida, which was developing a drug for kidney disease. The trial did not meet its primary goal. Shares of Tricida slumped 94 percent, and everything went south for the company, which eventually had to file for bankruptcy. Interestingly, the same day that Tricida's stock nosedived, the shares of another biotech company, Vaxcyte, soared after it reported positive drug trial data.[8]

Secondary Endpoint

Sometimes a drug company will have a secondary datapoint to measure the success of its new drug—an additional positive result—which could further enhance the potential and revenues from the sale of the drug. For example, if a drug being studied for diabetes also starts showing positive results in treating baldness, the latter becomes the secondary endpoint, adding tremendous value to the drug. Another hurrah!

Stock movement related to drug trials often needs to be explained in lay terms by journalists who are aware of every stage of the trial and its potential consequences, unsuccessful outcomes such as adverse effects, a lack of efficacy, or primary and/or secondary endpoints not being met.

"A bad research study could be written about in such a way as to sound very promising, but if the precise 'statistically significant' wording was not used, I knew to quickly find the negatives that needed to be headlined," recalled Bethany Harshaw Bantle, former news Headliner. "Watching the graph fall for a biotech company when they had deliberately attempted to mislead investors was always quite satisfying."

FDA Approvals and Actions

As mentioned above, the gatekeeper for drugs is the FDA. Health care companies are required to keep the FDA updated on all trials and on research and development. Based on requests and submissions, the FDA has the authority to grant certain status to expedite new drugs or slow down the study by requesting additional data. Any action by the FDA is usually a market-moving announcement.

Fast Track Designation

When issued by the FDA for a particular drug trial, fast track designation allows a pharmaceutical company to expedite its development because the medicine may be effectively used to treat a serious condition and could address unmet medical needs. The FDA's designation is an indication that this treatment should be made available to patients in need, and the drug company can meet with the agency to make it eligible for a "priority review." It will then be on the fast track for approval to be sold in the market if requested clinical data continue to support a successful outcome. The stock market usually rejoices on such news. For example, in April 2023, a small biotechnology company called Agenus was granted a fast track designation by the FDA for its colon cancer treatment, which was still in its Phase 2 trial, sending its shares up 12 percent. In the same month, another biopharmaceutical company called KALA received fast track designation by the FDA for a drug that could treat persistent corneal epithelial defects—an impaired corneal problem for people with eye diseases. Shares of KALA rose 5 percent after the company announced this news.[9]

Orphan Drug Status

Orphan drug status is issued by the FDA for a drug or product with the promise to treat a rare disease or condition. This designation qualifies companies for certain incentives, such as tax exemption during clinical trials. For example, a Japanese pharmaceutical company called Sumitomo Pharma received an orphan drug status from the FDA in April 2023 for its Phase 1 trial of a treatment for a rare bone cancer called Ewing Sarcoma. The status also allows for seven years of market exclusivity for the drug. Similarly, in September 2022, Nasdaq-listed Amylyx Pharmaceuticals received orphan drug status for its drug that slowed the progression of amyotrophic lateral sclerosis, which could potentially delay death. The news sent shares of Amylyx up nearly 14 percent in extended hours trading.[10]

Vaccine Rollouts and FDA Concerns

At no time did the world watch FDA responses to clinical trials as it did when the COVID-19 pandemic raged worldwide in 2020 and 2021. In July 2020, a vaccine partnership between Pfizer and the German biotech firm BioNTech SE received a fast track designation for a coronavirus vaccine, which was in Phase 1 trial to determine "safety" in adults. The vaccines, BNT162b1 and BNT162b2, were the most advanced of at least four vaccines being assessed by the companies in ongoing trials in the United States and Germany. Pfizer's shares were up about 2 percent, and US-listed shares of BioNTech were up about 6 percent when the announcement was made before the bell on July 13, 2020.[11] Soon, Pfizer and Moderna, another biotech company that was also developing a coronavirus vaccine, became the leading companies to provide vaccines to boost immunity against the COVID-19 virus around the world. As their revenues soared in 2020 and 2021, they started looking for options to keep a steady monetary stream as variants became milder in 2022 and after.

In April 2023, Moderna reported mixed results for its messenger-RNA (m-RNA) shot for flu, but the outcome suggested there were not enough influenza cases to determine whether the result was "statistically significant." This did not help the shares, as investors were watching and wondering what else could Moderna do besides produce its one-time wonder vaccine for COVID-19. Moderna, too, was seeking to capitalize on its ability to replicate the m-RNA technology that worked well for its COVID vaccine, including signing partnerships with other pharmaceutical companies to work on new drugs.

Shares of Moderna had experienced an unprecedented rise of 434 percent in 2020, thanks to its successful vaccines. And then, in 2021, the shares rose an additional 143 percent. But in 2022, as the pandemic eased and demand for vaccines waned, Moderna's shares fell 29 percent. As of late 2023, the drug company was under pressure from the financial markets to prove its worth again after its blockbuster vaccine success.[12]

HOUSING

Quite like retail sales, housing data are revealed monthly, when real estate companies are expected to report data on new home sales in the

United States. These data are a barometer for the housing market and mortgage rates.

Key Performance Indicators used to measure home sales performance in the United States include home prices, how long a house stayed on the market before being sold, and mortgage and foreclosure rates. Whether people are buying or selling homes, home sales are a big reflection of demand and supply. One reason the sector is watched is because housing stocks are usually preferred as long-term investments. Journalists who cover the housing market are always conducting research, and they also look at how real estate investment trusts (REITs) are performing.

REITs hold a portfolio of housing companies, and their share movement is an indication of how the housing market is doing. For example, Kimco Realty Corporation, which trades on the New York Stock Exchange under the ticker symbol KIM, owns more than 400 properties across prime locations in the United States. In April 2023, BlackRock announced that it was buying 10.2 percent of KIM. At the time, there was a shortage of housing inventory because high demand caused home prices to soar in 2022.[13] Shares of KIM rose 2.25 percent after the acquisition as markets interpreted the BlackRock investment as a high demand for housing portfolio.

Analysts look at several key indicators to measure how the property market is doing, and journalists feed off the expert opinions of portfolio managers and economists, pushing the same thought processes to the financial trader. The next subsections outline the KPIs that analysts, reporters, and traders watch when housing companies and REITs release their monthly and quarterly financial statements. These metrics are leading indicators that also get headlined by newswire reporters.

New Home Sales

New home sales include newly constructed homes in a particular region and the demand, or lack of, from buyers.

Existing Home Sales

Existing home sales indicate the level of activity in the secondary housing market.

Days on the Market

Days on the market indicate how long a home has been listed for sale on the market, and provides insights into demand from buyers.

Inventory Levels

Inventory levels indicate the number of homes listed for sale at a given time, and provide insights into supply from sellers. High inventory levels indicate a buyers' market and more negotiating power for buyers.

INSURANCE

The payment of insurance premiums and payouts for claims are two primary activities for insurance companies. Also watched closely is whether any one-time or unusual catastrophic event occurred that would cause many claims to be filed and consequently cause significant payouts. Metrics for the insurance industry include the following.

Net Written Premium

Net written premiums include amounts received for premiums on insurance policies minus any premiums that are returned.

Catastrophe Losses

A catastrophe is defined as a natural disaster that results in any of these scenarios: $25 million or more in insured damage, at least ten deaths, injuries to at least fifty persons, and at least two thousand filed claims and/or homes or structures damaged.[14]

Total Combined Ratio

The total combined ratio is a measure of underwriting profitability; it is derived from incurred losses and expenses divided by earned premium. A ratio below 100 shows that the company is generating underwriting profit, while a ratio above 100 would indicate that it is paying out more for claims than it is receiving from premiums for policies.

MEDIA AND TELECOM

With respect to media and telecommunications, we are covering media, publishing, streaming, and telecom, and how the advent of technology has changed how people communicate and consume information. Technology has brought about the digital delivery of information and entertainment, which has caused an overlap of the services provided by traditional (or legacy) media and digital media companies. Digital media emerged from technological changes that coincided with the prolific use of smartphones and mobile devices, and also with advancement and digitization of telecommunication providers.

Options for getting information and entertainment have changed—for example, from a television screen to a mobile device, from viewing that could be shared in the presence of others and confined to what is on TV, to worldwide availability at any time for anyone. These options and delivery formats have merged the worlds of what is considered traditional/legacy media, digital publishing, streaming, and telecommunication. For example, Netflix provides content that is streamed or delivered via smartphones and other electronic devices through services from telecom companies. A physical newspaper is no longer needed for access to information, nor is access limited based on location or country.

Traditional/legacy media previously provided primarily news and information, and, based on the source, also entertainment. But like digital media, they can now offer products for direct purchase, and various services can be offered to subscribers and users, providing additional means of generating revenue. Both traditional/legacy and digital media companies are aiming to supplement and diversify their revenue source by figuring out innovative methods to boost their competitive advantage and lure more users and subscribers.

Case in point: ChatGPT. The initial $10 billion investment by Microsoft in this artificial-intelligence-driven writing algorithm sent its shares soaring as markets rejoiced about the possible future of Azure Cloud and the use of artificial intelligence in Microsoft's search engine.[15]

The *New York Times* is a major newspaper, but it offers separate subscriptions to sections such as cooking/food with access to recipes, various games, and sports content. And it tests household and other products, offers recommendations of the best in class, and gets a percentage of any sales of products made directly from its site based on the recommendations—a service that is also accessible only through a subscription. Television was limited to simply broadcasting advertisements. But now, with the use of a QR code in some advertisements, anyone watching can directly access a product or service immediately and initiate a purchase.

Apple is a technology company known for its mobile devices and software, but it also offers subscriptions to news and music, and it produces movies and serial programming. These overlapping services have made advertising and paying subscribers extremely critical sources for generating revenues for the companies, even as the revenue generation and subscriber growth chasm widens between legacy and digital media entities.

Advertising Revenue

While Walt Disney, a huge traditional media and entertainment company, earned total revenues of $40.89 billion in 2022, the digital publishing company Alphabet surpassed that considerably. Its main brand and unit, Google, generated $191.70 billion in advertising revenue, far ahead of other media companies in 2022. This was followed by Meta, which recorded $113.6 billion in advertising revenue. In contrast, a traditional media company such as the *New York Times* generated ad revenue of $520 million.

The example of the *New York Times* shows how consumers have migrated to digital sources for news and entertainment. Advertisers can use data analytics to hold media houses accountable for spending to boost impressions (views) and click-through rates. The global advertising revenue for traditional print publications has been on a downward spiral because of the rise of the digital consumption of information.

Amazon and Netflix are other examples of digital media firms that benefit from enhanced data capabilities that can be used to anticipate and offer content that users and subscribers may prefer. They are expected to surpass traditional television ad revenue in 2025, according to a report by PwC on the global telecom and entertainment and media outlook for 2023–27.[16]

Journalists, therefore, now look not only for KPIs but also for unexpected mergers and acquisitions or collaboration deals in the media and digital publishing industry. For example, the saga of Elon Musk taking over Twitter and renaming it X required adept reporting and analysis by journalists, especially given the significant impact on Twitter's financials as top advertisers slashed their spending after Musk's takeover, according to Reuters.[17] Another digital media platform that is closely watched is TikTok, which is owned by the Chinese company Bytedance. It is highly anticipated that the company will announce its initial public offering at some point, with its annual growth rate expected to be greater than Instagram, Facebook and YouTube.[18]

Subscription Revenue

The more offerings a media company provides, the higher the chances of it luring a consumer of its content to become a subscriber. Consumers seek engaging experiences and programming, prompting media companies to offer a wide range of services, such as streaming, gaming, and e-sports. In mid-January 2023, Netflix and World Wrestling Entertainment (WWE) signed a $5 billion, ten-year deal for streaming of its live WWE Raw show. The deal signaled Netflix's entry into live sports.[19]

Subscriber numbers are a critical component of revenue for some media companies because they may also determine pricing power—the leverage and flexibility the company has to change prices, usually by increasing them, based on operational targets and costs. Subscription revenue, however, may make up a smaller portion of total revenue compared with ad revenue based on the business model and operation of the media company. Subscribers are needed to drive advertising. Subscriber growth and advertising revenue have a dependent, symbiotic relationship for most companies.

According to a report by Salesforce, more than 65 percent of consumers subscribe to at least one streaming service.[20] But many are quick to unsubscribe if there are not new and innovative offerings, resulting in a significant churn rate, another KPI monitored by journalists. In April

2022, when streaming giant Netflix reported first quarter results that included the loss of 200,000 subscribers, its shares plummeted 35 percent, causing a $50 billion decline in the company's market value. Later, in the fall of 2022, during its third quarter, when the company reported a gain of 2.4 million net subscribers, its shares rose 14 percent on the news. And in the first quarter of 2023, Netflix's stock fell as much as 10 percent immediately after it reported earnings that included a number of subscribers below analysts' estimates. It recovered about half those losses the next day, however, as it closed just over 4.5 percent lower. In the fourth quarter of 2023, its higher-than-expected subscriber growth, which resulted in earnings that beat estimates, and strong earnings guidance for the first quarter, caused the stock to rise more than 8.5 percent in after-hours trading. It traded up to 14 percent higher when the market opened and closed with a gain of almost 11 percent.

AT&T, a traditional telecom company, also saw its stock fall sharply after reporting first quarter results in 2023 on fewer "postpaid wireless mobility subscribers." Those results, along with "free cash flow" that was also well below expectations, caused its stock to decline by over 11 percent. Free cash flow, which is a measure of the financial health and profitability of a company, was particularly important to analysts because AT&T was not showing subscriber growth. With the possibility of worsening economic conditions forecasted for later in 2023, the concern was that the company's results could deteriorate further.

Media companies must constantly innovate to provide a variety of services that are profitable while also ensuring that advertising revenue increases. This is reflected in financial statements under "average revenue per user (ARPU)," which is the revenue that can be attributed to a single subscriber based on the difference between what the subscriber pays for the service—the direct revenue from the subscriber—and spending or costs to gain or keep the subscriber.

Media companies also rely on various methods to attract advertisers—traditionally based on subscriber numbers and demographics. But with the prolific use of digital devices, innovative methods such as influencer marketing, live streaming of events to promote products and services, and publication of sponsored content are all increasingly being used as means of advertising. The Salesforce survey also showed that 65 percent of media and entertainment professionals reported that their companies had partnerships with influencers to promote products and services to attract users to their platforms. Whether a traditional/legacy, digital media, or telecom provider, the company's performance will be largely dependent on subscription growth, advertising revenue, and spending costs.

RETAILERS

While each company has to declare quarterly or half-yearly earnings, some retailers have added pressure to report monthly sales. For journalists covering the retail sector, it is an endless stream of work because the health of a retailer can also be indicative of the health of its economy. If retailers declare better-than-expected sales, this shows that people have the money to purchase products. Positive or negative coverage of retail sales performances or trends often leads to analysis and insights by journalists about affordability and purchasing power—all of which affects investor sentiment, leading to buying or selling in the stock market. Reporters are always quick to interpret and analyze data and its significance and write insightful pieces about consumer behavior and spending, which can further affect how investors react in the market.

Same Store Sales

Same store sales is a metric used in the United States for monthly retail sales of all the stores that have been operational for one full year. Same store sales are a key performance indicator for markets. If a retailer's monthly results are better than those of a year ago, or better than what analysts were expecting, it shows that consumers are buying their products. For example, home improvement retailer Home Depot reported better-than-expected same store sales in December 2019, sending its shares up 3 percent in premarket trading, and journalists wrote about how this was a sign of strong consumer demand for housing supplies.[21]

In their stories, journalists highlight the "why"—what is making this retailer perform better than its competition, for example. Such positive news can increase the demand for the retailer's stock and drive up its share price. Similarly, if same store sales are not as expected, the negative news can reduce demand for the shares, trigger selling, and cause a decline in the share price.

Another important news element the market watches is forward-looking statements. Any outlook or forecast provided by the company can provide insight into the retailer's ongoing and future performance potential, which can result in changes in its stock price. Conversely, skepticism about the future or any hint of things going awry can suggest to the market that the retailer may not be able to drive sales at a good pace in the future, negatively affecting the share price of the company.

Black Friday, Cyber Monday, Prime Day, and Holidays

Black Friday marks the beginning of the holiday season and is the day after the Thanksgiving holiday, which is the last Thursday in November, in the United States. It is also the day when retailers mark down their products to offer huge discounts and sales. The charm of December holiday season kicks in, and customers begin to think of Christmas and shopping for gifts, which is what retailers are aiming to provide by enticing shoppers with discounts, for strong sales to lead to increased revenue.

Why is it called "Black Friday"? The answer goes back to pre-technology days, when ledgers were maintained by accountants in various colors; red indicated an operating loss and black meant profits. The term was coined to indicate that sales promotions, deals, and discounts could end up turning a company's books from losses (red) to profits (black) for the year. In the days when sales were only done at physical stores, in many instances people would line up overnight or hours before the stores' openings to take advantage of hefty discounts.

There is also the question of brand loyalty; some customers wait for Black Friday sales at their chosen outlets to bag amazing deals on their favorite products. If the company does not live up to the expectations of such consumers, it could lead to disappointment and a negative market reaction. For example, in November 2022, ahead of Black Friday, the stock of the iPhone maker Apple fell 2 percent on news that production had been adversely affected at its Foxconn factory in China due to

COVID-19 and a shortage of workers.[22] It did not help that investors were also nervous about inflation and a possible interest rate hike by the US Federal Reserve.[23]

The Monday after Black Friday has also turned out to be a huge bonanza for online retailers. Cyber Monday, as it is called, is the day when online deals are prolific and shoppers spend to avoid crowded stores. They also snap up last minute discounts on residual sales that retailers may highlight after Black Friday shopping. It was this Monday that stood out in 2020, when COVID-19 scared shoppers away from stores, so they all went online, instead. Cyber Monday sales reached $10.8 billion in 2020, up 15 percent from a year ago, and was the biggest US e-commerce day ever, according to Adobe Analytics Data.[24]

Then there is the Prime Day sales event by Amazon, which initially took place on July 15 to celebrate Amazon's birthday, and then switched to October, before returning to mid-July again after COVID. It runs over two days and is packed with deals for Prime members of Amazon.[25]

As online shopping became a craze, the success of Black Friday led e-commerce companies to want to replicate similar promotions online. Cyber Monday and the weeks leading up to Christmas play an oversize role in the sales performance of retailers and how the market reacts to news regarding their financials. This holiday season period is considered the most crucial period for retailers, both for those online and for brick-and-mortar stores.

Journalists who cover retail keep tabs on prior year and year-to-date performance so they can make a quick comparison when new sales figures are released. They are also aware of analysts' expectations for a particular retailer's performance. Shopping, or a lack thereof, during the holiday season is a noteworthy indication of consumer spending and economic growth prospects.

Back-to-School Season

Back-to-school is the period from early to late August before most schools in the United States resume classes. It is considered the second-biggest sale season after the holiday period that follows Thanksgiving into the New Year. Before back-to-school sales actually begin, news organizations prepare their reporters to get pre-sales stories ready, which are more forward-looking and alert the public and markets about what to expect for back-to-school merchandise, how expensive they may be, styles that are trending, and what it means for consumer spending.[26]

During the COVID-19 pandemic, the back-to-school season faced a lot of uncertainty for retailers because classes were online, with children studying at home in their pajamas. COVID-19 hit the bottom line of many retailers: some reduced their workforce and cut salaries, while others went bankrupt. US companies like GAP Inc., Children's Place, and Urban Outfitters saw weaker-than-expected sales as families abandoned their usual back-to-school shopping. It was all doom and gloom for reporters as they wrote about the lack of sales during what would normally be a fairly busy season in America, and all of that spilled into a negative reaction from the markets. GAP shares hit a 52-week low in early April 2020.[27]

SUGGESTED ACTIVITIES

1. Why are the monthly same-store sales figures compared with year-ago figures and not with those of the previous month?
2. Typically, which one brings in more money for Media companies—advertising or subscription revenue, and why?

How Alibaba's Merry-Making on Singles Day Got Smashed within a Week in 2023

The world's largest online shopping festival happens on November 11 every year in China. It all began in 1993, when a bunch of single men at Nanjing University earmarked that day to celebrate their single status. The "Singles Day" is a spin on the four single numbers, 11.11, in the date, and Chinese trivia also notes that the number 1 resembles a stick or bare branches—*pinyin* in Chinese, which is slang for an unmarried man. Many bars and restaurants host singles parties on this day in China, and some also believe it is a perfect day to proclaim their love for someone or propose marriage. It is a national holiday, and has become a "bargain hunting bonanza," with discounted prices everywhere.

Alibaba, a multinational e-commerce and technology company, cashed in on this opportunity in 2009 by launching the Singles' Shopping Festival on its e-commerce platforms Taobao and TMall. In 2019, online shoppers in China spent $60 billion in 24 hours. A year later, when the world was reeling from the pandemic and almost everyone was shopping online, Chinese consumers spent $74 billion on Alibaba's retail platforms. In 2022, the total value of goods sold during the "Double 11" shopping bonanza was $157.97 billion, according to Bain, the consultancy firm.

Publicly listed American companies, too, have a presence on Alibaba's Tmall marketplace and reap benefits from this mega sale event. In 2023, whopping sales were experienced by Apple, L'Oreal, and Nike, with the shoe company declaring that demand from Gen Z consumers grew by 45 percent during this period. Alibaba's rival company, JD.com, said Apple sold more than 1 billion yuan worth of products in a minute on that day.

Alibaba lists its shares in the Hong Kong Stock Exchange as well as the New York Stock Exchange. Despite all the merry-making after its Singles Day sales in November 2023, it experienced market rejection within a week after it put out a press release announcing it had scrapped plans to spin off its cloud business amid uncertainties, because of restrictions by the United States on semiconductor chips. It goes without saying that the press release got ample love and attention from news Headliners. Alibaba's shares in the United States fell 8.5 percent and down 10 percent in Hong Kong, as the market viewed this as an unstable business environment for the company.

6

MERGERS, ACQUISITIONS, AND RESTRUCTURING

What is your growth strategy? That is a question journalists, analysts, and portfolio managers frequently ask senior executives, especially at the end of an earnings period, because companies must find ways to boost their businesses, both organically and inorganically. More often than not, a growth strategy involves expanding the business by purchasing a subsidiary of another company, buying a smaller rival, divesting and/or spinning off a poorly performing unit, or introducing new products.

To expand its profit-making ability, a company needs enough capital to invest in new ventures and products. The company may procure funds by streamlining businesses, which means selling or exiting units, closing stores, reducing inventory, firing employees, and the like, all of which have an impact—positive or negative—on earnings. In the long run, however, streamlining a business or reorganizing it will likely lead to cost savings that can enable companies to invest in areas that show potential for growth.

Any new plan or strategy announced by a company is an opportunity for a journalist to dig deeper into its finance and operations. Positive news that involves growth is often communicated to the press at media events or in exclusive interviews. News that could affect markets negatively very often ends up carefully buried in the middle or at the bottom of a press release.

For example, a General Motors press statement on November 26, 2018, carried the headline, "General Motors Accelerates Transformation," and the first few paragraphs focused on how the largest US automaker was "optimizing capital expenditures to drive annual run-rate cash savings of approximately $6 billion by year-end 2020" and that it was "continuing to take proactive steps to improve overall business performance." While there is no disputing that this scenario was indeed likely to happen from an operations standpoint, journalists focused on the restructuring actions—plant closures and job reductions, found at the bottom of the press release.[1]

While mergers and acquisitions (M&A)—along with reorganizing or restructuring businesses—may eventually lead to growth, securing cash may not always be easy. Plans could fail and lead to a threat of bankruptcy.

The market is quick to pick up on telltale signs of a looming bankruptcy—an inability to secure additional credit, use of a valuable asset as collateral, lenders seeking payment and defaults on loans. This could also explain why companies are cautious about releasing press statements that indicate internal turmoil. Instead, the news is often found in annual statements and government filings, such as Securities and Exchange Commission (SEC) filings in the United States. In this chapter, we look at two growth strategies, M&A and restructuring, and how any hint or suspicion of either activity can move markets.

M&A

One of the first things business reporters understand when they start digging into documents related to mergers and acquisitions is this: almost never is a deal ever a "merger of equals." More often than not, it is one party either buying the other one or owning a larger stake in the company. One way to determine which company may have the upper hand is from the new executive positions—which company's official is being named CEO, or is slated to take over after the transaction is approved or completed.

Among the ten largest M&A deals worldwide, as of December 2022, seven involved American companies.[2] However, on top of this list sat a deal in Europe that underwent unexpected twists and turns—giving sleepless nights to journalists who had to keep up with the details—before an agreement was finally signed. This was the acquisition of the German company called Mannesmann AG by Britain's Vodafone Group in 1999 for $190 billion—the most expensive M&A deal in history, and an unsolicited one. The deal almost did not happen. The first time the management of Vodafone approached Mannesmann with a proposal, the German maker of steel pipes and telecommunications rejected it. Vodafone doubled its offer, and finally, after three months, the board of Mannesmann agreed, creating a new company with a market capitalization of $350 billion.[3] Let us use this example to explain what an unsolicited bid is, and compare it with a hostile one, another type of M&A strategy.

Unsolicited versus Hostile Bids

Vodafone made an unsolicited bid to buy Mannesmann. In other words, Mannesmann was not looking to be sold or soliciting an offer to be bought, but Vodafone needed to expand further into Europe, so it made an "unsolicited" bid. The management and board of the German company rejected the offer, calling it "brutal behavior" and "predator capitalism."[4] The works council, a group that represented Mannesmann employees, even organized a brief strike to protest the takeover.

The company even adopted its "Declaration of Düsseldorf," in which Mannesmann's works councillors, or the elected representatives for about 75,000 of its employees in Germany, declared that they were strongly against the offer and saw it as a "flagrant disregard of our company culture."[5] A week later, the president of Vodafone, Chris Gent, sent an open letter to employees of Mannesmann assuring them that no one would lose their jobs.

After a bitter three-month battle, Mannesmann succumbed as Vodafone went hostile, going straight to shareholders with an offer they could not resist—58.96 Vodafone shares for each Mannesmann share they held, an 84 percent premium on the value of Mannesmann's stock.[6] Vodafone agreed to hold 50.5 percent of the company, making it the bigger stakeholder. The deal created the world's largest mobile phone operator.[7]

Companies make unsolicited offers to buy other companies for many reasons: for access to a unique tool or product, to expand in another region, to increase market share, or to limit competitors by creating a larger company.

Unlike the Vodafone-Mannesmann case, which was an unexpected, unsolicited bid and a hostile takeover, a solicited bid is a friendly acquisition approved by managements of both sides. For example, when Facebook acquired WhatsApp in 2014, it was a friendly takeover with no resistance from the management of WhatsApp. Both companies stood to benefit: not only did WhatsApp get $19 billion, it had an instant opportunity to expand its users; and for Facebook, it was also the instant acquisition of a large data set of 450 million users worldwide.

Any news about M&A can cause market activity to increase significantly, especially if it is unsolicited or hostile. The subsequent direction of the share prices of both companies indicates market sentiment about the bid. For example, when Men's Wearhouse made an unsolicited proposal to buy Jos. A. Bank in 2013, the shares of both men's retailers rose—Men's Wearhouse went up 27.8 percent; and Jos. A. Bank, 6.4 percent—indicating that the market was in favor of this deal. (Ironically, just a few weeks before this, Jos A. Bank had made an unsolicited bid for Men's Wearhouse, which the latter rejected.) After six months, Men's Wearhouse sweetened its offer to $63.50 per share, up from its previous offer of $57.50, for its smaller rival Jos. A. Bank.[8] Shares of Men's Wearhouse jumped 7.5 percent, while Jos. A Bank's shares increased 9 percent on the new offer, and the deal was sealed.

Underscoring the need for accuracy and interpretation, news Headliner Karen Mielcarek recalls how she handled a press release on a merger: "I crafted a headline that accurately portrayed what the company was saying, so I had the confidence in my interpretation, but after I sent that out . . . I watched the stock drop more than nine dollars in about 10 minutes. I remember thinking 'I really hope I'm right or else I just tanked a stock.'" Mielcarek was relieved that her interpretation was accurate when the companies announced two weeks later that they had cancelled the merger.

Poison Pill

A poison pill is hard to swallow, and that is exactly the strategy a company can use to prevent another company or shareholder from making an unsolicited attempt to buy it. It is incorporated in the bylaws and protects the target company from being acquired by capping the acquirer from buying more than the designated number of shares to launch a bid, so the would-be acquiring company is not able to cross the ownership threshold. This poison pill strategy also enables the shareholders, other than the bidder, to acquire more shares at a discount, thereby diluting the shareholding of the bidder and making the bid less appealing. This strategy is also called a shareholder rights plan.

For example, the auction house Sotheby's had a poison pill in place as part of its shareholder rights plan. So, when Third Point, a hedge fund owned by one of its billionaire investors, Daniel Loeb, attempted to increase its stake to more than 10 percent, the poison pill was triggered and other shareholders were allowed to buy more shares of Sotheby's, raising its valuation. Loeb took Sotheby's to court to challenge the shareholder rights plan. As reporters kept tabs and wrote about the court case, shares of Sotheby's took a beating, falling 16 percent in a span of five months. But they rose nearly 2 percent in May 2014, when news of a settlement was flashed on screens, saying Loeb could now raise his stake in the company to 15 percent from the 9.6 percent cap, making it possible for him to join Sotheby's Board of Directors.[9]

White Knight

As the term "white knight" suggests, this is the company that rescues a target company (like a knight in shining armor) from an unsolicited offer by striking a friendlier deal, which is a more suitable alternative to an unsolicited or hostile bid. A white knight is the savior company, and this is a preferred option for a target company that is facing a hostile bid.

In 2006, the European pharmaceutical giant Merck AG made an unsolicited bid to buy the smaller German drugmaker Schering, which Schering rejected. Then arrived the white knight, Bayer AG, offering €86 per Schering share and outbidding Merck's €77 proposal.[10] The market welcomed the Bayer-Schering combination because Bayer's growth would benefit from its acquisition of Schering's top-selling birth control drug, Yasmin, and its multiple sclerosis treatment, Betaseron. An interesting coincidence is that it was the American drug company Merck &

Co. that ended up buying smaller rival Schering-Plough, which was an affiliate company of the German company Schering many years ago.

Accretive or Dilutive

An important bit of information that reporters are keen to check in an M&A press release is whether the deal will add (i.e., be accretive) to the acquiring company's earnings or hurt it (be dilutive). For instance, the friendly drug deal that happened when Pfizer bought Wyeth in 2009 had quite a few interesting facts that prompted journalists to analyze the acquisition carefully. One of them was that the deal was not "immediately accretive" to Pfizer's earnings—it would only add to its profits in the second year.[11] This meant that there would be some monetary damage to Pfizer's balance sheet in the near term, but it was worth biting that bullet because Wyeth would bring in a host of new medicines and vaccines before Pfizer's blockbuster cholesterol drug, Lipitor, lost its exclusivity status in the market. Pfizer even had to reduce its dividend payout to pay for the deal, and it announced job cuts as it closed some manufacturing facilities. Luckily for the drugmaker, it received additional funding through credit facilities to offset the impact of cost cutting.

Pfizer thought it was doing the right thing in buying Wyeth and increasing its repertoire of drugs, especially when its blockbuster medicines were reaching patent expiration. But Pfizer's shares fell 10 percent on the back of the announcement, as traders saw near-term losses from the deal.

M&A Advisers

Does the market care about which financial firms provide advisory services in an M&A deal? You bet it does. These are provided by reputable investment banks that advise companies for a sizable commission. If they have a track record of success and the market is interested in an M&A proposal, other stakeholders will start buying the shares of the companies, anticipating a final deal that will benefit all parties.

So, bearing all the above points in mind, Headliners will have a few "macros," or saved templates, that allow them to push out short news headlines the moment a press release arrives on their screens. These days, an algorithm will do it for them, of course.

Here are examples of typical M&A headlines—the key is to type clearly and precisely first, and interpret later:

ABC TO BUY XYZ
ABC TO BUY XYZ IN A STOCK AND CASH DEAL
ABC TO BUY XYZ FOR $25/SHR
ABC TO BUY XYZ FOR $980 MLN
ABC SAYS DEAL TO ADD TO EARNINGS IN TWO YEARS
ABC TO TAKE ON $XX DEBT OF XYZ
ABC SAYS COMPANY YY IS M&A ADVISER

When the first draft of the story urgently goes out in less than 10 minutes, the reporter should have ideally calculated the "premium," and that is a formula that most journalists who cover M&A know by heart:

PREMIUM = (ACQUISITION PRICE PER SHARE – (MINUS) XYZ CLOSING PRICE), DIVIDED BY XYZ CLOSING PRICE.

So if ABC offers to buy XYZ at $25 per share, and XYZ's stock closed yesterday at $22 per share, this means ABC is offering to buy XYZ at about a 14 percent premium.

RESTRUCTURING

While "reorganization" and "restructuring" are often used interchangeably, the dictionary definition highlights a slight difference. Restructuring is to change the makeup, organization, or pattern of something; and reorganization could include the financial reconstruction of a business concern (*Merriam-Webster*). More often than not, when there is a merger or acquisition, the companies need to reorganize and restructure, often resulting in redundancies or job losses. Since both words refer to changing the existing structure of something, whether financial or not, here we use these words interchangeably as having the same meaning.

When a company releases news about a restructuring, it tends to highlight its cost savings, as seen in the example of General Motors given above. A journalist is interested in knowing what is being cut, and what changes are being made to achieve cost savings. "Restructuring," "reorganizing," "streamlining," and "downsizing" are all words that indicate significant changes and possibly a company's shift in strategy.

When a company streamlines its operations, it means there will be expenses for items such as severance, supplier and/or vendor contracts, and inventory, all of which can be written off by the company as a one-time charge. Depending on the company's business and the action announced, journalists will want to know a number of things: How many plants or stores will be closed? How many workers will lose their jobs? What costs or one-time charges are expected? How will the action affect the outlook or forecast for the next earnings period? This last question will be intriguing to a stock market trader because any change in a company's forecast or outlook is a reflection of its future strength and financial health. This is exactly why it is very important to "stick to their wording" while headlining a press release—this is the kind of instruction every Headliner will receive. In those speedy seconds of making news judgments, you really do not have time to figure out whether the company "means something" or is "hinting at something else," and precision is key.

"I remember 'precision of words' being something our team leader would repeat to us: both in how we used language and how we needed to be investigators into the wording of what we might be reading," said news Headliner Bethany Harshaw Bantle. "Obviously, exact figures and facts would move the markets, but looking out for the tiny, seemingly insignificant wording in a carefully crafted press release could lead to us gathering news that another agency hadn't paused to investigate."

Companies are just as aware of market reactions to news and hire copy writers who understand the subtle art of wrapping bad news inside a bouquet of flowery writing. Digging that out and interpreting what they actually mean, especially while rushing in and out of press releases could be a recipe for disaster. This is why sticking to their precise wording is the best thing, and later jumping back in to call their investor relations or corporate communications person would be the next best thing.

"At a basic level, a (press) release might list restructuring as a positive, and detail some new hirings or company divisions. But if we called and asked how many positions were being cut, we could gain some information that was not in the original release. They were typically hidden in less obvious wording, but trying to think why the author of a press release might choose certain wording could lead to a bigger story. The lack of word precision could also lead investors down an incorrect path," reiterated Bantle.

"I can remember sending a headline and then watching the share price rise or fall in an unexpected way and having the sinking feeling that my less-than-precise wording may have caused that!"

The market always seeks clarity: Will the impact of the restructuring be accretive or dilutive to earnings? The news could also be taken as reassurance that the company is on track to sustain itself and increase revenue, as traders are well versed about a company's operations and its industry. For example, General Motors' streamlining of its operations in November 2018 was seen as a turning point in the North American auto industry, according to a Reuters article.[12] The restructuring, which involved reducing slow-selling sedans and slashing its workforce, was understood by traders as shifting capital to drive innovation and create electric vehicles. Shares of General Motors did not fall that day; they rose almost 8 percent after the announcement.

JOINT VENTURES, CONTRACTS, AND LICENSES

While M&A deals make headlines, the markets are also always interested in partnerships between two companies. Why do companies want to partner with others? In short, they want to expand and have their products reach more consumers or clients. It could be by entering another market, benefiting from a new product that would complete its existing product line, boosting distribution, adding an asset that complements its existing one, or even just for the advantages of brand alignment. Partnerships are more amicable than M&A deals because both companies continue existing on their own terms but can still benefit from each other; this is a mutually beneficial agreement to boost revenue, which is easier than a complete buyout. There are many ways to do such deals, and often companies involve M&A advisers to help draft a legal agreement to ensure that no one gets a raw deal.

A joint venture is when two companies partner to start something new because one company could not do it alone. For example, Google and NASA have been working together on many things since 2005: Google Earth, Mapping, and the like.[13] Markets love this kind of partnership; it shows the promise of new things to come. The companies can also decide to create a new company to focus on new ventures without channeling resources away from the parent companies. A disadvantage of this kind of joint venture can be governance. A lack of good leadership or management can cause problems in executing the agreement, so the market is always looking to see who will lead the new initiative.

An example of a successful partnership is MillerCoors—a joint venture created by Molson Coors and SABMiller to distribute beer in the United States and Puerto Rico. The companies expected savings of $500 million a year because of this venture, the creation of more jobs, and projected additional revenue of $6.6 billion. Shares of both companies soared when the joint venture was announced in 2007 after news reports showed that beer sales had been flat in the United States and the venture would help them succeed in the market.[14]

A strategic partnership such as MillerCoors is mutually beneficial. Other such examples are of Google partnering with Luxxotica, an eyewear company, to invent the Google Glass. Samsung partnered with Spotify to bundle audio streaming into its Android phones. Microsoft formed a joint venture named Caradigm with General Electric to provide technology and data to improve health care.

Many partnerships are also struck in the form of contracts, where the agreements have an expiration date, which may be renewed. There are set deadlines and Key Performance Indicators to assess whether the partnership is working.

Mergers and acquisitions are typically a lot of fun to cover: the story brings a reporter closer to their sources (after all the calls, emails, and texts), and the learning that comes as the drama unfolds is considerable. The anecdotal example given below is one that corporate journalists will never forget, for it had all the makings of an edge-of-the-seat thriller, as Elon Musk provided enough material to keep journalists and investors awake at night.

SUGGESTED ACTIVITIES

1. If Company M offers to buy Company P in an all-stock deal on Monday for $14.50 per share, what is the premium if Company P's stock closed at $9.89 on Friday?
2. Find at least two market reactions, one where a company's stock price went up and one where it went down, after it announced it was restructuring its business.

Markets Went on a Roller-Coaster Ride as Elon's M&A Drama with Twitter Unfolded

The Twitter M&A saga began on January 31, 2022, when a delayed SEC filing by Elon Musk revealed that he had gradually increased his Twitter stake to 5 percent, giving him voting rights on the board. Musk soon started tweeting about the lack of "free speech" on Twitter, and then, on Saturday, April 9, 2022, five days before proposing to buy Twitter, he asked his followers this: "Is Twitter dying?" He pointed out ten celebrity accounts—which included those of himself, Barack Obama, Justin Bieber, and Taylor Swift—and said, "Most of these 'top' accounts tweet rarely and post very little content."

On that Monday, shares of Twitter opened about 2 points below their Friday close as shareholders, influenced by Musk's remarks, offloaded some shares over the weekend. On April 4, 2022, an SEC filing revealed that Musk, the world's wealthiest person, who had 80 million followers on Twitter, had boosted his stake to 9.2 percent, owning a $2.9 billion stake, making him the largest shareholder of the social media platform.[15] Shares of Twitter surged as much as 27 percent on the announcement, which journalists dug up from an SEC 13D filing.

On April 13, 2022, another 13D SEC filing revealed that Musk had not only boosted his stake but was also proposing to buy Twitter at a 54 percent premium on the share price on January 28—the day when he had slowly increased his stake to 5 percent in the company. He also said he would like to take the company private so it could become a platform for free speech. Twitter stock jumped 5 percent after journalists flashed news headlines that Musk was offering $54.20 a share, an 18 percent premium over the previous day's closing price!

Some shareholders rejected the offer, while others were interested but wanted more on the table. Twitter adopted the 'poison pill' strategy to prevent a hostile takeover by Musk, who had secured funding of $46.5 billion from lenders for the deal. He also sold Tesla shares to raise another $8.5 billion. Finally, the Twitter board agreed to sell the company to him on April 25, 2022, for $44 billion.

Shares of Twitter Inc. rose more than 5 percent, to $51.70 per share, as the markets felt the deal was cemented.[16] But, on July 8, 2022, Musk backed out of the deal and placed it "temporarily on hold" because he was suspicious about "spambots" on Twitter.

Twitter shares fell 1.7 percent in premarket trading as markets got confused whether he would really pull out of the deal. With all the drama, the stock had erased all its gains in the weeks since Musk had disclosed his stake in the company, and it was trading at $36.80 per share on May 27, 2022—well below Musk's offer price of $54.20 per share.[17] Twitter hired lawyers and sued Musk, who then countersued.

What followed were nearly six months of disputes and recriminations between Musk and Twitter's board members. He finally closed the deal on October 27, 2022, for the original offer price of $44 billion, and he immediately fired Twitter's top four executives, including its CEO and the CFO, leaving 75,000 employees in limbo about their future. A day prior, he had walked into the Twitter office carrying a kitchen sink. He posted a video with a tweet—"Entering Twitter HQ—let that sink in!"

The owner of Tesla and SpaceX paid $54.20 to shareholders, and he turned Twitter into a private company named X Corp.[18] "The bird is freed," Musk tweeted when the M&A deal closed on October 28, 2022.

7

THE STOCK MARKET AND BEYOND

Sometimes, there is nothing rational about how and why markets move. It may depend on the "sentiments" of the moment, or irrational reasoning, and either can account for stock market volatility. Artificial intelligence, stock trading bots, and various algorithms are already performing some functions of financial traders, but an investor will still be a person with fluctuating sentiments and concern about their investments—or so we think.

This chapter looks at factors inside Wall Street (or any other stock market), as well as those beyond Wall Street, and how sometimes even journalists cannot understand why stocks move a certain way. The stock market does not always operate with logic.

INSIDE WALL STREET

A bit of trivia: Did you know that Wall Street got its name because of a wall in the seventeenth century built by the Dutch to keep the British away? The wall no longer exists, but the street's name stayed. This street in Lower Manhattan houses the New York Stock Exchange. For some reason, someone decided it was OK to refer to the New York Stock Exchange or the stock markets as Wall Street. Here are some company actions and events that impact "sentiments," and therefore move markets.

Initial Public Offerings

Public trading of company shares on the exchanges begins with an initial public offering (IPO), when the stock is offered on the exchange for the first time. Anyone can buy shares of a publicly traded company by having an account with a brokerage firm.

The price range of an IPO is usually set the day before the first trade. The price is very important because it reflects the amount that could potentially be raised from the initial offering. It is also an indicator of the success of an IPO, depending on the closing price at the end of the trading day, which every company hopes will be higher than the price at the start of trading. For a high-profile, highly anticipated IPO, the firm—or underwriter—that brings it to market carefully monitors trading and, if necessary, buys shares to prevent the closing price from falling below the IPO price. What often happens with IPOs is that the share price may experience somewhat of a surge—typically moving higher on the first few trading days from anticipation, excitement, and the availability of public participation. In the media, the IPOs of highly anticipated companies—especially those seen as unique and/or having a first advantage in a particular business—for example, Facebook (now Meta Platforms) and the rideshare and delivery company Uber Technologies—will be reported on and followed closely on at least the first few days after they start trading. How a newly listed company opens and closes on its first day of trading is indicative of the demand and sentiments of investors about the future of the company. For example, a private jet charter company called flyExclusive did not fare too well on day 1 of its market debut in November 2023; its shares opened at a price of $11.98 and closed at $6.85. Company officials blamed the stock's fall on "pressure from New York Stock Exchange officials that required flyExclusive to create more trading liquidity."[1]

The path to the first trade for an IPO begins with the company and its bankers marketing and publicizing the coming offering through what is called a "road show" over several months. The road show allows them to carefully time the IPO to capitalize on momentum that will, at least initially, propel early trading of the stock to push its price higher.

Secondary Offerings

An IPO, as the first availability of the stock, is the primary offering. After an IPO, in the future the company can issue more shares to raise funds via a secondary offering, also called a follow-on public offering. Shares sold in a secondary offering may either be newly created or existing shares owned by the company. A secondary offering of a company's shares may also be done with shares sold by shareholders to other investors. In those transactions, all proceeds go to the selling shareholders.

When new or additional shares are sold, they increase the total number of shares—or the "float"—in the market and have a dilutive effect on the ownership interest of shares owned particularly by large investors. Secondary offerings by existing shareholders are not dilutive because they do not increase the total number of shares already in the market. An increase of shares from a secondary offering may cause a decline in the stock because it "dilutes" the ownership interest of shares and decreases the earnings per share. Here is an example: A company with an initial public offering of 50 million shares, and earnings or net income of $25 million, will have earnings per share of 50 cents. If the company issued, say, about an additional 10 million shares, it would increase the total shares outstanding to 60 million, and earnings per share would decline to 42 cents, with net income of $25 million unchanged. An investor whose share ownership provided an interest of 2 percent would see their stake decline to 1.7 percent after the offering. Terms of all offerings, including IPOs, are outlined in a prospectus and/or a filing with the US Securities and Exchange Commission (SEC) in the United States.

Separate from the effect on earnings per share, a secondary offering or sale of shares may be viewed as negative by the market if it is thought to be a precursor to bad news or results from the company. Investors and journalists will try to gain insights, or rationalize the reason for selling, especially if certain company officials are among those selling stakes. Secondary sales may also affect the price of a stock based on the pricing compared with the current market value of the stock. If priced significantly or even reasonably below the current market value of the stock to generate high interest and sales, it could cause the price of the stock to fall as it adjusts to the secondary offering price.

However, sentiment toward a secondary offering can also be positive if the company is viewed as having high potential for growth. Issuing stock to raise money would therefore be justified and would further support the company and its growth aspirations, which could increase interest in buying the stock.

Dividends

A dividend is a distribution of a portion of earnings that some publicly traded companies make to shareholders. It is viewed positively when a company declares that it plans to begin to pay a dividend, because it means the company has more than enough funds for its operations and is financially sound and strong. The initial announcement from a company that it plans to start paying a dividend is important and is news that is greeted gleefully by investors and the stock market. The type of dividend (cash or stock) and the amount are important elements in a business story. Also important are details such as the regularity of the dividend (quarterly, semiannually, or annually), the date of the first payment, the date of record (which determines who is entitled to receive the dividend), and the ex-dividend date (the final date the stock can be purchased to be eligible to receive the dividend).

Separate from regular dividends, a company may also declare a "special dividend," which is a one-time distribution. This can also be done by a company that pays dividends regularly. A special dividend sends a positive signal to markets because it is an indication of financial strength and may likely give the stock a boost.

Once a company declares a regular dividend, the expectation is that it will keep paying it. A change that can be made is to increase the dividend, which is likely to have a positive effect on the stock. If, however, a company suspends or reduces its dividend, that is likely to cause a decline in the stock because of the negative financial implications. As mentioned above, dividends are paid based on earnings and the ability of a company to share profits with shareholders. So announcing a pause or lower dividend payments would indicate that the company can no longer allocate profits or funds for that purpose. It could be that funds are needed for different purposes for which the company needs to conserve cash, or it is not generating a profit to be able to pay a dividend—these are all some reasons that get investigated by journalists covering the company. Any reason given or hinted at by the company is newsworthy because it will indicate the strength of its business and operations and could cause analysts to reevaluate the ratings of the stock.

Preferred Dividends and Stocks

While regular dividends are part of a company's income statements, there are also "preferred" dividends that a firm gives out—which, as the word suggests—to "preferred" shareholders. Common shareholders are last in line to receive any assets from a company, especially if it should unfortunately file for bankruptcy.

Basically, large and profitable companies that have more than enough cash for their operations will seek to distribute some to shareholders. They are stable companies with consistent share prices that may not rise or fall significantly, but their constant dividend payments make them safe bets for shareholders.

Preferred stocks, on the contrary, are equity securities with features of stocks and bonds. Preferred stocks pay dividends that are higher than regular dividends and are paid out to shareholders who have preferential rights over common shareholders and get priority over liquidation proceeds if the company goes bankrupt. It is very rare, however, for journalists to write about preferred stock payments—except in cases where a significant amount of capital was invested by a known name.

Stock Buybacks

Another action that can be as positive as initiating or increasing a regular dividend is when a company announces a stock buyback or share repurchase. This means the company will act as an investor and purchase its own shares at various times at market prices. The total amount to be spent or value of shares to be bought will also be announced. Buybacks often cause an increase in share prices because they indicate that a company is financially healthy. One of many reasons companies do buybacks is because their stock is usually trading at a price that is below what is believed to be their true value and that of the company. So shares can be purchased at a lower cost, boosting their value to the holder when they move higher.

According to *Forbes Advisor*, some companies that executed the largest buyback programs in 2023 were Apple—$90 billion, for 3.4 percent of shares; Chevron—$75 billion, for 21.7 percent of shares; Salesforce—$20 billion, for 10.9 percent of shares; and Applied Materials—$10 billion, for 9.7 percent of shares.[2] At the end of November 2023, General Motors also announced a $10 billion stock buyback—the largest in its history—as well as a 33 percent increase in its dividend. The news caused the stock to trade at a high of 12 percent above the previous day's close. It ended the day with a gain of 9 percent on a volume of almost five times the prior trading day.

Stock Splits

A stock split refers to an action—a forward or a reverse split—that changes the number of shares outstanding and the price at which the stock trades but does not change the value of the existing shares held by shareholders. The most common forward stock splits are 2-for-1 and 3-for-1. But there are also 3-for-2 and 5-for-4 stock splits. Whichever is declared, holders get the multiple accordingly—for example, a 2-for-1 split doubles the number of shares one holds, but the stock price is halved—so the overall value of existing shares held remains unchanged.

Let us do a little math here to explain the points above. You are a shareholder with 100 shares valued at $50 per share, so you have shares with a total value of $5,000. The company announces a 2-for-1 split, which means each share has been split into two. Now you have 200 shares (instead of 100), but each share is valued at $25, not $50 anymore. But the total value of $5,000 has not changed. The advantage you have is that the forward stock split increases the number of shares you hold as well as those outstanding in the stock market, which means there are more shares available for people to trade. Sometimes it is difficult for average, main street or retail investors to invest in high-profile, profitable companies that are leaders in their sectors because of a high stock price. A stock split makes it less expensive, more affordable, and appealing to purchase for those investors.

The announcement of a stock split includes the date applicable for holders of record, the distribution date, and when the split-adjusted shares will begin trading. Forward stock splits often generate excitement and buzz, resulting in shares trading at a higher price after the announcement due to optimism that the price will go even higher over time. In March 2022, when Amazon announced a 20-for-1 stock split and an up to $10 billion buyback program, its stock rose 6 percent in after-hours trading.[3] If the split were applied to Amazon's stock at the time, the price would have changed from $2,785.58 per share to $139.28 per share, a much lower price, making it affordable for a retail or individual investor to acquire the shares.

A reverse stock split is the opposite of a forward split and is usually done because a company wants to boost a low stock price, by declaring, for example, a 1-for-5 split—for every 5 shares held, an investor will have the equivalent of 1 share. So 20 million shares outstanding would be reduced to 4 million. But again, the total value of existing shares held would be unchanged, as well as the market capitalization of the company. Here is the math again, to simplify: 20 million shares at 50 cents per share are valued at $10 million. A reverse 1-for-5 split will result in 4 million shares at $2.50 each, and the value will remain $10 million. Reverse stock splits are usually done to maintain the minimum share price of $1 per share required to stay listed on a US stock exchange.

Panic Selling

Buying and selling of stocks is the key activity that makes equity markets. On most days, buying and selling happens with normalcy, whether indexes go higher, lower, or are mostly unchanged. But certain news can trigger extreme concerns, which can occasionally cause widespread selling, leading to a significant decline in stocks—beyond any decline or even a sell-off that happens from time to time. Significant market declines could occur for many reasons—for example, disappointing earnings results, warnings about expected or upcoming results, negative news about one or more market sectors, analysts' downgrades, negative economic news, and geopolitical events.

A decline of stocks in the market for a day or more, while not a favorable situation, is considered orderly if the reasons previously stated can account for market activity. When the market falls because of heavy selling that is largely unexplained, it is considered irrational and can often be attributed to a rumor or hearsay about an impending announcement, resulting in panic and extreme selling activity because of fear and/or uncertainty about the future.

A well-known decline in the stock market occurred on October 19, 1987—known as Black Monday. The Dow fell over 20 percent at the end of trading that day. The crash of the US stock market that day spread globally, leading to steep declines in other markets around the world. With analysis over time, the market's worst day ever at that time has been attributed to certain trading activities. The sell-off was seen as cascading into panic selling or herd behavior once it started. As it worsened, there was speculation about the reasons and whether the markets would close or pause trading. A large number of mostly sell orders caused price imbalances at the open, so some stocks were not available for trading. That caused more anxiety among traders and investors, leading to more intense pressure to sell. A primary cause of the decline, however, was program trading, in which buy/sell orders were initiated automatically by computers for quantities of stocks, such as those in a benchmark index, when certain price levels were reached. One type of program trading that played a major role was portfolio insurance—gradually selling amounts of stock when the price is falling and doing the opposite, buying when the price of the stock is rising, but this was done through buying and selling stock index futures. One of the problems seen with portfolio insurance in 1984 was, "if a large number of investors utilized the . . . technique, price movements would tend to snowball. Price drops would be followed by sales, which would lead to further price depreciation."[4] This seemed to have played out on Black Monday and exacerbated the drastic fall of stocks. Margin calls for investors to add cash or securities to their margin account to maintain a value to cover their obligations were also cited as a factor. On the trading day before Black Monday—Friday, October 16— "triple-witching"—which is the simultaneous expiration of stock options, stock index futures, and stock index options contracts—also played a role by causing volatility close to the end of trading and in after-hours trading.[5] A record volume of 338 million shares were traded on the New York

Stock Exchange, and the loss of 108.35 points of the Dow would be the largest ever, before the next trading day, Black Monday.

The terrorist attacks on September 11, 2001, also led to a very sharp decline in stock markets worldwide. In the United States, the attacks happened about 40 minutes before the markets were due to open. The decision was made to close the exchanges, so no trading occurred. The severity and unprecedented nature of the attacks, which caused the horrific loss of thousands of lives, led to the markets being closed for an entire week. When trading resumed, the Dow fell 7 percent on the first day and 14 percent for the week, the Standard & Poor's (S&P) 500 Index declined 11.6 percent, and the Nasdaq was down 16 percent. Airline and insurance stocks had the worst declines. American Airlines Group, Inc., fell 39 percent by the end of the first day when trading resumed, and United Airlines Holdings, Inc., fell 42 percent.[6]

Similarly, when the COVID-19 pandemic started in March 2020, the S&P 500 fell 66 percent by March 23, 2020, from its peak recorded a month earlier. The sectors and industries that saw the worst impact initially were energy, industrials, and finance. Health care and consumer staples, in contrast, were better performers. They traded at low points of 72 and 76 percent, respectively, of their peak reached in February.[7] So, despite steep market declines from time to time, one-time disruptive events are likely to cause widespread panic selling and have a greater negative effect on stocks and companies that have a direct relation to the event.

Short-Selling

Short-selling is betting that a stock will fall or decline to a certain level. Investors who engage in short-selling borrow shares and then sell them, betting that their prices will fall from the levels at which they were sold. If or when the stock price falls, the investor then buys the stock at the lower price to return it to the lender, making a profit from the difference between the higher price at which it was sold and the lower price at which it is repurchased. Short-selling is risky and is not recommended for the average investor. It is done through margin accounts, which have specific regulatory requirements.

High volumes of short-selling of a stock can put pressure on the price, causing it to fall. Often, during the course of a trading day, when there may be no specific news about a stock or industry and no company announcement or event that produced news, short-selling may be the reason for a significant decline of a stock. Short-selling affects individual stocks but does not have a similar impact on the broader market in a similar way as panic selling and disruptive events.

Analysts' Ratings

Having in-depth knowledge about a company is critical for making an informed decision about whether to buy its stock. Analysts obtain information about the company and its operations that is not available in company reports, SEC filings, and other sources in the public domain. They conduct interviews with company managers and key personnel; with company or sector business partners, such as suppliers; and they extensively research a company to be able to critically assess its current operations and outlook. Analysts then produce research reports about the company and give recommendations for its stock: buy, hold, or sell (the latter is rarely given). These three main recommendations also include additional subcategories, such as strong buy, accumulate, overweight, underweight, and neutral, which are also assigned based on expectations of whether the stock may outperform or underperform.

An analyst recommendation of "buy" for a well-known or high-profile stock can cause the stock to move higher. The opposite reaction can be triggered by a sell, hold, or underweight recommendation. Based on the reputation developed from their reports and recommendations, as well as correct calls about stocks, an analyst can earn high respect from investors, resulting in much attention and news reports about their recommendation. These analysts are often on CNBC and Bloomberg TV sharing their viewpoints about markets and the expectation for a specific company's stock.

Stock movements based on analysts' recommendations are also more likely if more than one analyst issues the same recommendation for a stock. It is not unusual, however, for analysts to have different recommendations for a stock. In such a case, during the course of the day, the stock could trade steadily or show volatility, going up and down depending on the analyst's recommendation that holds sway in the market.

Trading Halts

Significant or notable market activity, when indexes move up or down, results from the collective movement of individual stocks. While buying and selling occur mostly uninterrupted, subject to the decisions of buyers and sellers and what they think, there are times when action will be taken to pause trading in a stock. This action, shown as a HALT—yup, in all caps on screens of traders—temporarily stops trading in a stock. Often, beside the HALT notification is a reference suggesting the reason, such as "News Pending," resulting in anticipation or rumors that cause significant movement in the share price of the stock after trading resumes. This can be negative or positive news. After the news is released, the stock will resume trading within a few minutes. A "trading halt" is a mechanism that helps to maintain orderliness of trading in a specific stock and the broader markets before significant and unexpected news is disseminated. It is also used when there is a significant imbalance between buy and sell orders and if there is an extreme move in the price of a stock for no accountable reason.[8]

Circuit Breakers

Stated simply, a circuit breaker stops trading for all stocks in the entire market and halts trading activity of any sort on the stock exchanges. While a HALT is issued for individual stocks because of pending news, the purpose of a circuit breaker is to pause trading to avert continued, widespread panic selling.

The first circuit breaker was set up after the stock market crash on Black Monday and was also used during the COVID-19 pandemic. In the latter instance, uncertainty caused a sharp drop that met the parameter for triggering a circuit breaker. In the United States, a circuit breaker is activated if the S&P 500 index falls first by 7 percent, then 13 percent and 20 percent.[9]

BEYOND WALL STREET

Be it Wall Street in the United States or Dalal Street in India, these are trading arenas comprising stock exchange floors where market traders used to once-upon-a-time scream numbers, yell on phones, gesture codes with fingers, and place orders on computer terminals. While a lot has changed with technology, and the trader's "pit" is no longer an arena, it is important to note that factors influence stocks that are not always linked to companies and their decisions. News that emerges from sectors beyond Wall Street, or any other financial district in the world, whether corporate or noncorporate, can make an impact on the sentiments of investors and, therefore, their investment decisions.

The other securities that affect the wallets of many shareholders include bonds, warrants, dividends, debentures, and derivatives, to name a few. Some of these are fixed income securities, for which the amount that investors receive is fixed. Let us take a look at why a business journalist who largely covers stocks should be interested in events that happen outside stock markets.

Bonds

When stock prices rise, bond prices generally fall. One of the first things financial journalists learn is the inverse relationship between bonds and stocks, and that a big difference between them is ownership. With shares, you invest in the equity market. With bonds, you invest in the debt market.

While stocks are made up of shares of a company, bonds are the money lent to a company or government by investors. While share prices can fluctuate, bonds give a fixed interest over time for a set period, including the principal amount at the end (maturity), and the return is often better than what a bank provides, which is why, for many investors, bonds are a safe haven.

But bonds are not always low risk. If the bonds were purchased from a company that goes bankrupt, that is the end of payments. But that is also true for shares.

In order to make money from shares, you need to sell them at the right time. With bonds, you are guaranteed a set amount every year (the yield) for the entire period of the bond.

In the United States, investors can invest in Treasury bonds and notes, which pay interest every six months until maturity. For Treasury bills, the payment is done only upon maturity. For corporate bonds, it depends on how a company has organized its debt payments; it could be monthly, quarterly, or even half-yearly.

Typically, when the stock market is strong, many people shift their investment strategy toward equities as bonds react inversely. When stock markets are bearish, people tend to be more cautious and head to save in the lower but steady returns of bonds.

How do stock market reporters interpret bond markets and look for stories in this sector? The demand for bonds is also linked to central bank decisions about interest rates. For example, if an investor bought a bond before the US Federal Reserve cut interest rates, the new bonds in the market will have a lower yield and the investor's bond will be more valued.

In 2022, as the world emerged from the COVID-19 pandemic amid rising inflation, the Fed raised interest rates. The economic worry was so high that both shares and bonds fell.

Credit Ratings

Another important debt to which reporters pay close attention—there are teams that monitor this in newsrooms—is corporate debt, or the ability of a company, or even a country, to pay back the debt it owes, and in which others have invested.

A credit rating—which is given by an agency such as Moody's Investor Service, Standard & Poor's Global Ratings, and Fitch Ratings—indicates whether a corporate bond is investment grade (i.e., it has a higher credit rating with lower risks) or high-yield (a lower credit rating, with higher risk). The latter are also called junk bonds.

Rating changes by the agencies help investors to decide where they may get higher returns—equities or fixed-income securities. Actions taken by rating agencies (e.g., Standard & Poor's, Moody's, and Fitch) on a company's credit rating are often done after market-moving news breaks but are important as they give investors a more complete picture of a company's value, said Susan Abbotts, a former news Headliner at Bloomberg News who specialized in covering actions by rating agencies. "Because of this, I took pride in my job and ability to provide this side of breaking news to our customers," Abbotts added.

Even the biggest blue chip companies sometimes need to borrow money to expand further or to pay back a loan. Journalists are quick to write stories about such fixed income securities that companies are likely to float. For example, in August 2022, Bloomberg broke a story, based on information in an SEC filing, about Apple seeking to do a capital raise for $5.5 billion through a corporate bond, which would mature in anywhere from 7 to 40 years.[10] The company said it needed the money for "general corporate purposes"—a common phrase companies use that reporters should investigate further. In Apple's case, plans for the funds included buying back shares and paying dividends. Big banks such as Goldman Sachs, Bank of America Securities, and JPMorgan led the offering.

This was not the first time Apple was issuing a bond to raise capital. In July 2021, the company offered notes worth $6.5 billion in four parts.

Shares of Apple dipped a little when news of the capital raise was made public, offset only by Moody's long-term rating of AAA—the highest—given to the smartphone maker because it had the lowest level of credit risk. Moody's had given the same rating to Microsoft and Johnson & Johnson, indicating that these companies are in a position to fulfill their debt obligations.

When it comes to the debt owed by countries, the markets watch what the big three credit rating agencies do—and usually, after one agency acts, the others follow. For example, both S&P and Fitch downgraded US credit ratings in 2021 and 2023, respectively. And then, in November 2023, Moody's Investor Service downgraded its outlook for the US government's AAA rating to "negative" from "stable." Reasons cited by Moody's were high budget deficits and the lack of confidence in the US government reaching a consensus on a fiscal plan.[11] The markets were unfazed by these rating changes.

Similarly, Moody's downgraded China's outlook to "negative" from "stable" in December 2023, citing hidden debt in local and regional governments on the mainland.[12] S&P and Fitch did not change their ratings, however, and this led to some experts calling Moody's reaction a "politically biased" move.[13] China's financial markets remained largely stable after this news.

Abbotts recalled the financial crisis in Argentina during 2001, which followed those of Russia and Brazil and made investors wary of the increased risk of investing in developing countries. "During this time on the Headlines desk, it felt very unsettling to watch Argentina unravel in such a large-scale, all-encompassing manner," Abbotts said. The country's gross domestic product plummeted and inflation skyrocketed, foreign investors and investment left the country, and the social and economic situation declined drastically and led to social upheaval. The entire government was forced out of office.

This turmoil led to numerous cuts of the country's ratings by rating agencies in 2001. "Over the course of that year, downgrades to Argentina's ratings by Moody's and S&P were so frequent as to become practically commonplace," Abbotts recalled.[14] "Each time, I would run the headline and cue the assignment desk for a follow-up with my familiar call: ARGENTINA CUT . . . again."

Debentures

Debentures are like bonds or notes that a company or country puts out as a debt offering to get long-term financing. Treasury bonds (T-bonds) and Treasury bills are debentures. For example, the T-bonds issued by the US Treasury are used to help finance big projects such as infrastructure or to fund government operations.

The primary fact any journalist needs to know about a debenture is that the company is required to pay interest on it before any dividend payment can be made to shareholders. It is, therefore, a more secure investment. If the company goes kaput, debenture holders will still get their payments. There have rarely been any stories written about shareholders who held debentures and lost a lot of money after a company went bankrupt.

Commodities Markets

Commodities can be classified as hard, soft, and energy. Hard commodities are metals, nonferrous and ferrous, such as gold, silver, and copper. Soft commodities are largely food and beverage related, such as agricultural crops, fisheries, drinks, and livestock. Energy is a commodity that consists of oil, coal, natural gas, and renewables.

Raw materials used in the production of any goods or services are also called commodities. Usually, the supply chain for a company begins at the point where raw material is sourced, further developed, packaged, and turned into a finished good that is ready for sale through retail or wholesale channels. At any point along the supply chain, when a disruption happens, it makes an impact on productivity and sales, and therefore affects company stocks, a particular industry, or financial markets as a whole.

Consider the example of Apple again. The company manufactures its iPhones in factories in China, where raw materials—such as copper, glass, plastics, rare earth elements, gold, steel tin, and zinc—are brought in to create the gadgets. During the COVID-19 pandemic that began in 2019 in China, the Foxconn factories of Apple were disrupted as China went into lockdown and workers were not allowed to assemble the products. Raw materials were also not reaching factories on time. The shortfall in iPhone production meant that demand in the United States could not be met, which meant lower sales and caused the share price of Apple to decline.

The prices of commodities typically increase when the inflation rate rises, and therefore, the price of the finished goods also goes up. It is eventually a game of supply and demand. An economy that is doing well may lead to increased demand from buyers for commodities such as oil and natural gas. But often, supply can be hindered because of unexpected circumstances, such as natural disasters or wars, and this can in turn affect the financial markets at large. For example, when Russia invaded Ukraine in 2022, it destroyed granaries and crops, affecting sunflower oil production by the world's largest exporter of that commodity. The global shortage of sunflower oil resulted in soaring prices for cooking oils and also led countries like Indonesia to restrict its own exports to keep up with domestic demand. The British retailer Tesco placed a cap on the number of bottles of edible oil customers could buy.[15] When journalists wrote about this, readers discovered that sunflower oil was Britain's favorite choice for frying—no wonder fish and chips were tasting differently all of a sudden.

Futures and Options

Besides the impact on the stock market, commodities trade on the spot or cash market via derivatives, such as futures and options contracts. The sale and purchase of commodities is generally carried out through a "futures" contract to hedge the risk of losing money. Journalists that cover commodities are always checking futures and options trading on commodities exchanges.

A commodity futures contract covers the purchase and sale of physical commodities—such as cobalt, zinc, and gold—for future deliveries on a commodity exchange. Everything about a futures contract is about the "future," but the terms have been agreed to at the time the contract is entered into—a future seller is expected to deliver a specific quantity of the raw material at a stipulated price to a future buyer on a particular date. This locks in a price for a product, as the price of commodities can always fluctuate because they depend on supply and demand. An options contract is linked to an "option," meaning the contract holder has the option, not an obligation, to buy or sell an asset during the contract time, not necessarily on a particular date. The buyer is not required to exercise the option, so it is low risk, but they will lose the premium they paid for the contract.

Commodities are bought and sold on special exchanges around the world. In the United States, the four big exchanges are the Chicago Board of Trade, the Chicago Mercantile Exchange, the New York Mercantile Exchange, and the Commodity Exchange Inc.

Agriculture

An agriculture correspondent typically works within the commodities team because whatever food comes from the farm to the table is a commodity. Food prices are Key Performance Indicators of the economy at large. Inflation is an indicator of the level of commodity prices, which makes an impact on the purchasing power of consumers. A drop in food prices is seen as a positive sign for lower inflation. However, lower prices could squeeze the profit margins of companies along the food supply chain.

The Russia-Ukraine war in 2022 is an example of how external factors can affect the economies of many countries. Both countries are major exporters of wheat, sunflower oil, and other crops. Exports of such commodities took a hit because of the war as supplies were abandoned or halted, leading to shortages and therefore increases in the prices of the affected commodities.[16]

Oil Markets

When the price of crude oil increases or decreases, individual companies are affected as input costs and the overall production of finished goods is affected, causing profit margins to rise or fall, which in turn can also cause an increase or decrease in share prices. The sectors that are immediately affected by changes in oil prices are airlines, oil refineries, and logistics and transportation companies. An increase in oil prices leads to higher gasoline and transportation costs.

Oil prices affect the imports and exports of a country. When oil prices decrease, imports become cheaper for a country, and stock markets may do better. Conversely, when oil prices increase, goods coming into a country become more expensive.

Journalists and beat reporters analyze how the price of oil can affect the goods and services of companies, and their stories often explore the relationship between energy prices and commodity sales. For example, stocks of transportation companies may be negatively affected when oil prices increase because they rely on fuel. When oil prices fall, costs of production and transportation also fall, so more assets can be transported at a lower price.

Metals

What is interesting about precious metals, like gold, is that they respond inversely to interest rate moves. When stock markets fall, the prices of gold and silver rise, making them a safer haven as investment assets than other securities. Gold is often used by investors to hedge against unexpected events that could lead to declines of other assets. Commodities reporters look at the bullion market to check daily rates of gold.

When economies are shaky, investors typically withdraw assets from stock markets and may invest in gold to protect themselves from losses during periods of market volatility. As sales of gold increases, the higher demand also causes an uptick in the price of the yellow metal.

Cryptocurrencies

As of March 2023, there were about 22,932 cryptocurrencies in the world, with a total market capitalization of $1.1 trillion, according to CoinMarketCap.[17] It all began in 2009 with Bitcoin, which had traders and journalists alike trying to figure out this new world of blockchain and crypto exchanges and payments. What is significant to note is that some publicly traded companies decided to invest in cryptocurrencies from the onset or early stage, maybe because they were prescient or maybe just because they understood blockchain and what it meant for the future.

Unfortunately, a lot of the profits made by those companies and individual investors were wiped out in two years when the operations of FTX, a digital currency exchange, came crashing down.[18] Reporters had to educate themselves about this new world of nontangible monies. Everyone was on top of the FTX story, which soon became a riveting saga of money, youth, and debauchery—some even called it crypto's "Lehman moment."[19]

What also came out of this were a lot of "explainers" by journalists to educate readers about so-called valuable things that are not only intangible, but they also actually do not exist in some cases. FTX was a high-yield exchange where people could sell digital assets such as bitcoins and ether, among others.[20]

Some reporters dug deep into the founding of FTX by Sam Bankman-Fried, who received endorsements from sports celebrities and politicians as the crypto market boomed. The year 2021, when the COVID-19 pandemic was at its peak, was also the year of the crypto, when Bitcoin, which was trading at $10,000, almost touched $70,000 in November. Many people who spent considerable time staring at their screens because of lockdowns wanted a piece of this seemingly easy money-making tech asset. In 2024, the value of Bitcoin had reached $73,000.

There were acronyms galore—BTC (for Bitcoin), dApp (a decentralized application), DAO (decentralized autonomous organization), ETH (Ether), ICO (Initial Coin Offering), and so on—that were flung into every news story, and further digging revealed new surprises from FTX. Coindesk, a digital media website, linked Alameda Research to Bankman-Fried's FTX and then to FTT, the digital token.

It was all a big maze. And while the future of cryptocurrencies is hard to fathom right now for a majority of consumers, it is clear to say that investors are weary of fraud, but some have still enjoyed positive returns, laughing their way to their banks.[21]

Cryptocurrencies as an alternative to cash or cash-based payment systems is an interesting, ongoing development in the twenty-first century. The SEC's approval of bitcoin exchange-traded funds at the start of 2024 marked their official entry as legitimate investments in the stock market.[22] As with any new type of investment, it can be expected that bitcoin exchange-traded funds will only attract more money in years to come, making them, in time, just like other regular investments.

SUGGESTED ACTIVITIES

1. Find a recent IPO listing and write headlines based on the share movement on its debut day.
2. Research any sovereign rating change by Moody's, Fitch, or S&P and write corresponding headlines.

How Panic Selling—Even of Invisible Things—Can Drag Markets Down (Acronym-Fest Alert!)

What FTX promised its investors was a much bigger return on investment than a bank. But greed is what brought the downfall of many affiliated with the company. They all—including various celebrities and politicians—put their trust in a thirty-year-old man named Sam Bankman-Fried, even though he was speaking a language they did not understand. Big venture capitalists, too, were swayed and invested billions in the man's crypto exchange, where invisible and cryptic things could be traded.

The price of bitcoin was at its peak in 2021, just a few points below $70,000, but it gradually declined, as did other cryptocurrencies. However, in FTX's land, all was very well. Until one day, it was not. That was the day when Coindesk, a digital news website, investigated Alameda Research, a company owned by Bankman-Fried that held a lot of FTT, a cryptocurrency created by FTX. FTT was minted by FTX and given out as rewards to customers.

Enter CZ. Also called Changpeng Zhao, the CEO of another crypto platform called Binance. CZ happened to have bought FTTs, too, but the Coindesk story led him to offload all those tokens.

Panic selling followed, and the price of FTT dropped drastically. More panic ensued as crypto investors started withdrawing from FTX, too—$6 billion worth of withdrawals in 72 hours.[23]

About eight months after the FTX saga, in June 2023, news came out that CZ's company, Binance, by then the world's largest cryptocurrency exchange, had also mishandled funds. The SEC claimed in a lawsuit that Binance had violated securities laws, and like Alameda Research, CZ was allegedly siphoning funds to a company called Sigma Chain.[24]

A day after Binance was in the line of fire from the SEC, the regulatory commission targeted another crypto company—Coinbase—accusing it of illegally operating without registering with the regulator. Shares of Coinbase fell 13 percent, dragging other crypto stocks down with it.[25]

8

SHAREHOLDER ACTIVISM

There is a saying that "it takes money to make money." Accumulating large quantities of stock and gaining clout to occasionally assert for change within a company is most often done by individuals who possess a lot of money. Buying and selling stock, funding start-ups, and/or buying out companies is the world of private equity, venture capital, and hedge funds. This chapter looks at the differences between these entities and the impact they can have on markets.

PRIVATE EQUITY

The private equity market refers to the activity of private equity (PE) firms and investors. PE investors are accredited, high-net-worth individuals who own or have interests and/or stakes in various high-yielding firms and funds. A PE fund can be described as a group of investment funds that are engaged in one or more of these: (1) invest in or seek to buy or acquire private companies that are not publicly traded; (2) conduct buyouts of publicly traded companies and then take them private; and (3) provide equity or financing to both public and private companies.

KKR & Co. and Blackstone Inc. were listed as the top two biggest PE firms by *US News & World Report* in 2022, based on money raised over five years.[1] Both Blackstone and KKR, as well as the Carlyle Group (listed at number six), are listed on the New York Stock Exchange, which means that their shares are available to the public. The average investor can thus own shares in these publicly traded companies and therefore a stake in a PE firm. Otherwise, only individuals with millions of dollars can invest in or have a stake in these firms.

When a company, especially one that is public, receives private equity financing, the headline may be "ABC PE FUND REPORTED TO OWN X% STAKE IN X COMPANY," or "ABC PE FUND SAID TO OFFER $X MLN FUNDING FOR STAKE IN X COMPANY." But when PE deals are made, the specific terms are often not made public, so the amount of financing and the ownership/stake are not officially disclosed. According to *Forbes*, the value of PE deals reached a record in the third quarter of 2021 and was more than $787 billion for the year.[2]

Whenever PE funds or investors are involved in any deals or provide any financing, it usually elicits a reaction—often positive—from the market. Although no investment activity can guarantee a profit, the overarching perception is that PE investment activity will turn a big profit by generating a positive return on investment. So it is often viewed as positive when companies get PE funding, or if there is even the perception of a PE firm being interested in a company. PE interest in a company may also be seen as positive if there is an indication that the objective is to bring about change in the company, to create efficiencies, or to scale up operations.

In 2023, traders and journalists discussed PE financing at length after the failure of three significant banks and ongoing concerns about the state of regional banks in the United States. The high interest rates charged by banks also prompted fears that companies would find it difficult to get loans. So market watchers believed that PE investors could possibly fill the financing gap, giving rise to "shadow banking"—an alternative banking activity that lacks proper regulation and scrutiny. This chatter generated separate concerns that unbridled growth of shadow banking could spawn problems that might negatively affect the broader economy.

VENTURE CAPITAL

While PE investments have a known effect on financial markets and mid- or large-cap companies, smaller companies seek venture capital (VC), which is capital or funding provided to start-up companies, or companies that are in the first or early stages of operation. Start-ups that attract VCs are seen as having the potential for exponential growth. While many do not achieve this expected prolific growth, some start-ups are called unicorns—privately owned and valued at over $1 billion—with a transformative economic impact domestically and on a global scale. Well-known companies such as Apple and Google received VC funding well before their technology and products were widely available. Some prominent innovative companies, such as Uber and Instagram (before being acquired by Meta), received VC funding along with strong backing from individual investors. In 2023, VC investment in start-ups was $170.6 billion, down from $242.2 billion in 2022, according to "The PitchBook—NVCA Venture Monitor" from the National Venture Capital Association and PitchBook.[3]

PE firms and venture capitalists profit by selling the companies they invested in or taking them public. When the latter occurs, it is almost always a big success because PE investors would be the first on board to acquire shares in the company at its lowest valuation. Some of the early indications of a potentially successful initial public offering include an increase in the higher end of the proposed price range—the eventual price at which shares get listed; the upward movement of the share price after trading begins; and the profitable closing price at the end of the first day. The share price is monitored by market watchers over the weeks and months to follow, generating headlines if it trades significantly higher, stays relatively flat, or declines below the offer price. VC funding highlights the possibility of a future listing, and it also provides an early spotlight on an emerging technology, sector, or idea that in time could have significant domestic or worldwide impact.

It should be noted that while VC funding may come from PE firms and investors, it is different from PE investing. The latter provides funding to larger, more established companies, while, as said previously, VC offers financing to companies that are in an early, formative stage.

Here is a short list of top VC firms and some of the companies they funded:

- Andreesen Horowitz: refers to companies it funded as "Builders We've Backed." These include Airbnb, Coinbase Global, Lyft,

GitHub (acquired by Microsoft), Oculus (acquired by Meta), Pinterest, Roblox, and Skype (acquired by Microsoft).[4]

- Accel: UiPath, Squarespace, Bumble, RiskRecon (acquired by Mastercard), CrowdStrike Holdings, and Pismo (acquired by Visa).[5]
- Bessemer Venture Partners (Motto: "We partner with audacious entrepreneurs building enduring businesses): Shopify, LinkedIn (acquired by Microsoft), Pinterest, Twilio, Yelp, and Twitch Interactive.[6]
- Founders Fund: SpaceX, Palantir Technologies, Stripe, Facebook (now Meta Platforms), Affirm Holdings, OpenAI, Spotify, Lyft, and The Athletic (acquired by the *New York Times*).[7]
- Sequoia Capital (Motto: "We help the daring build legendary companies): Apple, DoorDash, 23andme Holding, Airbnb, Dropbox, and Citadel Securities.[8]

HEDGE FUNDS

Like PE and VC investing, which are both exclusive to high-net-worth investors, hedge funds are for ultra-high-net-worth and accredited investors—the latter is a status granted by the Securities and Exchange Commission (SEC). The aim or objective of hedge funds is apparent in their name—to hedge positions so that a profit is made irrespective of how the market behaves. The mechanism or method for that strategy clearly involves more than just buying, selling, or holding a position in a stock.

So what is involved in a hedge fund's strategy? Although there is not much transparency in their activities, it is plausible to assume that their trading activities include various options and derivatives. Sometimes, information reaches the market about the position a hedge fund has taken, which may cause a particular movement in a stock. An unexplained or significant movement of a stock may also give rise to speculation that it is due to some hedge fund activity, which then warrants further journalistic investigation.

PENSION FUNDS

Another large holder of money that can have a significant investing impact are pension funds, which hold assets from which a specific group of workers receive benefits during retirement. Pension funds are mostly public in the United States, monitored and run by states/government entities, which have the responsibility to administer the fund and make payouts to retired workers. The California Public Employees' Retirement System (known as CalPERS) and the California State Teachers' Retirement System (CalSTRS) are two of the best-known public pension funds in the United States. In Canada, CPP Investments is the largest pension fund.

Pension funds need to manage their assets to remain solvent, but they must also stay healthy with increasing value to afford payouts as needed by former workers. Pension funds in the United States are insured by the Pension Benefit Guaranty Corporation, which guarantees that the pension fund will have money needed for its obligations if it faces financial difficulties.

To increase their assets, pension funds may invest or pool their assets in a hedge fund, PE fund, or VC investments. But a big difference between pension funds and investments they may make to maximize returns is that they have an obligation as fiduciaries to manage their assets in the best interest of pensioners—the people who get payouts from the funds. Risk is therefore an important factor that pension funds must balance in making investments. So, while they may seek higher returns in alternative investments with private equity, hedge funds, and venture capital, it is incumbent on pension funds to invest prudently and not risk a significant or even moderate percentage of their assets.

Transparency is also required by pension funds, which means it is known or publicized more when they acquire a stake in a stock or mutual fund, or reduce or exit a position. Because of the fiduciary obligations, such moves can be perceived by markets as indicative of the outlook of a stock—whether it has peaked, has a potential for further upside, or may signal a concern or lack of conviction in the company.

Pension funds—along with PEs and VC entities—have the clout to get more information about a company's operations from meeting privately with management, suppliers, and others that may have business dealings with a company. The information they obtain is used to make investment decisions, which could spark movement by a stock.

Based on their clout and influence to buy, sell, and hold investments, PE firms, hedge funds, and individuals with high net worth may engage in investing that makes them "activist investors." This means they specifically acquire a significant stake in a company with the intention to cause considerable change, touted as seeking improvements or efficiencies to increase the company's profitability. An activist investor makes their intention known, and a company will usually issue a statement based on the specific objective of the activist investor. The objectives can include seeking one or more board seats, new management, different capital spending priorities, the sale of a unit deemed to be a drag on the company's profitability, or even the sale of the entire company. By acquiring and publicizing a stake in a company, the activist investor's aim is to gain leverage to force the change they want.

One such prolific activist investor is Carl Icahn, a legendary businessman born in 1936 who is known for campaigning to bring about change in companies. An example of his activism was his opposition to Illumina acquiring Grail, a cancer-detection company. Icahn had a partial victory when one of his three nominees was elected to the company's board in a shareholder meeting in late May 2023. His nominee replaced Illumina's chairman, who was not reelected. Icahn, who was seeking a management change, was unsuccessful in achieving that objective because the company's CEO won reelection to the board. Icahn cited "failed oversight" in opposing the continuing efforts by Illumina to complete the acquisition of Grail. European antitrust authorities and the Federal Trade Commission also opposed the acquisition, both citing negative effects on competition. Icahn decried the company's decision to continue to pursue the deal because of the cost to the company. Not long after Icahn revealed his 1.5 percent stake in Illumina and his objective, the company had offered a board seat for one of his nominees and for an independent candidate, but Icahn had rejected the offer.[9] In mid-December 2023, Illumina announced that it would divest Grail after a court ruling sided with the Federal Trade Commission's finding that the acquisition would hurt competition in the sector for cancer detection tests.[10] With this development, Icahn indicated he would continue his plans to seek change at Illumina to accomplish a third goal to "remove . . . legacy-conflicted directors."[11]

The size of the stake amassed by an activist investor, their overall objective, and the response of the company, are developments to be followed until there is a resolution. And an ending or resolution is an outcome in which the fight or differing objectives is recognized as over by the parties. The activist investor may get their objective in full or part, could withdraw their action, or there could be a settlement with the company. While journalists and markets follow these maneuvers closely, a final outcome may or may not cause a notable stock reaction because markets may account for a result over time based on speculation of how the dispute may end.

Nelson Peltz and his Trian Fund Management firm engaged in a prolonged challenge to gain influence to bring about change at the Walt Disney Company. His actions and the responses of the company and shareholders are examples of the maneuvers and back-and-forth frequently involved in proxy fights by activist shareholders.

SUGGESTED ACTIVITIES

1. Identify firms and/or start-ups that recently received funding from venture capital firms. What made them attractive candidates for funding?
2. Research a proxy battle that was successful and one that was not. Identify factors that contributed to the different outcomes.

No Fun for Disney with Challenges from Activist Investors

The Walt Disney Company, which is in the business of delivering entertaining, fun, and joyful experiences that put smiles on faces, experienced the very opposite with challenges from activist investors. Trian Fund Management's cofounder, Nelson

Peltz, acquired a significant stake in the company and proposed two directors, including himself, for nomination to Disney's board to change how the company does business.

Trian cited the lack of performance of Disney's shares, underperformance of its total shareholder returns, and poor corporate governance as reasons to nominate Peltz for election to Disney's board.[12] This came after talks between Disney and Peltz failed to satisfy or resolve Peltz's concerns. After Peltz announced his intention, Disney issued a statement in which it said the executive chairman of Nike, Mark Parker, would be named chairman and would "chair a newly created Succession Planning Committee of the Board" that would advise the board on that matter.

Disney also responded to Trian saying that it "remains open to constructive engagement and ideas that help drive shareholder value." The statement also noted that there had been a dialogue with Peltz in the last few months and that the company "does not endorse the Trian Group nominee, and recommends that shareholders not support its nominee, and instead vote "*for*" all the company's nominees." Disney also noted that it is "the envy of the industry" and mentioned actions by its CEO to implement changes related to streaming and its network properties.[13]

In February 2024, Trian issued an announcement congratulating Disney and said it would withdraw its nomination of Peltz. Trian cited recent initiatives of Disney as "a win for all shareholders (and that they) broadly align with our thinking."[14] But in late November, a day after Disney announced two new directors—James P. Gorman, Morgan Stanley's chairman and CEO; and Sir Jeremy Darroch, former group chief executive of Sky—Trian said it would go directly to shareholders to seek the change that it was advocating. Trian said it had given Disney "the opportunity to prove it could 'right the ship,' . . . but billions in shareholder value had since been lost."[15]

As the saga continued, each party gained support from other large shareholders. Disney said Peltz was acting in partnership with a former Disney executive, Isaac Perlmutter, who the company said owned 78 percent of the shares that Peltz was claiming as beneficial ownership. Disney further noted that consideration about Peltz and any other nominee should include the fact that Perlmutter had been dismissed from the company and had expressed negative opinions about Disney's CEO.[16] Disney confirmed in December 2023 that Trian intended to nominate two individuals for election to the board at the 2024 annual shareholder meeting.[17] And from January to March 2024, Disney gained support for its nominees from

Investment Firm ValueAct Capital, Blackwells Capital LLC, Disney heirs, and the filmmaker George Lucas.

Disney in turn planned to consult with ValueAct as it executed a transformation to changing technologies. Disney also cited ValueAct's record of cooperation with companies it invests in, and said, "We welcome their input as long-term shareholders." ValueAct said it believes "Disney can lead the media industry forward," as the industry undergoes technological change to digital platforms, and that it was "excited to partner with Bob (Iger) and the Board to help create long-term sustainable shareholder value."[18] Shareholder Blackwells Capital LLC also informed Disney of its intention to nominate three individuals for election as directors but indicated that they would support the company.[19]

The decision rested on the votes of shareholders leading up to and at the company's annual meeting on April 3, 2024. Disney reported that voting results showed its "full slate of 12 directors has been elected by a substantial margin over the nominees of Trian and Blackwells." The stock closed 3 percent lower at the end of trading that day. Disney, of course, was happy and relieved, saying, "With the distracting proxy contest now behind us, we're eager to focus 100% of our attention on our most important priorities: growth and value creation for our shareholders and creative excellence for our consumers."[20] At the end of May, it was reported that Trian's Peltz sold all his Disney shares.

Divergent outlooks and advocacy of different ideas takes away from operating with clarity, affecting how well a company may achieve its stated objectives, which over the long term will affect its performance and value. Disney's stock price traded mostly over $100 per share at the start of 2023, with pullbacks on some days into the high $90 range, before Trian announced its proxy fight. By the summer, Disney's stock had declined to the mid- to high $80s, and remained mostly in that range until November, when it climbed back to over $90 into the start of 2024. After reporting first quarter earnings on February 7, 2024, the stock traded almost 14 percent higher intraday and closed up 11.5 percent from the previous day. It would continue to rise, closing at $122.82 the day before the shareholders' meeting, which turned out to be the highest it had traded in a year.[21]

9

ECONOMIC INDICATORS

The stock market consists of shares issued by publicly listed companies, so it may be natural to think that announcements from those companies are solely responsible for decision-making by traders. However, this is not true.

Other factors play an equally important role in how investor sentiments are affected, resulting in the buying and selling of company shares. These include geopolitics; new leadership of a country; natural disasters such as earthquakes, fires, and tsunamis; war and conflict; disease outbreaks; and refinery shutdowns or oil leaks—all of which are covered in the subsequent chapters. Here, we focus on the bigger picture: the role of macroeconomics.

Economic factors—such as demand and supply of raw materials, prices of goods and services, inflation, unemployment, and central bank decisions—are all indicators of the health of a country and the overall conditions in which its companies conduct their business. The impact of external factors depends heavily on the kind of business a company does. For example, excess snowfall results in increased business for companies that provide heating services or winter clothing. And a disease outbreak would translate into big profits for a pharmaceutical company that launches a new vaccine as investors would rush to buy shares of such companies. In the same scenario, however, excess snowfall can also delay sales of seasonal clothing, resulting in a backlog of inventories in warehouses, causing a drop in sales at a department store or beachwear apparel company. In a similar way, travel companies can be negatively affected during a pandemic.

When central banks make decisions about increasing or decreasing interest rates, their deliberations include considerations about purchasing power, as both the inflation and unemployment rates need a good balance for healthy spending by consumers. The day when major decisions are announced by central banks, be it on interest rates or steps on cooling inflationary pressures, is a stressful day for an economics reporter who gears up to be locked inside a room with fellow journalists.

Here is a sneak peek of the situation, in almost poetic words, as shared verbatim by an experienced reporter who wrote stories about central bank decisions, and requested not to be named: "We walk through the central bank's grand entrance, badge in hand, and go through security, the weight of history seeping through its tall columns. We make our way down circular marble steps, trying to take care not to slip up, so as not to put a bad omen on the upcoming lock-in. Down in the depths of the bank, you put your mobile, laptop, and any other connection to the wider world in a locker, and make your way to a room where several computers are set up for news outlets to share the central bank's next interest rate decision with the world. With the phone lines off, you are handed piles of documents to sift through. Like a detective in a bunker, you look through the documents, searching for any new expectations, additional words, changes in language, anything that gives the reader the sense of what the central bank is thinking and what is new. With a set time to complete the task and set up the news alerts that could affect maybe thousands or millions worth of dollars of trades worldwide, you work as fast and as diligently as you can as a bank staff member reminds you how much time you have left. Thirty minutes, . . . ten, . . . five minutes left; . . . publish! Your gut is cold with every news alert that hits 'the terminal.' As the live press conference starts on a screen, one person types furiously, while the other 'double-eyes' the news alerts, looking out for any errors, as we watch the currency graph go up and down based on the headlines. As it all wraps up, the heart palpitations subside, and you are left feeling completely depleted with a foggy brain. You have survived another lock-in."

Let us take a look at some economic indicators that can move shares of companies, and what better measurement to start with than gross domestic product (GDP).

GROSS DOMESTIC PRODUCT

GDP refers to the goods and services produced inside a country within a certain period, which are for sale, and it measures the monetary value of those goods and services. In other words, it measures the output of a country and the value it produces within a year or a quarter compared with the similar quarter of the prior year. Basically, it is a reflection of the income made by everyone—individuals and companies.

An increase in GDP means more is being produced and the economy is in good health, which means that businesses are also generating or manufacturing more products. That is a hurrah for stock markets because it shows people are getting employed readily and are spending happily, resulting in a good flow of money within the country.

On the flip side, a shrinking GDP indicates all is not well, and one of the biggest indicators is declining employment or lack of jobs. A negative GDP means that production has declined compared with the last reporting period, which means businesses are not doing well. Investors therefore want to reduce their positions in the stock market or sell the shares of companies in sectors that are having a tough time.

The word "recession," and market conversations about a "looming recession," can unnerve investors. These typically mean that for at least six months or more, a country's economic activity could be slumping, fewer people are getting employed, the values of investments and personal income are declining, and the overall production of goods and services has dropped. Some economists believe a recession occurs when a country has faced an economic slump for two consecutive quarters, indicated by declining GDP; in other words, it would be hard for any country to find its way back to expansion after a slump of six months.[1] To get an economy on a path to growth and back on an upward trajectory takes time and is often difficult for policymakers to achieve. Any indication that a country may be heading toward a recession signals gloom, and could lead to a drop in financial markets as many people start to offload shares and seek investments overseas or choose to retain cash or gold in their home country.

There are also many things that GDP in different countries does not measure, such as where is the factory of a certain company located because that output will be taken into consideration in the country where raw materials were gathered and items produced. Stories about the economy and economic performance are usually done by experienced reporters and subject matter experts in newsrooms, who often have a prewritten piece ready based on interviews and polling done by their teams.

This "polling team" in a newsroom or a news agency is either a specific team or a group of reporters and/or interns who do quick polls with analysts, economists, and other market watchers. They also take notes, while talking with them, that are often used in stories to inform readers about what pundits are expecting. They then publish the data or results of the poll with a short story that gives the GDP predictions. The same may also be done for a poll on whether interest rates will change and by how much, or the numbers expected for the Consumer Price Index and/or Producer Price Index, as well as the Purchasing Managers' Index (PMI). The markets—equities and fixed income—will often move based on what the market predictions are, which is based on the consensus results of analysts, economists, investors, and others. When the actual numbers arrive—usually by phone from a reporter who is inside a government office or in an email—the headline has to be precise and quick.

"One person would have fingers hovering above the numerals while another would be in the queue waiting for something like a jobs number to come from the government," recalled Bethany Harshaw Bantle. "It was always a game trying to predict which number would come first. Which number on the keyboard should your finger be ready to hit first? A misclick of a key would result in firing off the wrong number or having to backspace, losing a fraction of a second and thus losing the race. When done correctly, though, you and your partner might have a second to celebrate before a rush of earnings dropped into the queue."

INTEREST RATES

Financial markets—whether equities or fixed-income securities—can be immensely affected by central bank decisions. Whenever there is any tightening of rates, it puts pressure on stocks because investors expect a decline in economic growth.

Rising interest rates also put pressure on the real estate markets because they make mortgage rates higher, and other debt more expensive. As borrowing costs rise, companies may put expansion plans on hold. Any such announcement would be watched carefully by the market. A cut in interest rates, conversely, indicates more spending power for companies and consumers.

For journalists, it is all about predictions that are based on what economists and other experts are expecting. The statements that companies put out on the "macro environment" and how they will navigate it are also very useful information for reporters. Companies may indicate their cash reserve levels, mention whether clients plan to cut back on projects, and note if there may be job cuts or plant closures.

For example, e-commerce and technology companies, such as Apple and Amazon, flourished during the two years of COVID-19 as the world went online to shop for everything from groceries to toilet paper. But when vaccinations took effect and economies opened up, many faced growth slowdown, and it took time for supply chains to get back to normal. As currencies weakened against the benchmark dollar, tech companies took a slight hit, too, albeit they stayed resilient despite headwinds as the world that had gone into lockdowns had started relying on them.[2]

March 20, 2024, was a significant day for Japan, an aging country known for its negative interest rates, when the Bank of Japan raised interest rates for the first time in seventeen years.[3] The Nikkei hit an all-time high as markets factored in wage increases as corporations boosted salaries to balance the rise in consumer prices.

THE JOBS REPORT

The jobs report is also referred to as the employment report or the nonfarm payrolls report (it does not include jobs in farming areas, which are released separately by the US Department of Agriculture). The US Bureau of Labor Statistics releases this report every month. It is an indication of economic strength if it shows more people were employed from month to month. Because this report is all about the economy, it includes many data points, and so it also results in news stories about wages, hiring trends, areas where jobs are increasing or decreasing, and working hours. The jobs report in the United States also includes a survey of 60,000-plus households to show movement in and out of jobs, self-employment, and income status.

Journalists and traders alike check to see if the numbers "met" or "beat" expectations by analysts, or consensus estimates. Similar to GDP, the consensus estimates would have been reported by news publications after an informal poll of analysts and economists. This allows reporters to write in-depth stories about the sectors they cover and further analyze for the markets what this could mean for the future of the companies in that sector. The employment report highlights not just the health of the economy but also the health of the consumer who is employed and is in a position to earn and spend money.

The other indicator that directly affects consumers and their standard of living is the inflation rate. If unemployment and inflation are both high, that is bad news for the economy, and will force a central bank to intervene and take some action on the interest rate, such as lowering it, to cool down the situation to ease the cost of borrowing for businesses and consumers. The market can swing any which way, depending on the economic conditions and how traders perceive the data from the jobs report in relation to inflation and interest rates.

Here is an example: The US jobs growth in October 2023 was nearly half of what it was in September, and the unemployment rate was up slightly—not a good sign for the economy. However, inflation was still high. The markets went up that day, not down, because despite the slightly higher unemployment rate, the labor market remained fairly tight.[4] Continued high inflation meant that the Federal Reserve would not raise interest rates, which was a relief for the markets.[5]

Central banks are always trying to balance two economic indicators, inflation and unemployment, so purchasing power is maintained. In fact, there was an online game that lecturers in business and journalism schools ran in class to teach students how inflation and unemployment are two of the biggest economic indicators that help the Federal Reserve in setting monetary policy. That game—called "Chair the Fed"—allowed students to increase or decrease the Fed Funds Rate as macroeconomic factors on the screen kept changing. The online game was unfortunately removed in June 2021.[6]

INFLATION

Too much money chasing too few goods—that was how inflation was best described at one point. But this indicator now reveals that too much money can also chase too many goods, as purchasing power increases and some strata of people are in positions to pay premium prices for goods. The rate of inflation is a big indicator of the economic health of a country and the direction its financial markets could take with the release of inflation data. Higher prices for goods and services are less of a problem when consumers have high employment rates and are willing to spend. Reporters will often track the price of a finished product along supply chains to investigate how pricey the raw material may have become because of inflationary pressures.

Rising inflation can have a huge impact on corporate margins. Investors who are risk averse may be quick to get rid of shares of companies that are experiencing eroding margins, leading to a drop in their stock.

The year 2022 saw high inflation as the world recovered from COVID 19 and concerns about a recession loomed everywhere. In the United Kingdom, for example, inflation soared to 11.1 percent from January to October 2022, the first time in forty-one years that it went that high, staying in the double digits each month during that period. It was not until April 2023 that the number dropped to single digits, at 8.7 percent, giving the country a sense that conditions were cooling after being hit by a severe cost-of-living crisis.[7]

The Consumer Price Index and the Producer Price Index

Inflation is measured using the Consumer Price Index and the Producer Price Index. These two key data figures are analyzed very carefully by traders, as they show two ends of a spectrum: the average change over time in prices of goods and services for consumers, and the average changes in selling prices received by domestic producers for their output.

When the price of raw materials goes up, including oil prices, it has a ripple effect on the end product and the price that consumers pay for the final product. Both these indicators reflect the prices of items from milk and eggs to homes and cars, and they help central banks to assess the health of the economy.

MANUFACTURING AND INDUSTRIAL PRODUCTION

The Purchasing Managers' Index is based on a monthly survey sent to managers of select companies, or people who purchase goods and services in a supply chain, across various sectors. The survey is sent by the Institute of Supply Management every month to assess five things in a company: new orders, inventory levels, production, supplier deliveries, and employment. The index is scored from 0 to 100. Anything above 50 is a positive indication that traders view as "expansion," while under 50 is considered a "contraction."

Why is this important for the stock market? Because it covers many business sectors and companies, and also indicates what this means for future production. It is an indication of the health of a company, or companies—are there enough new orders coming in every month, do they have ample inventory, are there any roadblocks in supplier deliveries, are people losing their jobs? Each of these can be a story for a reporter to follow and to delve more deeply into any related issues and causes. Sometimes the root cause across industries can be the same, for example, during the COVID-19 pandemic, which caused a supply chain crisis in many sectors.

What do reporters do with this information and how do traders benefit? Take China's Purchasing Managers' Index numbers, for example, released in May 2023 for both manufacturing (factory activity) and nonmanufacturing (travel, retail, etc.) sectors. There was a drop in the monthly figures for both numbers compared with April. The job of the reporter is to find the "why." What happened in China? Was it not supposed to be self-reliant and producing innumerable goods effectively? Chasing the why resulted in a big revelation: youth in China are not finding jobs.[8] The nonmanufacturing PMI includes travel, which went up quite a bit as soon as China opened up after the pandemic, but it started to decline as demand again fell. People were not shopping enough in China, and that showed up in the drop in retail sales. Industries also were not showing robust production, as demand had slowed. The story that reporters told traders was that China's economy was slowing as new export orders were declining, supply chains were taking a hit, and inventory backlogs were being reduced.[9] Asian markets tumbled on the news of China's PMI—the Hong Kong stock index dropped the most among all regional markets.[10] Other key macroeconomic numbers of interest to stock market investors are home sales and retail sales, which have been covered in previous chapters.

HOME SALES AND RETAIL SALES

For information about Key Performance Indicators for housing and retailers, see chapter 5.

CONSUMER CONFIDENCE INDEX

All the indicators described above drive one important factor: how confident a consumer is to spend money. The Consumer Confidence Index (CCI) survey is done on consumers to track and analyze their spending habits because it is a direct correlation to their income and purchasing power. In the United States, this survey is done by the Consumer Conference Board with help from data analytics company, Nielsen, and a number is released on the last Tuesday of every month. A CCI above 100 means consumers are confident and optimistic about their living standards. It is important to note that many economists and journalists call the CCI a "lagging indicator" of the economy because it has many attached variables and can change according to a consumer's financial or economic situation.

The postpandemic year 2022 was one of recovery for just about all countries, and many indicators showed struggling economies around the world as life gradually returned to "no masks." Budget cuts, production delays, inflationary pressures, interest rate hikes, and unemployment rates all pointed to negative trends, and markets wobbled throughout the year.

Stock market investors were hit in 2022 with one crisis after another that left them wondering where to place their money amid inflationary pressures, rising interest rates, continued COVID-19 woes, production losses, and the unexpected war in Ukraine. And then, in 2023, the world was glued to news sources to see whether the government in the United States would raise its $31.4 trillion debt ceiling or default on its loans, causing market volatility around the globe. The United States has had a debt cap in place since 1917, and the ceiling has been raised or suspended 102 times since World War II.[11] On May 31, 2023, the markets heaved a sigh of relief when the US House of Representatives passed a bill to suspend the debt ceiling days before a default.

Macroeconomic factors affect business productivity, and investors look for all signs of stability, so they get good returns from market securities. When an economy slumps, everything goes downhill for corporate sectors, and vice versa. A lack of production, a lack of resources, a lack of capital, and the like can lead to a drop in business performance, thereby affecting earnings and outlook. Inflation and unemployment data affect wages, which in turn affect an individual's spending power, and these can affect sales of retailers, homes, and other consumer-related sectors. Therefore, it is crucial for governments to be prudent about fiscal and monetary policies so economic indicators can stay on a steady track.

SUGGESTED ACTIVITIES

1. Research the GDP over the past year for any country. Compare the action by its central bank on interest rates during the same period.
2. Find the latest report on China's manufacturing and services (PMI figures). Compare with a similar report on the United States. How has factory output changed in both countries?

"Inflation Everywhere" in 2022: How Markets Relied on Central Banks' Decisions

Prices all around the globe shot through the roof in 2022 as the world recovered from the COVID-19 pandemic but faced increased prices for food and fuel, largely due to the war in Ukraine. Inflation was at a forty-year high in the United States, and major economies in Europe were on par with the United States. In Asia, while South Korea raised rates to stem inflation, Turkey insisted on cutting rates, even though their inflation rates were at their highest level, at 36 percent.[12]

Markets all over were watching central bank decisions. In the United States, the Federal Reserve hiked interest rates twice, with consecutive increases of 75 basis points to tone down inflationary pressures and ward off a recession, especially after seeing one quarter of negative GDP.

"In taking the benchmark overnight borrowing rate up to a range of 2.25 to 2.5 percent, the moves in June and July represent the most stringent consecutive action since the Fed began using the overnight funds rate as the principal tool of monetary policy in the early 1990s," wrote CNBC's Jeff Cox.[13] But what made the markets react was a forward-looking statement by then–Federal Reserve chairman Jerome Powell: "As the stance of monetary policy tightens further, it likely will become appropriate to slow the pace of increases while we assess how our cumulative policy adjustments are affecting the economy and inflation."[14] Fears of recession were eased when Powell assured markets that there were too many "areas of economy" that were performing well.

Stocks rallied, with some hitting all-time highs that day as the Dow Jones Industrial Average jumped 436 points, or 1.4 percent. The Standard & Poor's 500 gained 2.62 percent, while the Nasdaq Composite climbed 4.06 percent. Markets made merry: shares of the tech giants Meta, Amazon, and Apple soared; retailers rejoiced as Walmart jumped 3.8 percent; Costco and Ross Stores gained 2 percent each; and Chipotle rose nearly 15 percent.[15]

10

INVENTIONS AND INNOVATIONS

Anything new and promising is exciting. An announcement about a new technology or an innovative idea that is intended to propel a business forward will attract attention from the public at large and investors, who are always seeking to invest in innovators and the next new technology or big idea.

If Elon Musk's Space Exploration Technologies Corporation, or SpaceX, was a publicly traded company (it was not at the time of the writing of this book), maybe every rocket launch, and every tweet that followed, would have moved shares of the company. As one of the highest-valued start-ups in the world (valued at $150 billion as of mid-2023), there have been incessant chatter and rumours about a potential initial public offering (IPO).[1]

Whether the mission is to take humans to Mars or hold meetings in metaverse, traders in stock markets are hawk-eyed about the investment that a company pours into a new innovation, analyzing what it might mean for the company's balance sheet as well as market returns. A journalist with a technology beat has to keep abreast of not just a company's new products and technical expertise but also its funding capabilities to support research and development on innovative products.

Technology reporters have to keep their fingers on the pulse of companies that promise to deliver innovative products, watching their progress and capital expenditures. In 2021, for example, despite supply chain woes brought about by the COVID-19 pandemic, the big five US technology companies—Amazon, Apple, Alphabet, Microsoft, and Meta—generated combined revenue of $1.4 trillion, which was more than Mexico's gross domestic product.[2]

PATENTS

Brands and patents are intangible assets that help to define businesses and can even be lucrative sources of revenue. Many companies are known not by their management but by the brands and patents they own. Companies seek patents for new designs and products to gain a competitive edge. A 2023 study done in Singapore on world-renowned brands concluded that the companies with the most valuable brands and patent portfolios outperform their peers and that these are key reasons for higher revenue, profits, and market capitalization.[3] Journalists who cover companies need to educate themselves about ideas and inventions pursued by companies.

While brands are every company's identity, patents are intellectual property (IP) that can be leveraged through licensing to boost revenue. For example, IBM received yearly royalties of nearly $1 billion in 2000 for licensing its patented products to others, which is a recurring net revenue stream for the technology giant. IP, which goes beyond patents, consists of legally protected assets that have achieved great, or at least some, commercial success for both large and small companies, making them a hassle-free addition to companies' bottom lines. Xerox, too, uses an IP strategy to boost its revenue, along with many other US technology companies, such as Microsoft and Dell, and the consumer products company Procter & Gamble, which owns the Gillette brand, known for its patented razors.[4] Patents are revered in the health care industry, where pharmaceutical companies can make billions with "blockbuster drugs," which have a huge impact because they treat chronic diseases and can generate at least $1 billion in annual sales for a company. Many of these drugs also have exclusivity in the market until their patents expire.

When a patent is nearing expiration, it can present a problem for the company if new products have not been developed to provide a revenue stream. A patent expiration means a company may have to deal with a possible rival generic, or copycat product, which will reduce its revenue and market share, because generic products can be bought at reduced prices by consumers.

Reporters who understand how companies use their patents on drugs are able to write insightful stories that go deeper into the issue to explain to readers how companies are capable of artificially inflating prices on their innovative and best-selling products. For example, the *New York Times* dug deeper into the drug maker AbbVie's competition while researching the patent expiration of Humira, its blockbuster anti-inflammatory medication.[5] Even though the drug's patent was expiring at the end of 2016, the reporter found that AbbVie had managed to manipulate the system to try and delay the onslaught of copycats from others in the market—such as Amgen, Pfizer, and Biocon—by using its IP protection to prolong its hold in the market. Similarly, reporters at Bloomberg and the *Wall Street Journal* wrote about "shields of patents that protect the world's best-selling drug" when Humira's patent did not expire in 2016.[6] When Humira's twenty-year, $200 billion monopoly finally ended, paving the way for cheaper drugs for patients in 2023, Humira's US revenue dropped 26 percent in the first quarter of 2023.[7] Shares of AbbVie tumbled more than 8 percent, even after the company raised its full-year profit forecast the day of its first quarter earnings announcement.[8]

NEW PRODUCTS

New products can have patents and carry the legal support of intellectual property. But these are tangible, unlike the intangible brand reputation and IP quality of a patent. Therefore, how investors and consumers react to this physically visible asset is key to how markets will react. So companies can often go gangbusters with their marketing and advertising, not to mention media conferences, to build hype around the product, which could highly influence its success or downfall when it is eventually launched and made available to the public.

There is no better example of product launch events than those by Apple and its late founder Steve Jobs, in his trademark black turtleneck and jeans. After launching the iMac in 1998 and the iPod in 2001, Jobs returned onstage in 2007 to launch the first version of Apple's iPhone, which he did after a two-hour speech and demonstration of the new product, saying it "would make history." He was not wrong. By the first quarter of 2022, the iPhone, with all its new versions, controlled 62 percent of the smartphone market, according to Counterpoint Research.[9] It also shows that by 2021, 52 percent of Apple's revenue came from its iPhones.

Apple is skilled at launching new products by creating euphoria that keeps consumers excited and yearning to own the latest version of a gadget. Even after Jobs passed away, his successor, Tim Cook, continued launching new products to much fanfare—Apple Watch, AirPods, Smart Speakers, and, in early 2024, the augmented reality Vision Pro headset.

For reporters who cover technology companies that are arch rivals, such as Apple and Samsung, watching the excitement build around new products and writing about it is a thrill on its own. It becomes more than just a story about products and innovation; there are feelings and emotions involved, too, as customers become obsessively loyal about respective brands. Like them, journalists too join the throngs waiting in line outside Apple stores when a new product comes out. While COVID-19 diverted everyone's attention to online shopping, some people still lined up, maintaining safe distances, when Apple launched the iPhone 13 in 2021.[10]

For the stock market, a surprising thing to note is that Apple shares have not historically done well on the launch date. That is because the gains were already made in the excitement and lead-up to the event, all of which would have been covered by journalists, so nothing new really occurs on the actual launch day. Shares of Apple typically rise 13.9 percent more than the Standard & Poor's 500 in the three months leading up to the launch, according to Bernstein Data.[11]

NEW TECHNOLOGIES

When it comes to technology companies and their Key Performance Indicators, journalists look at two contributions to revenue: service and product.

Service Revenue

As the words "service revenue" indicate, this is the money earned by a company for providing services to customers. For technology companies, this can include many items, such as subscription fees, licensing fees, monthly retainers, monthly or weekly installments, and advertising revenue, which can be a line item under service revenue in a financial statement. Service revenue also reflects customer demand and retention, especially when there is an increase in subscription renewals.

Markets and reporters look for "churn," which is the rate at which customers stop doing business with the company; this is a measure of dissatisfaction with the company's service, which in turn affects service revenue. Reporters are always checking subscription renewal, churn, reviews, and social media posts and comments to gauge customer satisfaction.

Many technology companies offer "freemiums," where the basic features are free and then customers pay for premium service. The rate at which that conversion happens is also an indication of how good a company's service is and how reliable a customer feels the product is. The subscription-based revenue model provides a recurring revenue stream for companies.

Constant innovation in its service stream is something synonymous with Apple. In the first quarter of 2023, Apple reported better-than-expected results because of the "best ever quarter" for its services businesses across the iCloud, the App Store, and its credit card business.[12] A month later, as its key services business continued to do well, boosting its overall sales, Apple became one of the most valuable companies in the world, surpassing a $3 trillion market capitalization, as of June 30, 2023.[13]

Product Revenue

Every new product matters to the market, and product revenue is the total revenue earned by a company from selling a product during a specific period of time. It is the value that each product contributes as a line item to the company's overall revenue. Some companies are one-product wonders, such as Crocs, which makes comfort footwear designed with holes; its entire revenue model is based on sales of these products, which are niche items with high brand loyalty among consumers.

But often, single-product companies eventually try to diversify because the love for that one product may not last. They then need to try to innovate and introduce new product lines (e.g., Bose, with its soundlinks, soundbars, and sound cancellation buds) or new versions of the old product (e.g., Apple, with iPhones, iPads, and iMacs), or just completely ditch the idea of a new product (e.g., Microsoft Watch).

FINTECH

When it comes to innovation and technology, another sector that has made remarkable and successful change is the world of finance and banking. Who would have ever thought that technology could enter, sustain, and profoundly reshape financial services and work in tandem with regulators? Financial technology (fintech) began with start-ups taking risks and pursuing growth as an array of funders were willing to invest in promising ideas.

From 2019 to 2023, there were more than 250 fintech start-ups with a combined value of $936 billion. And as of July 2023, publicly traded fintechs represented a market capitalization of $550 billion.[14]

"Our research shows that revenues in the fintech industry are expected to grow almost three times faster than those in the traditional banking sector between 2022 and 2028," McKinsey noted in an October 2023 report, which stated that emerging markets expected to play a growing role in fintech revenue growth.

INNOVATION AND SHARE PRICES

Since 1980, more than 40 percent of firms that transitioned to public equity markets in the United States were technology firms. The next subsections describe five innovative technology advances that not only moved stock markets but also changed the way the world started thinking and behaving. They all have one thing in common: the decision on how to operate was determined largely by fulfilling consumer needs. Therefore, each of them is as much a general story or people story as a business story.

Apple

Apple's flagship product is the iPhone, which it launched for the first time in 2007, and continues to modify with added features, such as advanced camera function, facial recognition, and augmented reality. The buzz that Apple creates around the launch of each new version (the iPhone 16 is the latest at the time of the writing of this book)—for example, when Steve Jobs pulled an iPhone out of his pocket to make a point about its size—excites tech journalists and markets as they seek to review and be first users along with consumers. On the day of the release of the first iPhone, January 9, 2007, Apple's stock rose just a little over 1 percent, but it surged 16 percent in the next month, as journalists wrote about consumer interest and markets saw the iPhone as an innovative, one-of-a-kind product that would have very high sales. By the end of 2007, Apple's stock was up 129.5 percent, which means it rose from $2.80 on January 9 to $6 on December 31, 2007. As of January 9, 2024, after many stock splits, the share price stood at $185.14, and Apple had sold 2.3 billion iPhones to more than 1.5 billion active users, according to Demandsage research.[15]

Netflix

Online streaming changed the world of media. This happened in 2007 as well, when Netflix moved from being a DVD rental company to an online streaming business with a subscription model, allowing consumers to have the joy of watching movies and TV shows whenever and wherever they wanted. Netflix continues to be innovative by creating its own exclusive content. The closing price of Netflix was $3.80 on December 31, 2007, and the price at the end of 2023 was $486.88.

Google

The Google search engine provided much-needed direction and navigation to a world that was trying to figure out what cyberspace was all about. The algorithm Google created was faster and more efficient than any other, and innovation continues as consumers adapt to personalized searches involving audio and images.[16] Google shares reached a high of $154.84 in January 2024 before its fourth quarter earnings announcement, in anticipation of double-digit growth.

Airbnb

Why did no one think of reusing homes before Airbnb created a platform that connected homeowners with travelers? Its continued innovation has led it to countries around the globe with hotels and inns too signing up to be listed on Airbnb. Founded in 2008 by three friends who rented out their apartment with air mattresses and breakfast to conference goers in San Francisco, Airbnb slowly disrupted the hotel and lodging industry. It also decided to become public through its IPO during the peak of COVID-19 in 2020, just when the hospitality industry was desperately trying to survive with lockdowns preventing travel. Lockdowns and restrictions forced some people to find getaway homes online through Airbnb. During its IPO, shares opened 113 percent above the listing price of $68 per share; and by the end of the day, Airbnb's market value had reached $100.7 billion, making it the biggest IPO in history, as of December 10, 2020.[17] The community-driven hospitality company's app had more than 2 million homes listed within a decade, and it keeps innovating, with new offerings, such as personalization and design that does "bespoke matching" of travelers with suitable locations. It has also launched a luxury service that is designed to lure the wealthy, in which inspectors check the quality and features of some homes to lure an affluent clientele.[18]

Uber

Like Airbnb, Uber was a community sharing service—connecting drivers to riders. The ride sharing platform allowed for a more affordable and convenient way to go from point A to point B than a taxi. Since 2009, it has continued to innovate by providing consumers with scooter rentals, package deliveries, and Uber Eats—food delivery. Its competitor, Grab, bought Uber's Southeast Asian operations, expanding Grab's services in the region. But Grab's stock slumped 70 percent because markets in Singapore were unhappy that Uber could not survive in the region.[19]

Innovations are everywhere, including in the market trading arena, where blockchain technology is being used to decentralize financial systems (DeFi), which allows investors to access trade assets and financial services in an efficient way. Algorithmic analyses of data, cryptocurrency exchanges, and automated trading have also revolutionized how stock markets work.

SUGGESTED ACTIVITIES

1. Research at least three recent innovations that resulted in an increased stock price for the companies. Why were they so important for investors?
2. If there was one thing you could change technologically in newsrooms, what would it be? Research to find out if it has already been done.

How Innovative Google Defied Negative Press and Came Out an IPO Winner

When Larry Page and Sergey Brin started working on a research project called BackRub (yup, that could have been the name, instead of Google), they had no idea an algorithm that ranked search results would one day shape how people lived and worked, becoming an obsessive habit for the world.[20] They ran their company from the garage of a friend named Susan Wojcicki (who later became CEO of YouTube), and they raised funds, including from a seed investor named Jeff Bezos. In 1998, Google was incorporated as a company, thanks to a $100,000 investment by Sun Microsystems' co-founder Andy Bechtolsheim. Then they hired Eric Schmidt, who, as CEO for ten years, further built the company, launching its IPO in 2004 at a price of $85 per share. There was a lot of furor over Google's IPO, including the consideration of a "Dutch Auction," in which a company collects bids from many investors and the lowest bid becomes the offer price for the IPO on the exchange. The dilemma about Google going public was written about a lot by journalists as the company maneuvered its way around how best to raise capital. "Don't bother to bid on this shot-in-the-dark IPO," wrote a *BusinessWeek* columnist. "How Miscalculation and Hubris Hobbled Celebrated Google IPO," was what the *Wall Street Journal* carried on its front page. Google's "limbo" and its potentially "unconventional IPO" provided fodder for journalists and excitement for financial traders. In a *Harvard Business Review* article in 2010, six years after the IPO, Eric Schmidt wrote: "I remember thinking as we headed down to the Nasdaq trading floor, '*We're screwed.*'"[21]

Despite the press's skepticism, Google's first trade on its IPO launch day started at $100, not $85—18 percent higher than expected. It closed at $100.30 that day. "There was an unbelievable amount of excitement in the press," wrote Schmidt. Since then, innovations have been limitless for this company that has changed how people gather information—Gmail, Chrome, Docs, Calendar, Maps, Android, Drive, Cloud, Books, Vault, Wear OS, TV, to all the expectations about artificial intelligence—underscoring why it may have felt the need to change its name to Alphabet in 2015, making Google a unit under its umbrella.

11

POLICY, LEGISLATION, AND THE COURTS

Financial markets need to operate within certain rules and regulations—for the sake of prudence. Given the complexity of trading, evolving strategies, and innovative financial products, it is necessary to maintain order in the markets to help deter stock manipulation and fraud. The US Securities and Exchange Commission (SEC) is responsible for the enforcement of rules in the stock market. Whenever the SEC announces an action against a company, it becomes pertinent news to investors, the media, and financial markets.

THE SECURITIES AND EXCHANGE COMMISSION

Timely filings or reports are one of the many methods used by the SEC to monitor the compliance of companies. If a company fails to be compliant with required filings, it could be subject to an SEC investigation and enforcement action, including trading suspensions and penalties.[1] For serious violations or activities that result in an investigation, the SEC may bring civil actions against a company in federal court and may work with the Department of Justice (DOJ) to seek criminal charges, depending on the severity of the violation.[2]

For any company, a serious offense may result in a warning letter, or Wells Notice, which is issued by the SEC to inform an entity of an enforcement action after an investigation—not a positive situation for the stock. Reporters are quick to report news of a Wells Notice because it means serious problems for a company. For example, on March 22, 2023, shares of Coinbase Global fell 13 percent after this United States–based cryptocurrency exchange platform disclosed that it had received a Wells Notice from the SEC related to its cryptocurrency products and activities that the regulator cited as not being registered or authorized. A likely headline would be, "COINBASE GETS SEC WELLS NOTICE." The company's shares fell 13 percent in after-hours trading.[3]

When the SEC decides to charge a firm because of a violation, it will inform the company and could also make an announcement, alerting the media when the violation is egregious. An order from the SEC will detail the violations and state any monetary amount reached in agreement with the company to settle the charges. The company may also agree to other remedial actions, along with cease-and-desist orders related to the matter. Sometimes, despite the SEC charges, a company still includes a statement saying it is "not admitting or denying" the SEC's findings. A case in point: In May 2022, the SEC charged Wells Fargo Advisors (an entity of Wells Fargo & Company) for failing to file Suspicious Activity Reports between 2017 and 2021, and Wells Fargo Advisors agreed to pay $7 million to settle the charges. The SEC's press release said, "In addition to the $7 million penalty, Wells Fargo Advisors, without admitting or denying the SEC's findings, agreed to a censure and a cease-and-desist order."[4]

While a Wells Notice is taken as a warning issued by the SEC for company violations, it is a subpoena that carries far-reaching consequences, because it includes the possibility of being summoned to court. During an investigation, before any charges are brought, the SEC may file a subpoena against a company and individuals—usually against the company's management. The subpoena will seek a court order for the company and/or individual(s) to provide documents and/or testimony related to an investigation. Whether it is a formal charge or an announcement of a subpoena, it is negative news for a company and its management, usually causing a decline in its stock.

For individuals, insider trading charges are among the most serious violations they can face from the SEC. Insider trading occurs when an individual receives material information that has not been made public and makes trades based on that information. It is inevitable that company officials will have significant knowledge and material information about the company's operations and results before it is released to the public. But trading on such information provides an unfair advantage.

Rules are therefore in place for certain company officials to buy and sell company stock on a schedule, and blackout periods are imposed—such as a certain number of days before the release of earnings—when they cannot engage in any trading. Insider trading charges may result in fines, and also criminal charges, and possibly even a jail sentence. For example, in June 2023, the SEC charged a former Pfizer statistician with insider trading based on information that was not yet released about Pfizer's successful study of the drug Paxlovid as an antiviral treatment for COVID-19. In its announcement of the charge, the SEC noted that Pfizer's stock rose nearly 11 percent on the news, which was the largest single-day price move in more than ten years. The SEC's announcement also alleged that the former Pfizer employee and a friend / business partner netted one-day investment returns on their trades of 2,458 percent and 791 percent, respectively.[5]

On a wider country level, in June 2023, SEC officials demanded to see audit papers of Chinese companies listed on US stock exchanges, with which the Chinese authorities had long been reluctant to comply, citing security concerns.[6] Finally, the SEC identified more than 150 Chinese companies as failing to meet US auditing standards, and five companies—all state-owned in China—agreed to delist from the New York Stock Exchange. This led to a decline in Chinese stocks around the world, especially those listed in Hong Kong.[7]

THE DEPARTMENT OF JUSTICE

Apart from fines and courtroom appearances linked to securities violations, companies could also face criminal charges by the Department of Justice for actions that violate laws. In January 2021, for example, the DOJ charged Boeing with "conspiracy to defraud the Federal Aviation Administration's Aircraft Evaluation Group in connection" with this group's "evaluation of Boeing's 737 Max airplane, which had two deadly crashes in which more than 300 people died. Boeing agreed to a settlement with the DOJ and to pay over $2.5 billion to cover a criminal monetary penalty, compensation payments to certain MAX airline customers, and to establish a fund to compensate beneficiaries of those who died in the two crashes."[8] In February 2024, the DOJ began another investigation of Boeing after a door plug completely detached from a 737 Max plane during the flight.[9]

Also, in July 2023, NextGen Healthcare agreed to settle allegations with the DOJ which accused it of violating the False Claims Act. The DOJ charged NextGen with misrepresenting some of the capabilities of its electronic health record software and providing illegal incentives for users to recommend the company's software. NextGen agreed to pay $31 million. Its stock ended the trading day up about 2 percent to $17.09. The positive trading could be attributed to a sigh of relief by investors after the matter was resolved, giving certainty about the status and finalization of the issue.[10]

Outside the United States, but involving a US company, the 1Malaysia Development Berhad (1MDB) case was about both politics and business as it revolved around a president, his associates, and Goldman Sachs, which provided banking and advisory services for 1MDB. To briefly summarize, 1MDB was an investment fund owned by the Malaysian government—it was created by then Prime Minister Najib Razak. The fund was established to be used for foreign investment and the development of public projects for the general economic benefit of the country. Goldman Sachs was an adviser to 1MDB for five years—between 2009 and 2014. Among the services the bank provided was conducting three bond deals that raised about $6.5 billion from investors and, for Goldman Sachs, fees of more than $600 million. 1MDB became embroiled in corruption when development projects failed to materialize and it became public knowledge that money from the fund was misused to keep the prime minister in power, was stolen by government officials and associates, and that bankers/employees of a local Goldman Sachs unit had paid government officials bribes to gain business contracts and had overlooked the misuse of funds. And this all happened without any action being taken, or questions asked, or suspicions raised, by the bank's control-and-risk mechanisms to escalate concerns or halt transactions and activities.

The DOJ charged Goldman Sachs with violating the Foreign Corrupt Practices Act, and in October 2020, the bank entered a deferred prosecution agreement in which it agreed to "pay a criminal penalty and disgorgement of over $2.9 billion." The DOJ said the bank also reached agreements with other authorities in the United Kingdom, Singapore, Malaysia, and elsewhere, and with domestic authorities in the United States.[11]

The 1MDB case underscores the importance of diligent corporate governance and how strict guardrails to monitor risk and adherence to compliance and regulations are mandatory and non-negotiable. For Goldman Sachs, 1MDB was a case from which its stock did not suffer significant or continued decline. The effect was borne personally by individuals who were prosecuted and by the company for the harm caused from tarnishing its reputation and negative publicity. Companies seek to portray and protect a positive reputation because reputational damage can lead to loss of business, which will affect profits and eventually the performance of the stock.

So, with the DOJ, the reason for any investigation or charges and the amount of a fine are the primary news. If a company pleads "guilty" in settling charges, that too is big news. What is definitely not news, however, is a statement from a company that may include saying that it "neither admits nor denies" certain actions related to the charges and settlement. That is the company trying to deny culpability or liability for its actions. But the charges and fine are what should be the determining factors.

REGULATORY AUTHORITIES

Political leaders exert power and influence by passing laws that regulatory authorities enforce, giving both the ability to move markets. Laws that are specifically related to certain industries and/or business activities will attract a lot of interest. On one hand, they will mean that business practices and processes will need to change to be compliant. But on the other hand, it also means operations may be affected negatively if the law seeks to curb or regulate, or positively if the law removes restrictions or introduces new rules that permit or expand certain activities. Laws are often developed and passed due to a crisis, or some business activity or scandal that shows lack of accountability, all of which usually cause a decline or even rout in the markets.

Traders, company executives, and investors will analyze and assess any legislation being considered before it becomes law to determine how trading activities may be affected. They will want to get ahead of any planned changes, especially if the anticipated changes are seen as potentially altering any aspect of business or trading activity. Being prepared to adapt and be ready for change is an essential strategy to maintain operations with as little disruption as possible and, hopefully, the level of profits.

In 2010, the US Congress passed the Dodd-Frank Wall Street Reform and Consumer Protection Act, which authorized the Commodity Futures Trading Commission to regulate the swaps marketplace—which was then valued at more than $400 trillion. The Dodd-Frank Act and added regulation came about because of the 2008 financial crisis, which was determined to be caused mostly by swaps. Swaps were not traded publicly and did not have any standard or regulatory rules or oversight.[12] The Commodity Futures Trading Commission charged three financial institutions in September 2023 for "swap reporting failures and other violations."[13]

In 2002, the Sarbanes-Oxley Act was passed to reform financial information reporting by public corporations. That law established the Public Company Accounting Oversight Board to establish and oversee rules for auditing, financial record-keeping, and certification by top company officials—CEOs, CFOs, and COOs. According to the new law, executives would be held criminally responsible if there was certain intentional or negligent conduct.[14] It came about in light of fraudulent financial record-keeping and erroneous reporting by companies—Enron and WorldCom were prime examples. Numerous news headlines and reports over time exposed the extent of inaccurate and improper accounting, causing the stocks of both companies to plummet, leading to billions of dollars in losses. Enron eventually declared bankruptcy in December 2001. It was the largest bankruptcy in the United States at the time.[15]

A bill with positive implications for the average American worker and that will likely be a boon to many financial companies, is the

SECURE 2.0 Act of 2022. This law brings several changes to retirement plans, such as the 401(k), which many large and mid-size companies offer to their employees. The changes are aimed at getting a greater number of workers to save more in preparation for retirement. Financial services companies anticipate benefiting from the law by offering new or expanded products and services, which will diversify and increase their revenue streams.

A regulatory body that is not often in the news, is not directly associated with the financial operation of companies, and that can be perceived as "boring"—but can also order companies to pay fines for violations of its regulations—is the Occupational Safety and Health Administration (OSHA), which is a part of the US Department of Labor. OSHA states that its purpose is to "ensure that employees work in a safe and healthful environment by setting and enforcing standards."

After over 200 inspections since 2017 of individual Dollar General locations and proposed fines, OSHA reached a settlement in July 2024 with the company. The terms required the discount retailer to pay $12 million and "make significant workplace safety improvements in stores nationwide."[16]

OSHA's activities may not result in frequent or occasional headlines because most public companies do not have workplaces that may compromise safety, such as those in construction and agriculture. But as the example of Dollar General shows, other work environments can also have unsafe working conditions that, if reported and not corrected, can result in fines from OSHA. Companies will sometimes see regulations as burdensome or unfair and seek to overturn them, taking cases all the way to the Supreme Court.

SUPREME COURT DECISIONS

A Supreme Court ruling in June 2022 that drew much attention was *West Virginia v. US Environmental Protection Agency (EPA).* The ruling was against the EPA, limiting its authority to regulate greenhouse gas or carbon emissions from coal and gas power plants, by generating power from alternative energy sources, such as wind and solar. The ruling stipulated that the EPA must first get approval from Congress before implementing climate change regulations to have power from so-called cleaner sources. Much of the focus on this decision was on the restrictive aspects for the EPA, but it was also noted that it was limited in scope to coal and natural gas. The ruling provided a short-term boost to industry stocks.[17]

Rulings from the US Supreme Court can affect business sectors, individual rights, and personal freedoms, all of which can have implications for the broader economy, although specific stocks may not be affected to cause noticeable market movement. The Court's ruling on June 23, 2022, to overturn the *Roe v. Wade* decision, which had given women the legal right to abortion in the United States, was viewed as one that could potentially affect the participation of women in the workforce over time.

The overturning of *Roe v. Wade* was seen as a setback for women and their personal autonomy. While such an issue may not directly affect financial markets, it has an impact on the broader economy. Before the reversal was officially announced, Treasury Secretary Janet Yellen, giving testimony before the Senate Banking Committee, told lawmakers that reproductive rights enabled more women to enter the workforce, and contributed to improving their lives, households, and the general economy. "*Roe v. Wade* and access to reproductive health care, including abortion, helped lead to increased labor force participation," Yellen said. "It enabled many women to finish school. That increased their earning potential. It allowed women to plan and balance their families and careers."[18]

Women engage in more than 75 percent of what is called "unpaid care work" worldwide. Unpaid care work includes cooking, cleaning, and other household chores, and being a caregiver. And unpaid care work supports the global economy—the total value of unpaid care and domestic work is estimated to be between 10 and 39 percent of gross domestic product—a higher contribution than sectors such as manufacturing, commerce, or transportation. The International Labor Organization estimates that care work would represent one-tenth of the world's economic output if it were valued equally as other work.[19]

For any direct impact on the market, the rollback of abortion rights was seen as possibly benefiting stocks of certain companies, such as Pfizer, which makes Depo-Provera, an injectable contraception product. Shares of Evofem Biosciences, a small company that makes an alternative birth control product, rose 30.6 percent after the Court's ruling on abortion. The stock had fallen more than 90 percent, trading below 40 cents before the ruling. It continued the positive uptrend and reached a high of $1.57 in early July 2022. But by the end of the month, it lost much of those gains and retreated to 80 cents a share, possibly on profit taking. Another small stock in the reproductive health sector, Femasys, also rose about 40 percent in the weeks after the decision on *Roe v. Wade*.[20]

What was seen as a political ruling by the Supreme Court occurred in 2000 to resolve the stalemate in the aftermath of the Bush-Gore election. It took five weeks for a winner to be declared, which happened on December 12, 2000, after the Court ruled against a recount of votes that were cast in Florida, which would have included the murkiness of looking at punched paper ballots or "chads" to determine valid votes.

Uncertainty is something that markets fear, and that is what was felt during the very unusual, long duration before George W. Bush was declared president in 2000. The financial world cares about election results because they can be harbingers of the long term—of future policies, legislation, and regulations—based on campaign ideas of the president and the majority in Congress. Policies, legislation, and regulations can affect various sectors and will also be viewed, along with the party administration, as probusiness or not.

In 2000, the Standard & Poor's 500 fell 7.8 percent from Election Day to the end of the year. While the unresolved election played a part in that downturn, other factors also accounted for the decline: low earnings and volatility in the technology sector, a profitability concern that was heightened by volatile dot-com stocks, an economic slowdown, and higher interest rates aimed at reducing inflation.[21]

While the stock market is not the measure of the economy, it determines the value of many companies—from large ones that have outsize roles in the economy to those classified as mid-size and small. In developing policy and legislation, governments need to strike a balance between regulations that implement standards for businesses and protect consumers. Businesses and industry lobbyists will always seek what is most in their favor, but regulations are important to conserve the integrity of markets and business operations in general.

SUGGESTED ACTIVITIES

1. Look up statements from regulatory agencies and write headlines from related press releases where a public company was reprimanded with a fine.
2. Use the New York Stock Exchange and Nasdaq historical stock website to check the movement of a company stock after regulatory action was announced; see www.nasdaq.com/market-activity/quotes/historical and www.nyse.com/market-data/historical.

Violations, Diplomacy, and a CFO Arrest

It was a nexus of politics, business, and diplomacy—the arrest of a top executive in a foreign country. Meng Wanzhou, the CFO of Huawei Technologies and its founder's daughter, was detained on December 1, 2018, by the Canadian authorities at the request of the US government.

Huawei's CFO was arrested at Vancouver International Airport, where she was changing flights on a business trip from Hong Kong to Mexico City. Canadian police detained her with the expectation that she would face extradition to the United States on charges that she had played a role in helping or enabling Huawei to violate sanctions placed on Iran. Neither Canadian nor US officials immediately disclosed her arrest—the news broke a few days later—and they also did not readily give details about the reasons for it, partly because a judge had granted Meng's request to prohibit publication and the release of information about the case.

Huawei, a Chinese technology company that sells telecom equipment and smartphones worldwide, had restrictions on the equipment and devices it could sell in the United States because of national security concerns. Telecom and technology companies were duly warned against doing business or entering into any agreement with Huawei for sales of phones or related equipment.[22]

In a statement issued a week after her arrest following a hearing in a Canadian court, Huawei said it was "not aware of any wrongdoing by Ms. Meng." And a day before the hearing, top officials in China and Ottawa requested the release of Meng and asked for an explanation for her detention. A day after the hearing, China's Foreign Ministry officials had a meeting with the Canadian ambassador in Beijing in which they voiced strong disagreement, requested that the ambassador send a "strong protest" about the matter, and warned that there would be consequences if the CFO was not released immediately. But a week after being arrested, Meng remained in detention.

On December 10, China retaliated and detained a former Canadian diplomat and an entrepreneur on espionage charges. Days later, Canada condemned the detention of the men as "arbitrary." A day after the detention of the two Canadians, Meng was released on $10 million bail and ordered to wear a tracking device at a mansion she owned in Vancouver, as the case continued for her possible extradition to the United States to face charges. The main Asian indices—Japan's Nikkei, Hong Kong's Hang Seng, and China's Shanghai Composite—all sold off after news of the arrest was made public days after it actually occurred.

Concern about possible escalation to a trade war caused volatility in the US stock market after the news was widely reported the week after the arrest. Stocks of companies that were suppliers of technology, semiconductors, and networking equipment to Huawei were most affected, with Broadcom Inc., Qualcomm Inc., Intel Corp., and Advanced Micro Devices among the stocks that declined the most. At the time, uncertainty about the eventual outcome and speculation meant that the revenue of those companies could be hurt severely if restrictions were placed on their business as suppliers to Huawei, or worse, if they would be banned from engaging in business with Huawei.[23]

The Department of Justice brought a total of thirteen criminal charges against Huawei, certain of its affiliates, and Meng. Lawyers took legal action to have her freedom restored and possible extradition removed, but she remained in Canada for more than two and a half years after her arrest. During that time, along with the Canadian diplomat and entrepreneur who were detained and charged in China, another repercussion was that a Canadian ambassador to China was somewhat pressured into resigning after making a statement that seemed to oppose or question Meng's detention.

A hearing on Meng's extradition did not occur until August 2021. She was eventually released in September 2021, after reaching a deferred prosecution agreement with the US government on fraud charges. The DOJ said she "has taken responsibility for her principal role in perpetrating a scheme to defraud a global financial institution."[24]

The agreement reached included the withdrawal of the extradition request and the release of two Canadians detained in China. The day after the agreement, both Meng and the two Canadian men returned to their respective countries.[25]

12

SUPPLY CHAINS AND GLOBAL TRADE

The interdependence between countries for supplies and raw materials was never as evident as it was during the COVID-19 pandemic. Companies around the world faced staff shortages, factory closures, and manufacturing delays as the disease upended daily lives and altered routines everywhere.

This global disruption showed that certain sectors fared worse than others, however. Among the hardest hit were the food and manufacturing sectors, which rely heavily on supply chains that include the movement of goods between different countries. While China took the heat for the origin of COVID-19 and the first recorded illness, the country also became embroiled in aggressive trade disputes with the United States, its biggest trade partner.

Soured or souring international relations can create mass unrest, derail investor sentiments, and lead to currency fluctuations, keeping reporters and traders on their toes. Social unrest in authoritarian regimes can scare investors because outcomes of decisions can be unpredictable, thereby affecting financial markets. An interesting point was highlighted in a paper from the International Monetary Fund that looked at a data set of 156 types of social unrest in the world and concluded that stock market movements are "large and negative" in countries with a more authoritarian regime.[1]

TRADE DEALS AND TRADE WARS

Usually, the Top News Desk at a publication handles news related to international trade deals and disputes. The Headlines desk in a newswire agency is always on alert during global conferences and high-level meetings between dignitaries from different countries because one never knows what agreement may be reached, or even about a resulting debacle or fiasco spurred by an errant comment by a representative that could be worthy of a headline or a blog write-up.

Trade disputes between the United States and China are a prime example of how tariff impositions and threat exchanges can happen, as seen during Donald Trump's presidency in 2018. Tariffs imposed by the United States hurt many Chinese firms listed on the US stock exchanges due to the reliance on supply chains between the two countries.

When President Trump threatened to impose an additional $200 billion in levies on Chinese goods in June 2018, a year before the COVID-19 outbreak, the news roiled global stock markets as investors feared that this could result in a trade war.[2] The Dow Jones Industrial Average dropped 400 points in early trading, wiping out one year's gain, and closed down 237 points at the end of trading on June 18, 2018. Companies with operations in China received this news with trepidation: shares of Apple, known for its factories in China, fell 1.5 percent, and Caterpillar Inc., a construction, mining, and industrial equipment manufacturing company with operations also in China, fell 2.7 percent.

Global markets experienced a nosedive as the spat between the two countries increased and reporters and traders updated readers and clients, respectively, as shares reacted everywhere. Trump's proclamations provided fodder for journalists, who scrambled to get quotes from economists and industry pundits as investors bailed out of various markets—stocks, foreign exchange, and oil. Chinese stocks recorded their steepest fall, as the benchmark Shanghai Composite Index dropped 3.8 percent, to 2,907.82—its lowest in nearly two years. The yuan also fell to its lowest level against the dollar in five months, and oil prices dropped as investors feared the dispute would hurt economic growth. In Europe, all the major markets fell, with the FTSE closing down 0.4 percent, France's CAC down 1.1 percent, and Germany's DAX down 1.2 percent.[3]

In August 2022, Nancy Pelosi, then speaker of the US House of Representatives, made a controversial trip to Taiwan, a self-ruled island that

China claims to own.[4] The trip, which happened during a sensitive time, when China was supporting Russia in the Ukraine war, was not viewed favorably by Beijing. China proceeded to undertake military exercises around the island, and it also suspended some important dialogues with the United States.

CHINA'S ROLE IN GLOBAL MARKETS

As is well known, news from or about China has a direct impact on market sentiments. What happens between the United States and China affects not just shares of US companies but also hundreds of Chinese companies listed on the New York Stock Exchange (NYSE), Nasdaq, and the NYSE American Exchange.

As of January 9, 2023, 252 Chinese companies, with a total market capitalization of $1.03 trillion, were listed on the three exchanges.[5] Many of the shareholders in these companies are people in China, foreign traders, and US institutional investors. Goldman Sachs estimated in March 2023 that US institutional investors held about $200 billion worth of American Depository Receipts in Chinese firms.[6]

News that involves China—whether macroeconomic concerns on inflation or political uncertainty—can lead to equity market drawdowns around the globe. Journalists also need to keep themselves abreast of international affairs and events that can lead to fluctuations of the yuan against the dollar, as that too can cause broader market reactions. For example, when the United States announced a sale of $180 million worth of submarine-launched torpedoes to Taiwan, this news led to a decline in global markets over concerns of a new security crackdown by Beijing.[7]

National security allegations have often led to retaliatory moves by China, such as raiding offices of global consulting firms to crack down on companies with overseas investors.[8] Amid an environment that is not transparent, international journalists in China need to rely heavily on unnamed sources to disseminate news globally.

Similarly, Huawei Technologies, the Chinese manufacturing company, was not allowed to obtain supplies from any American company because the United States claimed it was engaging in cyber espionage. These crackdowns and stipulations happened amid the tension surrounding COVID-19 and China's alleged role as the source of the virus, which led journalists and traders to believe that United States–China tensions could become a headwind for stock markets.[9]

Journalists covering technology also keenly observe Chinese companies trading in the United States that could potentially experience significant stock movements as a result of any slight issue in the United States or in China. E-commerce companies—such as Alibaba (NYSE), Pinduoduo (Nasdaq), and JD.com (Nasdaq)—cater largely to the Chinese market and are headquartered in China, but they reap the benefits that come from being listed on a US exchange. Investors can cash in during periods of market euphoria and better international relations, but they can also lose out when there are negative sentiments during a downturn.

COVID-19 AND SUPPLY CHAIN DISRUPTIONS

National lockdowns during the COVID-19 pandemic created a situation in which manufacturing took a beating. People responsible for connecting one end of the supply chain to another found themselves helplessly confined as travel and movement became restricted. Many activities—from manual labor in most factories to transportation by railroads, shippers, and airlines—came to a grinding halt or slowed considerably. While many traditional sectors that employed manual labor were adversely affected, employment opportunities were generated in high-tech industries that enabled people to work remotely.

Journalists on the ground were frontline workers braving disease and disruption to tell the story of the supply chain's breakdown. The lockdown and halt in the transportation of goods, including from China—the main exporter of goods to the United States since 2009—was particularly severe for retailers. Investors became anxious and markets were turbulent, fluctuating significantly as news of the outbreak in China emerged and the severity of supply chain disruptions became evident.[10] A key concern for investors was how such disruption would cause inflationary pressures.

As the trade rift widened between the United States and China, the latter lost its "top exporter" title in 2023, replaced by Mexico and Canada.[11] China exports to the United States between January and May of 2023 fell 25 percent, to $169 billion, according to US Commerce Department statistics. Data journalists pounced on this information, analyzed and opined about it, as global stocks dipped, influenced by the significant export downturn in China after the pandemic's onset.[12]

RETAILERS' RELIANCE ON OVERSEAS SUPPLIES

During the COVID-19 pandemic, shortages were seen in various products, such as meats, clothing, accessories, semiconductors, alcohol, steel and chemicals, and oxygen tanks.[13] In the holiday season in 2020, supplies of both real and fake Christmas trees were affected as tree growers could not find truckers to take them to market.[14] With nearly 30 million Christmas trees sold every year, as demand surged and supply was curtailed, so did the price of trees. Many presents under the tree that were to be shipped from China did not make it on time.

As e-commerce started thriving and holiday menus were decided, Amazon was doing everything to fill up positions to keep deliveries going, including spending "several billion dollars" to manage labor shortages and supply chain woes in the run-up to Christmas.[15]

With a high inflation rate in North America, Europe, and Asia, traders were beginning to worry about market volatility and the lack of sizable returns. With every bit of bad news about disease, death, and food insecurity, investors got nervous and put their money in safe havens like bonds and bullion (gold).

March 16, 2020, was when the coronavirus and its supply chain woes became a reality for investors as the disease dominated headlines in every newsroom.[16] The Standard & Poor's Index dropped 12 percent, and Nasdaq closed 12.3 percent lower, its worst day ever. The Dow suffered its worst loss since the "Black Monday" crash of 1987, when the US markets fell more than 20 percent in a single day. "The market didn't hear what it wanted to hear. I don't think that it wanted to hear that this was going to last until July and August, and now the market does the math," said BNY Mellon strategist Liz Young on CNBC's *Closing Bell.*

FOOD SECURITY CRISIS

Just when the world was figuring out how to fight COVID, a war started. Russia invaded Ukraine on February 24, 2022, causing inflationary pressures to gain traction worldwide. With food prices already high, prolonged disruption of exports from both Russia and Ukraine would lead to a new crisis. Journalists covering the war increased awareness of how it had disrupted supplies of wheat, barley, and sunflower oil, among other food products, especially to parts of Africa, Asia, and the Middle East, leading to concerns that it could cause millions to die of hunger. The UN's Food and Agriculture Organization estimated that the war could increase the number of undernourished people by 8 million to 13 million in 2022.[17] The conflict not only affected the availability of cereals and vegetable oils, but also caused interruptions of fertilizer exports and an increase in energy prices. The Food and Agriculture Organization's Food Price Index, which tracks monthly changes in international prices for a basket of commodities, showed that the February index was at the highest level since its inception in 1990.[18]

An advanced and modern country like Singapore in Southeast Asia, which was still importing 90 percent of its food, was in a for a reality check as it felt the pinch of the trade slowdown. Its overreliance on imports led Singapore to implement a 30/30 program: to produce 30 percent of its produce in-house by 2030.[19]

Food distribution is not just about hunger—it is an economic and social issue. More than 12 percent of Americans experienced food insecurities in 2022, according to government data.[20]

How is food a stock market issue? When families struggle to feed their own, it affects their spending and investments, and in turn corporate results and investor sentiments. Companies in the food and agriculture industry are affected because demand for their products falls as consumer affordability declines, dragging down profits, which sends distress signals to stock markets. For example, in 2023 rice production dropped drastically, driving up prices to a decade high because of the war in Ukraine, import restrictions by rice-rich India to meet domestic needs, and crops destroyed due to bad weather in China and Pakistan.[21]

Investors like to put their money in sectors of high demand, and this is what happened with agricultural Exchange Traded Funds (ETFs), which are open to the public. As demand for food grew in countries suffering from food shortages, commodity-linked ETFs saw an uptick. According to Lighthouse Reports, investors had pumped $1.2 billion into two major agricultural ETFs between January and April 2022, compared with $197 billion for all of 2021.[22]

Much of the information on world trade supply often comes to reporters at global economic conferences, such as the Group of Twenty Summit, the World Economic Forum's meeting in Davos, Asia-Pacific Economic Cooperation, and the Jackson Hole Economic Policy Symposium in Jackson Hole, Wyoming—all of which are attended by leaders and decision-makers who come together to find ways to collaborate on projects and policies that could have a positive impact on their societies.

NEWS FROM GLOBAL CONFERENCES

Here are three examples of annual meetings attended by dignitaries that draw the attention of journalists and financial markets.

The World Economic Forum

The World Economic Forum (WEF) is held at the beginning of every year in Davos, a popular ski resort in the Swiss Alps, to discuss next steps for issues that concern the world and its peoples. The WEF meeting is attended by presidents, celebrities, environmentalists, activists, academics, journalists, and business leaders. It is where powerful change is discussed. It is a rich story environment for reporters, as new ideas and strategies come to light and financial traders anxiously await and interpret news from the WEF on their web portals.

It is a meeting that can have contradictions and competing agendas, say some journalists. In his book *Davos Man*, Peter Goodman, a correspondent for the *New York Times*, talks about hypocrisy and cites how the same billionaires causing some of the world's biggest problems attend the WEF to discuss ways to solve them.[23] Ironically, in 2023, during the Davos summit where climate change and "Just Transition" were on the agenda, billionaires and politicians arrived in their private jets, becoming a talking point for journalists and consumers about how such jets are a big exacerbator of greenhouse gas emissions.

Jackson Hole Symposium

The Jackson Hole Symposium is an annual gathering of central bankers in the middle of every year at which thirty-seven to forty countries discuss methods and strategies to solve common issues through possible monetary intervention. In 2023, its overarching theme was "inflation," which was the top global economic concern as economies were recovering from the effects of COVID-19. Jerome Powell, then the US Federal Reserve chair, gave a speech in August that year at that retreat saying inflation "remains too high" and that interest rates were likely to remain high for some time.[24] He also expressed confidence in US economic growth and hinted that early signs of recovery were being seen in the housing market. As journalists headlined Powell's remarks, the markets cheered and stocks rallied across the United States, Europe, and Asia.[25]

Asia-Pacific Economic Cooperation

Asia-Pacific Economic Cooperation (APEC) is specifically for countries located around the rim of the Pacific Ocean, with the busiest container ports and international shipping, and aims to foster economic cooperation, while also establishing new markets for agricultural produce and raw materials. At its annual conference, APEC brings together heads of governments from the United States, Russia, Japan, China, Australia, Southeast Asian nations, and others. It is a great opportunity for correspondents to meet and interview high-level politicians and write important stories with global influence.

The 2023 APEC meeting in San Francisco was largely focused on tensions between the United States and China, as presidents Joe Biden and Xi Jinping were meeting a year after their last meeting at the Group of Twenty in Bali, Indonesia.[26] While friendly, light-hearted topics such as sending more pandas to the United States were discussed, hard-hitting discussions also topped the agenda. For example, China agreed to regulate exports of components that are used to make the opioid Fentanyl, which Biden hoped would decrease drug trafficking in the United States. Biden also highlighted how US companies—such as Apple, Amazon, Pepsico, Boeing, and Delta Airlines—had invested heavily in the region. Interestingly, CEOs of other companies, such as Tesla's Elon Musk and Citigroup's Jane Fraser, were also present at the APEC meeting, expecting and/or hoping–as journalists discovered—to have a personal or one-to-one meeting with Chinese president Xi.[27]

Every small thing said by a dignitary at a meeting or a press conference that can indicate change in a stance or policy, and thereby could affect international relations, is material to be headlined. Very often, if the meeting is open to the public, market traders are also glued to the television so they can make quick trading decisions for their clients.

"I remember during the US-led invasion of Iraq during the Gulf War, there was a press conference and they were about to announce something definitive," recalled Christina Pantin, a former senior editor with Reuters. "I remember sitting at the desk that was covering the stock market, and I think as soon as Secretary of State James Baker said the word 'Unfortunately,' the Dow just began to tank!"

SUGGESTED ACTIVITIES

1. What are the other industries, besides technology, that have been affected by trade disputes? Give examples of at least two companies in each sector.
2. Name at least three products that were affected by supply chain hurdles in the United States during the last two years.

How United States–China Trade and Technology Disputes Affected Chipmakers like Nvidia

As tensions continued and both countries engaged in tit-for-tat insults in 2022, the United States imposed a new restriction—that semiconductor companies in the United States would need a new license to sell chips to China—in an attempt to stop Beijing from receiving advanced US technologies to strengthen its military.

This was a big blow to Nvidia, the top artificial intelligence (AI) chip designer in the United States, and its shares fell 6.6 percent on the news. Shares of rival companies AMD and Intel slipped, too. A few weeks earlier, Biden had committed $280 billion to high-tech manufacturing and given tax breaks to companies that built computer chip manufacturing plants in the United States, to reduce reliance on China.[28]

Chips are used in many gadgets and as the world faced the COVID-19 pandemic in 2020 and 2021, more chips were required for laptops and webcams, which were being heavily used for remote work. To put restrictions on US companies on a product that was in heavy demand was not taken well by the financial markets.

News about the US restrictions on chipmakers, just when the world was opening up to resume normal trade after the pandemic, negatively affected investor sentiments and harmed chipmakers' stocks. For Nvidia, this move meant exports of its A100 and H100 chips, which were designed to speed up machine learning tasks, would be affected.

Chinese officials were upset at what Biden had done, saying that "actions from the United States deviated from the principle of fair competition and violated international economic and trade rules." The Chinese government put out a statement: "The US side should immediately stop its wrongdoing, treat companies from all over the world including Chinese companies fairly, and do more things that are conducive to the stability of the world economy."

Nvidia, the AI chip supplier to companies like Meta and Microsoft-backed OpenAI, kept bearing the brunt of this dispute. In 2023, the chipmaker said the US government had told the company to halt exports of high-end AI chips to China.

Nvidia did not let restrictions hinder its research and development, and it started making chips exclusively for the Chinese market. In March 2024, it launched its Blackwell chip series, and said it would market and distribute the chip through its Chinese partner. "Nvidia is easily the biggest single story in the stock market over the last year," Axios markets editors wrote in their February 21, 2024, newsletter.

News about chipmakers in the trade dispute saga became widely followed, and Bloomberg News reported in July 2024 that the United States has told its allies it will impose the most severe trade restrictions available—that is, a provision called the Foreign Direct Product Rule—if companies continue giving China access to advanced semiconductor technology.[29] A week after the Bloomberg story, Reuters did an exclusive piece, saying that Nvidia is working on a version of its new flagship AI chips for the China market that would be compatible with current US export controls.[30] Nvidia is a perfect example of how companies (in this case, chipmakers) become embroiled in a dispute between countries, and will do everything possible to survive.

13

DISEASE, DISASTER, AND DISRUPTION

Global disruption of any kind generates attention, and financial markets are one of the first places where reactions and indications of severity are felt. For financial markets, disruption, disorder, disagreements, and disturbances are unwelcome news because they mean the interruption of the usual routines and what is normal—and this creates uncertainty. Financial markets are never on any certain, straight path. So, they expect, and are comfortable with, periodic volatility—movement up or down, flat, or mostly unchanged—because there is a certainty that the breadth of market activity works and exists in a manner that is reasonably balanced. Occurrences of hostilities, conflicts, and disagreements between nations, and also domestically, are therefore certain to move financial markets.

Unpredictable and external factors that have increasingly been a cause for concern for businesses, and therefore markets, include the outbreak of diseases and natural and/or climate-related disasters. While businesses have insurance coverage for their operations and assets and even catastrophic insurance coverage, that still cannot offset the immediate repercussions from the loss of resources and ceasing of operations resulting from natural disasters. To a lesser extent—except for a pandemic—widespread disease can also disable normal business activities by affecting human resources—the people who are needed to work for the business to operate. This chapter examines how disruptions can change or alter business operations and have global implications, whether they happen as a result of a natural phenomenon or from differences between internal or external groups.

EPIDEMICS AND PANDEMICS

Like climate change, which is causing different and more frequent weather events, there is a growing fear that epidemics and pandemics could also become more prevalent. And the concern is that completely new ones may develop.

What became the first global pandemic in more than a hundred years started as a mystery or never-before-seen respiratory illness first observed in China. As more people became sick and awareness spread, the name "China virus" was used, until the scientific community used the characteristics of the illness to identify it as "coronavirus disease of 2019," abbreviated as COVID-19. As the disease crossed borders with global travel, and at its worst started to overwhelm hospitals and medical facilities even in countries with advanced health systems, many governments made the drastic decision to halt or curtail all but certain deemed "essential services" to limit person-to-person interactions. Most business activities, such as typical office work, were deemed nonessential. Businesses that could function without a physical location had their employees work remotely without commuting to an office. Lockdowns undoubtedly caused business activities to slacken significantly, which was immediately reflected in sharp declines in the stock market.

Using February 19, 2020, as the base level for the peak of the US stock market before the precipitous decline caused by the COVID-19 pandemic and government-ordered lockdown of all but essential businesses, the Standard & Poor's (S&P) 500 declined to 66 percent of its peak about a month later in March. The sectors that were first to experience significant declines were energy, which had low points of 44 percent; industrials, 58 percent; and financials, 57 percent of their index level on February 19. Energy stocks fell because of the lockdown that resulted in many businesses closing their offices for in-person work, causing less commuting and transportation that exacerbated a drastic decrease in the demand for oil. This in turn caused the price of oil and the stocks of oil companies to fall.

A year later, in February 2021, the energy sector had not fully recovered as the gains registered reached only 84 percent of its peak level. In contrast, the sectors that performed better were health care and consumer staples, which recorded low points of 72 percent and 76 percent, respectively, from their peak levels. There was a constant demand for health-related services and products and, consequently, stocks in those sectors would be among the better performers. Goods and services classified as consumer staples—essential items, such as groceries—were also top performers and had even higher demand because most people were confined to their homes.

By March 2021, the sectors with the strongest recoveries were information technology, up 133 percent; discretionary consumer goods, which increased 130 percent; and materials, which rose 124 percent. The positive performance of information technology companies was attributed to prolific use of their products and services by just about everyone. Discretionary consumer items—nonessential goods, such as clothes, automobiles, and restaurants—increased largely because of pent-up demand from the lockdown.[1] After reaching its low, the stock market was choppy, with periods of rapid rise and pullbacks—volatility that was not unexpected.

Such adverse reactions in the stock markets were not documented during other fairly recent pandemics and epidemics, but then those did not result in thousands of people being ill at the same time worldwide, in immense loss of life, or in hospitals being filled to capacity with sick people. During the Swine Flu pandemic from March 2009 to August 2010, the Dow rose over 40 percent.[2] Severe Acute Respiratory Syndrome (SARS) virus started in China in 2003 and caused the death of 774 people, but efforts to combat the disease prevented it from spreading and stopped a larger outbreak. The S&P 500 fell almost 13 percent during the outbreak of SARS, but it was still up over 20 percent that year.[3] Containment of SARS and the start of a period of economic growth in the United States accounted for SARS not having a negative impact. The Middle Eastern Respiratory Syndrome, which was identified in 2012, also did not have a tremendous impact worldwide and consequently did not affect markets. The Ebola virus killed thousands, mostly in West Africa, in 2014. It sparked fears of what would happen if the virus spread and was transmitted in systems and areas used by a mass of people—such as on subways, in airports and airplanes, and at theme parks. It remained largely in West African countries, however, with four persons testing positive in the United States and one person—an immigrant from Liberia—dying of the disease in the United States.[4]

While a pandemic or an epidemic may cause significant loss of life, they can be studied, and treatments and even cures can be developed. Pandemics and epidemics may emerge unexpectedly; but over time, scientists will likely identify patterns and traits and be able to make predictions. That is not so with acts of terrorism. Whether they are domestic or from an external source, they seem to occur randomly, and that terrifies people. Although many terror attacks are thwarted, unbeknown to residents, those that do occur garner the attention of everyone, including the markets.

TERRORISM

September 11, 2001, was a day of unimaginable horror and loss of life, when terrorists used planes as weapons to carry out an attack in the United States, hijacking four large jetliners and crashing three of them into iconic buildings. The assault caused the loss of 3,000 lives; the complete collapse of two skyscraper towers of the World Trade Center in New York City, which were once the tallest buildings in the world; and damaged a section of the Pentagon in Washington. A fourth plane that was hijacked with the intent to maneuver it to Washington crashed in Pennsylvania after passengers fought to overpower the hijackers. The nature and scale of the attack was unprecedented. The twin towers of the World Trade Center were located near Wall Street, and many financial firms had offices in the towers. Trading had not yet started for the day, but as the gravity and tremendous shock of the attacks were realized, US stock exchanges did not open that day. They remained shut for the rest of the week.

As the scale of the attacks became clear, markets around the world where trading had started also closed for the rest of the day. When the New York Stock Exchange opened a week later, stocks fell 7.1 percent on the first day. About $1.47 trillion in value was lost in that first week after trading resumed. At the end of the first week of trading, the Dow had declined more than 14 percent, the S&P had fallen 11.6 percent, and the Nasdaq was down 16 percent. Insurance and airline stocks had the steepest declines, particularly the stocks of the airplane companies that were used in the attacks—American Airlines and United Airlines. Stocks of insurance companies, which would pay out billions in claims, also saw severe declines.[5] Seeking a flight to safety, investors shunned stocks and bought gold, contributing to a price rise of almost 6 percent for the yellow metal. Gas and oil prices rose as more information about the attacks became known, and fears grew that the United States might retaliate and cause disruption in oil production and shipments from the Middle East.[6]

Similarly, oil prices and the effect of terrorism again became a global concern after October 7, 2023, when Hamas attacked Israel. When the stock markets opened that Monday, the S&P 500 fell 0.3 percent in early trading and energy stocks rose by about 3 percent. The Brent crude oil price had risen over the weekend but stabilized when markets opened and fell in the days after to just over $88, from just over $90.[7] In the next weeks, as Israel declared war and started a full onslaught on the territory of Gaza, which was ruled by Hamas and from where it carried out its attack on Israel, oil prices fell, trading mostly in the low $80 range in November.[8] At the end of 2023 and into 2024, prices were in the high $70s, with concerns arising not so much from the Israel and Hamas conflict, but from the attacks by the Houthis in Yemen on ships traversing the Red Sea. With ships facing higher insurance due to the risk of damage from war, along with increased fuel expenses to take a longer route around Africa, the risk to economies was that higher consumer prices would worsen inflation.[9] These incidents, and the invasion of Ukraine by Russia, accounted for intense reporting by journalists as the world recovered from the COVID-19 pandemic.

Attacks, invasions, wars, and conflicts among leading economies result in shocks to financial markets and just about all sectors of businesses. While information is gathered and analyzed for a comprehensive understanding of what happened and how, investors and traders want to learn more about winners and losers in money markets, such as the price of gold and oil immediately after 9/11, or the declining value of hotel and airline stocks during the pandemic. With the globalization of manufacturing and the movement of goods, cross-border effects are also analyzed when any terror or significant hostile event occurs, especially if it affects a Group of Seven or a Group of Twenty member country, or one that is strategically important because of a transportation route or as a manufacturing hub. Unexpected or sudden changes of governments are also disruptive because they bring uneasiness among traders and investors, and cause uncertainty in markets.

ASSASSINATIONS, ELECTIONS, AND COUPS

Similar to how terror attacks or natural disasters alter the state and welfare of people in a country, so do assassinations of political figures or officials, along with attempts to gain power forcibly outside legal jurisdictions established by countries. On August 13, 2024, a twenty-year-old white male with an AK-47 rifle climbed onto a rooftop, hundreds of feet from the site of a Republican campaign rally, and fired shots at then former US president Donald Trump in an attempt to assassinate him. He was campaigning as the Republican presumptive nominee for president in the upcoming election of November 2024. The former president was on stage and had been speaking for less than 10 minutes when he heard a whizzing sound and felt something hit his right ear. The country was very relieved that he was not seriously hurt, because he had fortunately just slightly turned his head to look at a screen to speak about the chart displayed on it. His right ear was injured, and the wound turned out to be not serious or debilitating. The shooter was killed by a Secret Service sniper.

The headlines below are examples of what would have been written as soon as news of the incident reached the media:

FORMER PRESIDENT TRUMP SHOT AT RALLY IN PENNSYLVANIA

TRUMP LED OFF STAGE BY SECRET SERVICE AFTER SHOOTING

TRUMP SHOT, WOUND NOT LIFE-THREATENING
TRUMP SHOT AT RALLY IN BUTLER, PA
TRUMP SHOT, CAMPAIGN SAYS "HE'S FINE"

Headlines would follow about the former president's condition and treatment, and this information dominated the news for the next few days. Information about injuries to others and specifically about how the incident unfolded, with direct quotations or descriptions from those present, was very important. In any breaking news situation, getting credible eyewitness accounts is crucial for getting details and establishing what the scene was like as the incident occurred.

This news cycle continued in the days ahead, as officials worked to ascertain a motive, get a profile of the shooter, and understand procedures and any security lapses or breaches that occurred. Because the incident happened on a Saturday evening, market reaction would not be seen until the following Monday. Contrary to what may have been expected, stocks rose overall, with the Dow Jones Industrial Average closing up over 200 points, the Nasdaq Composite adding 74 points, and the S&P 500 Index rising almost 16 points. While headlines would not be written to possibly explain the positive market reaction, it is important to understand why or to identify reasons for the market results. An explanation or perspectives from different market makers can be given in a story. In this case, the thinking was that there would be an outpouring of sympathy for the former president—even from some of his detractors—and that he would consequently gain even more support to give him higher odds of winning the upcoming election. His policies and ideas were also viewed as more business friendly, and this sentiment also contributed to the positive outcome in the stock market on the first trading day after the event.

An assassination was carried out against former prime minister Shinzo Abe of Japan on July 8, 2022. He had been Japan's longest-serving prime minister, and his fiscal and monetary policies to end deflation were dubbed "Abenomics." He was shot and killed at a campaign rally he was attending to endorse a candidate for the upcoming election. The benchmark Nikkei 225 Index fell as soon as the news became known, erasing earlier gains. The yen rose as investors sought safer havens as currency markets reacted to the loss of a man who had supported the need to keep interest rates low to help economic growth. While the yen's reaction was short-lived and many market pundits were unable to explain why it rose, it also shows that there is no constant to what market reaction and concerns may be when a significant event such as an assassination occurs. The general takeaway is for reporters to be knowledgeable about national and global politics, economic policy, and related factors that may be debated or matter to the economy at the time.

The same is true for government changes, whether they occur through due process in an election or through an unlawful action such as a coup. An analysis of how the country's economy has been performing, the policies that were implemented and/or had a role in the economy, and whether these policies were seen as negative or positive become pertinent news. With such facts, one can assess how a different government may change or continue with certain policies and programs, and the resulting impact, if any, on financial markets.

GEOPOLITICS

When Russia started a war against Ukraine in late February 2022, the World Bank was among the global entities expressing alarm that the conflict could disrupt production and transportation of grains and seeds from both countries, a scenario that could lead to food insecurity and hunger in lower-income countries. Could such a situation further increase perilous attempts by people on the African continent to migrate to European countries? Many in Ukraine—even the government—downplayed or did not want to believe the dire warnings from the United States about Russia's intentions. So when Russia struck, this led to a sudden and massive exodus—in the shortest time ever—of more than 1 million Ukrainians into neighboring Poland and thousands into other nearby countries.

Considering the factors that cause geopolitics to move markets—the disruption of specific commodities, goods, products, or services from the involved countries; the potential for significant harm and displacement of people; and the importance of the country regionally or strategically to another country or more than one country—not all hostilities will immediately affect markets. As an example, the conflict between Saudi Arabia and Yemen did not disrupt any global goods, services, or products, and so was a mute affair for markets. That changed somewhat in late 2023, when Houthi militants, who were fighting against Saudi Arabia, decided to show their support for the Palestinians of Gaza after Israel declared war on Hamas. The Houthis said they would attack ships in the Red Sea that were bound for Israel. Their action disrupted overall shipping on that route because they indiscriminately or wrongly identified vessels to attack. The same was true for the Azerbaijan–Armenia conflict over the Nagorno-Karabakh region, in which Azerbaijan reclaimed control, causing ethnic Armenians to flee. This breakaway region had existed with its own separatist government for many years. News of Azerbaijan's offensive briefly made headlines because of the potential impact, along with fear and uncertainty that it could possibly spiral. Other hostilities, such as Russia/Ukraine and then Hamas/Israel, dominated news cycles because of the geopolitics involved, along with the regional and internal politics of the individual countries.

BREXIT

A different confrontation between countries was illustrated by the majority vote of citizens in the United Kingdom in a referendum on June 23, 2016, to leave the European Union—a result dubbed Brexit. After the narrow 51.9 percent victory of the "leavers," more than $2.1 trillion was lost globally in financial markets the next day. The British pound also had one of its steepest one day declines—reaching a thirty-one-year low during trading but recovering to close at £1.368 versus $1.00, far below its prior value of £1.50. Politics played a primary role and led to the decision to sever trading agreements and the United Kingdom's bond as a member of the European Union. For markets, the matter of uncertainty loomed large, considering that the United Kingdom is a leading world economic and political power. How would a standalone UK economy fare? How exactly would the United Kingdom disentangle its relationship with the European Union? What terms would each party seek to sever the relationship? For financial markets, these and other questions indicated numerous uncertainties about the possible disruption of the production of a plethora of goods, continued provision of services, and the consequent effect on earnings potential, revenue generation, and companies' profits and losses. All these unknowns continued to jolt markets until reasonable agreements were reached to signal resolution and the return to stability.

Brexit can be seen as a once-in-a-lifetime change, but really it was about the uncertain economic future of a major country, the disruption of trade, and free movement of people across certain borders. Whenever any similar events occur for one or more member countries of the Group of Twenty, it certainly will be newsworthy.

THE CLIMATE CRISIS

Global climate change and the resulting effects from different weather patterns have definitely become disruptive, displacing people and interrupting business operations. Deleterious weather events—such as unexpected storms, droughts, stronger hurricanes, floods, longer seasons, more frequent and large-scale wildfires, and excessive heat—are all cited as evidence of climate change. The economic and/or market impact of climate change was at first seen as a lagging indicator for the economy—a condition that took time to be felt. But it has now become a real issue, affecting nations, regions, and cities, and upending industries, forcing adaptation and mitigation.

More frequent occurrences of major storms are seen as evidence of climate change. The US National Oceanic and Atmospheric Administration (NOAA) forecasted "above-normal hurricane activity" for the 2024 hurricane season in the Atlantic Ocean. The agency predicted there would be seventeen to twenty-five named storms, including eight to thirteen hurricanes, with four to seven of them being major hurricanes.[10] Forecasters were particularly concerned about how severe the season could become after Hurricane Beryl developed into a Category 5 hurricane in late June to early July 2024. It was the first time on record that such a strong hurricane formed so early in the season. It caused severe damage in several Caribbean islands, in parts of Venezuela and Mexico, and it knocked out electricity in parts of Texas for days, though it had weakened to a Category 1 hurricane when it hit that state.

NOAA also cited the previous 2023 Atlantic hurricane season as "above normal." The 2022 season was closer to average, with fourteen named storms that included eight hurricanes, of which two were major.[11] Globally in 2023, NOAA reported seventy-eight named storms, of which forty-five reached tropical cyclone strength—including seven Atlantic hurricanes and ten in the Eastern Pacific. Thirty were classified as major tropical cyclones, with seven designated as Category 5. The Western North Pacific Basin recorded seventeen tropical storms, with twelve typhoons and eight major typhoons. The Indian Ocean had seventeen tropical storms, of which eleven were cyclones and seven were major cyclones. In Australia, there were nine tropical storms, with five cyclones and four of them being major. The Southwest Pacific had six tropical storms, three cyclones and two major ones.[12]

Storms, of course, damage infrastructure along with farmland and crops, which means a loss of revenue and possibly decreased economic activity, based on the area and activities affected. When a storm affects the Gulf Coast, for example, offshore oil rigs must shut down. And after a storm weakens, it still causes fairly heavy rainfall that can lead to flooding. Along with the weather reports about a storm, reporters will need to know if any specific companies plan to temporarily stop operations, the estimated cost of any damage, and how their financial bottom line may be affected. The extent and effect of any significant flooding from heavy rain as the storm weakens should also not be overlooked.

Underscoring the negative effects of climate change, in a July 2021 report, the United Nations questioned whether some small island nations will be able to survive the climate crisis, noting research "indicates that low-lying atoll islands, predominantly in the Pacific Ocean, . . . risk being submerged by the end of the century, but there are indications that some islands will become uninhabitable long before that happens."[13] In 2024, Hurricane Beryl caused catastrophic, near-total destruction of one of the largest islands that is part of the island country of Grenada.[14]

The Intergovernmental Panel on Climate Change (IPCC) notes that there is very high confidence that as early as 2050, many low-lying cities and settlements, small islands, Arctic communities, remote Indigenous communities, and deltaic communities will face severe disruptions.[15] In the United States, coastal states like Florida could see the effects of a median sea level rise of 8-9 inches along different areas of the coast by 2040 under a moderate projection scenario, according to Resources for the Future. Median projections under the higher scenario expect increased sea level rises of 12 to 13 inches, and even more for the extreme scenario, with median projections of about 24 inches.[16] Although these projections are uncertain, Florida and its major coastal city Miami face enormous risks from increased flooding and damage to infrastructure as storms and hurricanes become more frequent and intense. Globally, coastal areas are home to "much of the world's population, economic activities and critical infrastructure," according to the IPCC, "with nearly 11% of the global population, or 896 million people, living on low-lying coasts directly exposed to interacting climatic and non-climatic coastal hazards."[17]

In the first week of February 2024, different but disastrous weather events—both seen as caused by climate change—affected the central coastal region of Chile in South America and Southern California in the United States. Chile had been experiencing a drought for several years. Over that first weekend, there was a scorching heat wave and wildfires broke out, killing at least 122 people in areas of the coastal towns of Vina del Mar and Valparaiso. In Southern California, high temperatures over the Pacific Ocean caused a strong storm called an "atmospheric river," which led to extremely heavy rainfall, resulting in severe flooding, landslides, and mudslides.

Climate change has resulted in extreme weather patterns, unusually heavy and record rainfall, as well as droughts, which increase the potential for deadly wildfires and lead to a scarcity of potable water that can affect farming and livelihoods. The economic impact of climate-related disasters and a global assessment of progress on renewable energies must therefore be on top of the agenda of countries, governments, corporations, small businesses, and individuals, and these are the concerns that Conference of the Parties (COP) events focus on every year. For example, during COP28 in 2023, which was held in Dubai, ironically—the United Arab Emirates is known for its expanding fossil fuel operations—stock market investors were looking for news about grid upgrades for renewables, infrastructure investments, methane capture and biofuel projects, and the carbon offset market.[18] A UN report also noted that specific funding—climate finance—was discussed more than ten years ago, with developed countries targeting a goal of mobilizing up to $100 billion a year by 2020, to support climate action.

Climate finance includes a broad range of spending on various initiatives and activities to help slow and mitigate the effects of climate change. The goals include limiting the level of global warming increase by reducing greenhouse gas emissions to zero, which means not adding any more new emissions to the atmosphere by 2050. This is the objective referred to as "net zero."[19]

Financial initiatives related to climate change and reaching net zero affect markets because they include green bonds—so called because the proceeds are committed to environmental projects—and investments and capital spending on renewable energies and related technologies. Investing in renewable energy or other sources to benefit the environment is also called "socially responsible investing." It is active investing that is part of environmental, social, and governance policies, which many companies have adopted, in part to show that they are concerned about the environment, but also due to shareholder outcry for change. Environmental, social, and governance investing and green bonds have become significant generators of revenue for some companies. In the future, they could grow to become data points that companies will report, and which reporters, traders, and investors will watch.[20]

For now, it is the green transition and innovation occurring in some industries that are moving markets. Electric vehicles, which produce no emissions, are now an important component of traditional automobile manufacturers. Tesla and Rivian Automotive are two automakers that make only electric vehicles, energy generation systems, and accessories. Tesla is a highly traded and closely followed stock. Toward the end of 2023 and in early 2024, it was dubbed one of the Magnificent 7 stocks, mostly responsible for the Dow and S&P reaching new highs in January 2024. It declined significantly after reporting lower-than-expected fourth quarter results, also in January 2024, because it warned of lower production growth. The stock recovered with moves higher in the second quarter, however.

Though Tesla was founded in 2003, its valuation now outpaces those of traditional automakers that have been around for much longer. The continued growth of electric vehicles, and whether traditional automakers can profitably pivot from gas-fueled vehicles to electric ones in the next few years, is certainly being watched by the markets.

The food industry is also undergoing change to mitigate climate change. Agriculture, particularly livestock, produces high levels of methane, which is a greenhouse gas. This has led to calls for lower meat consumption, which has given rise to plant-based meat. Beyond Meat, founded in 2009, manufactures and sells plant-based meat products that it markets as similar to beef, poultry, and pork products. Its products are sold in mass market stores such as grocery chains, fast food establishments, restaurants, and workplace cafeterias. Like the auto industry, traditional food companies such as Perdue Farms and its subsidiaries are also seeking to capitalize on any significant consumer shift away from animal meat by making products marketed and branded as "plant based." Markets would likely react if traditional meat consumption showed a gradual and continuous decline, even without an increase in sales of plant-based meats. Purely good intentions do not tend to move markets however, so plant-based meat producers will need to be profitable and generate results that make their companies and stocks attractive. Beyond Meat's stock tumbled from trading above $30 per share to single digits in 2024.

Electric vehicles and plant-based meat are completely different industries, but technological innovation is common to both. The ever-present use of technology in all aspects of life has brought access to information, products, and services literally to the fingertips of the vast majority of people. But it has also brought unforeseen risks from system failures, cyberattacks, and hacking. Technological innovation is now seen as evolving into the era of artificial intelligence (AI), with the promise of revolutionizing tasks performed by humans and industrial processes. But, as with the widespread use of computing, AI also carries risks.

CYBERATTACKS AND ARTIFICIAL INTELLIGENCE

A cyberattack is a technological threat that can upend nations and markets. At the end of January 2024, Christopher Wray, the FBI director, told US lawmakers that China "was ramping up an extensive hacking operation geared at taking down the United States' power grid, oil pipelines and water systems" if there were to be a conflict over Taiwan.[21] If technology was used as a weapon, through hacking, to cause major disruptions in businesses, then even markets may not be able to function. The immediate effect of a widespread hack affecting infrastructure and businesses would likely lead to panic and a selloff, and undoubtedly cause uncertainty, which is negative for financial markets. Companies that have reported instances of hacking have seen their stocks fall, based on how penetrative the incident was and the extent to which operations were affected. For example, on October 5, 2023, Clorox stock opened trading at $126, almost 4.5 percent below its close of $131.83 the previous day, after it reported that a cyberattack in August had significantly affected its operations and caused a decline in quarterly sales and earnings. It closed trading 5 percent lower, at $124.93, on an almost five-times-higher volume of shares traded.[22]

Artificial intelligence is another technology that could pose a threat. The public's initial interaction with AI was mostly through interactive chats on the websites of companies to get questions answered and as voice recognition assistants on smartphones and other electronic devices. But the introduction of more advanced AI, developed from large language models (LLMs), spurred much talk about machine learning blurring or obscuring what is real or true, and also concerns that it could surpass and upend human capabilities. Misuse of AI is a concern as people of all ages readily access tools such as ChatGPT, an LLM by OpenAI, which was launched in 2022, or Google's Bard, launched in 2023, which was later renamed Gemini. The use of AI to generate "deepfakes" and impersonations to advertise products with false information has led to concerns of misinformation and disinformation and demands for regulation. Google described its Gemini app as "the first model to outperform human experts on MMLU (Massive Multitask Language Understanding), one of the most popular methods to test the knowledge and problem solving abilities of AI models."[23] Gemini was described by media outlets as being able to respond to voice and text to carry out actions such as write an email, answer questions, generate images, and perform various other tasks—removing the need for individuals to use their brains to think and then take action, but to instead rely on an app. This capability of AI has many believing that one consequence of AI could be massive job losses, as it could be used for many tasks that humans now perform, such as administrative/scheduling functions and writing, including writing books. (The authors of this book conducted individual research to write it, without any use of AI.)

SUGGESTED ACTIVITIES

1. Research the assassination attempt on Ronald Reagan. What was the reaction of financial markets when that happened?
2. What is the latest AI technology that has received a positive reaction from financial markets? Discuss your views on this technology.

When Routines (and Toilet Paper) Disappeared, and a New Vocabulary Emerged

What is a pandemic really like? What changes, except for a large number of people getting sick and many dying from a disease that spreads rapidly, and for which there is no cure? Before 2019, the last global pandemic was more than a hundred years ago. Not many people thought they would experience one in their lifetime, especially given the advances in medicine. But in 2019, the coronavirus emerged and quickly spread worldwide, aided by global travel and an absence of early awareness of the disease outbreak.

The respiratory Coronavirus Disease 2019, which formed the acronym COVID-19, would eventually upend all daily activities—from work, school, and shopping to family visits and socialization. The drastic changes it brought also ushered in a new vocabulary. The first was curtailing gatherings, which became known as a "lockdown," so that many workplaces—especially corporate ones—ordered employees to work from home, giving rise to the jargon "remote work" and "work from home (WFH)." For jobs that required computers, the transition was not difficult.

What hurt many small and service-type businesses were restrictions on people congregating in a location. They had to pivot to online takeouts and deliveries to generate revenue as foot traffic decreased. Creativity became the name of the game, with many restaurants, for example, retooling their operations. But even businesses not associated with the delivery of services were forced to offer their services differently. Some hair salons, for example, offered to send packages to customers with instructions for selected do-it-yourself services, like hair coloring.

Luckily, some grocery and retail stores continued operating as usual, because they were deemed "essential"; and alcohol, too, found its way into this category. The employees of such establishments, along with medical personnel and first responders, came to be known as "essential workers." Many small businesses, however, suffered significant revenue losses and saw their businesses affected for several months.[24]

Demand exploded for products that were once an afterthought—such as Clorox, Lysol, and hand sanitizers—leading to severe shortages. Clorox, the company, reported that demand for its products rose 500 percent during the pandemic.[25]

Also, an unfathomable phenomenon happened worldwide in stores: the disappearance of toilet paper. Panic-stricken people who were forced to be in a lockdown feared some sort of a global Armageddon, and started hoarding toilet paper, boosting the average price of the tissue by $1.50 a package.[26]

Sales of toilet paper in the United States rose by an estimated 60 percent in March 2020 alone, compared with the same month a year earlier, according to Statista data. In Italy, revenues generated by bathroom tissue rose by 140 percent.[27]

In July 2020, Kimberly-Clark, a US company that makes the Cottonelle brand of toilet paper, reported better-than-expected earnings and boosted its outlook for the year; its shares rose 2 percent. One year later, the company raised the price of its toilet paper, citing higher demand for wood pulp, which is used to make paper.[28]

Whenever a company name becomes a verb, it can be taken as a measure of huge success. That is what happened to the company Zoom, during the pandemic. Everyone who now could not meet in person because of the lockdown turned to using a remote meeting software. While many businesses depended on software such as Cisco's Webex and Microsoft Teams, individuals increasingly used Zoom. It became common to say, "Let's do Zoom at X time" to arrange a meeting, whether work-related or a family gathering. Zoom's stock reached a peak of $538.99, its closing price on October 27, 2020.[29]

Many schools around the world were closed to keep the virus at bay, and education moved to "online classes." In a few places in the United States, however, officials disagreed with keeping elementary and secondary students out of school for a prolonged period and kept classes "in person."

Disagreement regarding schools, whether to continue in-person classes or have remote ones, was one of the most contentious issues in the United States during the COVID-19 pandemic. The other bone of contention hinged on safety regarding the spread of the virus–"mask" or "no mask"—a controversy that became political in the United States. Nevertheless, masks found their way into the fashion industry with different styles, colors, and patterns. Small businesses sprouted from home, offering masks, food, crafts, and the like.

Shoppers accustomed to well-stocked supermarkets were shocked to see empty shelves as supply chains and transportation were disrupted worldwide, affecting the movement of goods. And as supermarkets tried to do their part with maintaining safe distance between shoppers, "6 feet" markers and signs for one-way traffic on store aisles were stark reminders of the fast-spreading disease. Air travel became restricted, and subway stations became empty.

The gravity of COVID-19 had many thinking that wearing masks and keeping 6 feet distances would be a feature of life for the foreseeable future. But vaccines (and later boosters) were developed, boosting the business and stock performances of Pfizer, Moderna, and Novavax. (*Forbes* cited Moderna as the best-performing stock during the last two years of the pandemic.)[30]

COVID did not entirely leave us; its variants weakened over time. As the world returned to normal after two years, many phrases and much jargon stayed on for a while as the "new normal."

14

MILESTONES

As should be evident by now, market reactions have no method to their madness. While many times, markets react as one may expect after certain news breaks, very often there appears no logic to investors' sentiments. But it is a reporter's job to figure out what triggered a reaction after a headline moved: be it a quotation uttered by a newsmaker, a company's financials or internal turmoil, mergers and acquisitions or restructuring, macroeconomics, technology and innovation, policy changes and litigations, international relations, diseases, and disasters or disruptions.

Some headlines create waves and ripples around the world and become milestones that are used as benchmarks by market pundits. Here are some historical movements that will be worth your while to research.

HISTORICAL MARKET EVENTS

⬇ 1929: The Great Depression
⬆ 1949–56: Bull market period after World War II
⬇ 1971: Brazilian market crash
⬇ 1973–74: US miners' strike
⬆ 1982–87: Bull market credited to "Reaganomics"
⬆ 1987–2000: Tech bull run
⬇ October 19, 1987: Black Monday crash
⬆ 1995–2000: The dot-com bubble
⬇ 1997–98: The Asian Financial Crisis
⬆ March 29, 1999: The Dow reaches 10,000

⬇ 2000–2002: The dot-com bubble bursts
⬇ 2001: September 11 terrorist attacks
⬇ 2007–9: The Great Recession
⬇ 2010: European sovereign debt crisis
⬇ 2015–16: Chinese stock market crash
⬇ 2018: Cryptocurrency crash
⬇ 2020: COVID-19 crises
⬆ 2024: Broad US market rally after presidential elections

Newsrooms and Machines

The purpose of news—that of educating and informing the public, while also entertaining them sometimes—has been kept alive in most newsrooms. But with the advancement of technology, news websites have sprouted everywhere in the world. Not everyone who works as a journalist now needs a journalism degree, and not every news website needs to be run by a qualified journalist. However, those who understand and respect the ethics of the trade stay true to the profession by doing the job that is meant to be done—to inform and educate the public without a bias and tell all sides of a story to the best of their ability.

All this now needs to be matched with technology that is growing faster than expected, sometimes changing the nature of work inside a newsroom. But as with other industries, the media and publishing need to evolve and move with the times, as they did with telegraphs, telephones, radio, television, computers, social media, and now artificial intelligence (AI).

But with machines comes mania. When it comes to business and markets, some regulators fear that AI will be at the center of future financial crises.[1] Many are concerned that, as humans and machines work on the same trades simultaneously, there is a higher potential for glitches, thereby increasing the probability of market crashes.

Technological errors can have an impact on investor confidence. As was seen on January 24, 2023, a glitch on the New York Stock Exchange at the usual 9:30 a.m. ET opening time hurt the share prices of more than 250 stocks that opened well below their previous day's closing price. The trading of many stocks was halted, including big names like

McDonald's, Uber, Nike, ExxonMobil, and Prudential.[2] It was later discovered the trading glitch was a result of a manual error involving "the Exchange's Disaster Recovery configuration at system start of day."[3]

Financial traders and news consumers need to be more vigilant than ever as AI writes headlines, transcribes interviews, responds to queries, edits copy, verifies news, and turns into the new assignment editor.[4] "The complexity of AI increases platform companies' control over news organizations, creating lock-in effects that risk keeping news organizations tethered to technology companies," writes Felix Simon, a doctoral scholar at the University of Oxford, who wrote a white paper titled "Artificial Intelligence in the News: How AI Retools, Rationalizes, and Reshapes Journalism and the Public Arena," after interviewing 134 news workers across thirty-five newsrooms in the United States, United Kingdom, and Germany, as well as thirty-six international experts in industry, academia, technology, and policy.[5] "This limits news organizations' autonomy and renders them vulnerable to price hikes or the shifting priorities of technology companies that may not align with their own."

The demand for multimedia and vertical video stories has increased multifold over the years as new generations seek instant gratification due to low attention spans. At a time in the distant past in newsrooms, just adding graphics, pictures, and videos to a story was revolutionary.

"During the 2008 financial crisis, Reuters added financial graphics to their file," recalled Catherine Trevethan, a former news graphics designer. "We quickly learned that trying to capture the soaring crude oil prices was not going to work in a graphic format. Because the market moves so fast, it was better to focus graphics on the things that were moving the market rather than the actual prices. This gave the snaps (headlines) and news reports a visual context to why things might be happening in markets."

What the future holds for the news industry and its survival as data journalism and AI enhance storytelling capabilities—and headlining speed—is an interesting yet nerve-wracking thought. Will it increase the quantity of news headlines or improve their quality? Will Headliners continue to yell and scream during a press release rush, snapping fingers and furiously typing on keyboards, or will that soon become a thing of the past? Will the Headlines desk go into oblivion like the screaming traders on stock exchange floors?

Years ago, there was also a unit within editorial that only checked images or PDF files and faxes for headline-worthy information and converted them into text for subscribers. This was the Optical Character Recognition (OCR) Desk. Here is how former news Headliner Susan Abbotts recalled her time on this desk:

"I was an editor on the OCR Desk in my early days at Bloomberg News, and we would often receive embargoed stories via fax machine. The fax itself would be a regular press release, usually from the company's investor or public relations department, with a large banner across the top with the word 'embargoed' in capital letters and the time it should be released. The embargoed story was assigned to one of us on the desk, and that person was responsible for scanning the paper document into electronic form, checking for errors, and making corrections using optical character recognition software, then readying and sending the story as soon as the clock hit the embargo deadline. I remember how tension would build as the time drew close—you absolutely did not want to break the embargo (i.e., accidentally send it early), and you always wanted to be the first agency to report the news. So, for me, there was a competitive factor that I thrived on. It came down to watching seconds on the clock and having incredibly fast reflexes."

She continued: "That was twenty-eight years ago—a time when humans had to do the work. Eventually, subscription news wire feeds, such as PRNewswire and BusinessWire, automatically populated stories directly into Bloomberg. This made writing headlines and assigning stories faster and easier—a good thing, since the volume of financial and corporate news was rapidly growing each year."

The hunger for news and information will never subside, and there will never be a dearth of it, given that news is everywhere and as long as reporters are on the field doing their job, information will be disseminated. Now whether it is AI that disseminates that information or not, the world will depend on technological capabilities at the receiving end. And what if there is a dearth—or glitch—there? Oh well, that is another news item to headline and write about.

It seems, therefore, a suitable news item to share at the end of this book is a story about a technology glitch that ate up the glory of one of the biggest news items in 2012, and provided further fodder to newsrooms. Before that, one last quote from a former Headliner sums up the job of a Headliner and what you take away from it.

"The job really sticks with you! I still sit behind cars at a traffic light looking at the letters on the license plate and matching it up to a company stock symbol," reminisced Bethany Bantle, former news Headliner. "I felt smart and well-read for years, simply because I could understand the world and what moved markets."

How a "Technical Error" Ruined Facebook's Stock Market Debut in 2012

It was the biggest tech initial public offering in history—but a *tech glitch* spoiled the show. On May 18, 2012, Facebook made its stock market debut under the stock symbol FB on Nasdaq. Traders placed their orders in advance, and the exchange system was set to kick off Facebook's first official trading at 11 a.m. ET. However, there was a delay in the system, and the exchange announced trading of the IPO would instead occur at 11:05 a.m. But it was then delayed even further, to 11:30 a.m., preventing orders from being executed on time.[6]

The glitch, Nasdaq later announced, was due to a recalculation of orders by the system, as per a certain algorithm that was set up. Total chaos ensued on the stock market, as new orders or modifications could not be registered by the system or—in certain cases—were "botched up." Lawsuits soon followed. And ultimately, Nasdaq was ordered to shell out $62 million to companies that incurred losses that day.[7] Newswires flashed headlines endlessly, as neither journalists nor traders could fathom what was happening.

Still, 80 million shares of Facebook exchanged hands that day at an IPO price of $38. The high volume of trades, technical glitch, and pure chaos may have added to investor sentiments—shares of FB barely gained 23 cents at close of the markets on its very first day of trading.[8]

As a result of this market-quaking incident, Nasdaq upgraded its system's calculation process. A year later, Nasdaq was reprimanded by the Securities and Exchange Commission, which ordered it to pay a $10 million fine for disrupting the market.[9] At that time, it was one of the largest penalties a regulator had ever slapped on a single stock exchange. Reporters had a field day revisiting the infamous IPO "snafu" story when the commission slapped Nasdaq with that fine.[10] Facebook, which pivoted to foreseeing a future in the metaverse, rebranded on October 28, 2021, and changed its name to Meta Platforms Inc. with the stock symbol META.[11]

NOTES

FOREWORD

1. Paul Murphy, "Why Can't Fake News Creators Write Basic Financial News? (Updated)," *Financial Times,* November 22, 2016, www.ft.com/content/a5bf7719-3b35-3476-9ceb-14cb5e87392b.

INTRODUCTION

1. Reuters, *Reuters Handbook of Journalism,* "Accuracy Hallmark," www.reutersagency.com/en/about/standards-values/.
2. Alex Cook, "Every Generation's Top Investing Goal Is Retirement, but Younger Americans Have an Eye on Getting Rich," *Magnify Money,* www.magnifymoney.com/news/investing-by-generation-survey/.
3. "Global Female Leaders 2024," www.globalfemaleleaders.com/speaker/lauren-simmons/.
4. Zippia, "Stock Trader Demographics and Statistics in the US," www.zippia.com/stock-trader-jobs/demographics/.
5. Santiago Guzman, "How Technology and Innovation Are Evolving Financial Markets," *Forbes,* February 2023, www.forbes.com/sites/forbesfinancecouncil/2023/02/28/how-technology-and-innovation-are-evolving-financial-markets/?sh=28df46251cc2.

CHAPTER 1

1. History of Information, "Paul Julius Reuter Founds the Reuters News Service," www.historyofinformation.com/detail.php?id=46.
2. Reuters Communications, "The Long History of Speed at Reuters," October 2020, www.reuters.com/article/idUSKBN2761WD/.
3. Thomas L. Friedman, *The World Is Flat, 3.0* (New York: Picador, 2007) www.thomaslfriedman.com/the-world-is-flat-3-0/.

4. Steve Schifferes, "Here Is the US News from Bangalore," BBC, February 2, 2007, http://news.bbc.co.uk/2/hi/business/6289521.stm; Malini Guha and Edward Luce, "Reuters Expands India Offshoring Move," *Financial Times*, www.ft.com/content/189f2512-1896-11d9-8963-00000e2511c8.
5. Seth Sutel, "Stock Plunges After Hoax," CT Insider, August 26, 2000, www.ctinsider.com/news/article/Stock-plunges-after-hoax-11934287.php.

CHAPTER 2

1. Arjun Kharpal, "Global Chip Stocks from Nvidia to ASML Fall on Geopolitics, Trump Comments," CNBC, July 17, 2024, www.cnbc.com/2024/07/17/global-chip-stocks-from-nvidia-to-asml-fall-as-geopolitics-trump-weigh.html.
2. Federal Reserve Board, "Remarks by Chairman Alan Greenspan: The Challenge of Central Banking in a Democratic Society," December 5, 1996, www.federalreserve.gov/boarddocs/speeches/1996/19961205.htm.
3. Todd Benjamin, "European Markets Plunge; Greenspan Comments Revive Inflation and Interest Rate Fears," CNN Money, December 6, 1996, https://money.cnn.com/1996/12/06/markets/euroreax_pkg/.
4. CNN Money, "Dow Tumbles at Open; Greenspan Comments Shake Wall Street; Bears Running Wild," December 6, 1996, https://money.cnn.com/1996/12/06/markets/markets10a/.
5. PoundSterlingLive, "British Pound / US Dollar Historical Reference Rates from Bank of England for 2022," www.poundsterlinglive.com/bank-of-england-spot/historical-spot-exchange-rates/gbp/GBP-to-USD-2022.
6. X, "Elon Musk @elonmusk, January 26, 2021, twitter.com; Nasdaq stock historical data site, "GME Historical Data," October 2023, www.nasdaq.com/market-activity/stocks/gme/historical.
7. Nasdaq stock historical data site, "ETSY Historical data," October 2023, www.nasdaq.com/market-activity/stocks/etsy/historical.
8. X, "Chamath Palihapitiya @chamath," January 26, 2021, twitter.com.
9. US Securities and Exchange Commission, "SEC Finalizes Rules to Reduce Risks in Clearance and Settlement," February 15, 2023, www.sec.gov/news/press-release/2023-29.

CHAPTER 3

1. "Apple Stock Slumps Due to Production Delays of New iPhones in China," *Forbes*, December 4, 2022, www.forbes.com/sites/qai/2022/12/04/apple-stock-slumps-due-to-production-delays-of-new-iphones-in-china/?sh=44e061725042.

2. Vlad Savov, "Apple to Lose 6 Million iPhone Pros from Tumult at China Plant," Bloomberg, November 28, 2020, www.bloomberg.com/news/articles/2022-11-28/apple-to-lose-6-million-iphone-pros-from-tumult-at-china-plant?leadSource=uverify%20wall.
3. Matt Levine, "FTX's Balance Sheet Was Bad," Bloomberg, November 15, 2022, www.bloomberg.com/opinion/articles/2022-11-14/ftx-s-balance-sheet-was-bad?leadSource=uverify%20wall.
4. Ben C. Ball Jr., "The Mysterious Disappearance of Retained Earnings," *Harvard Business Review*, July 1987, https://hbr.org/1987/07/the-mysterious-disappearance-of-retained-earnings.
5. Paul R. La Monica, "Google: Party Over," CNNMoney, January 31, 2006, https://money.cnn.com/2006/01/31/technology/google_analysis/.
6. Sheila Dang, "Elon Musk Expects Twitter to Be 'Cash Flow Break-Even' Next Year," Reuters, December 22, 2022, www.reuters.com/technology/elon-musk-expects-twitter-be-cash-flow-break-even-next-year-2022-12-21/.
7. Chris Roush, *Show Me the Money: Writing Business and Economics Stories for Mass Communication* (New York: Routledge, 2010), chap. 4.
8. Securities and Exchange Commission (SEC), "Filings Website," www.sec.gov/edgar.
9. Annie Palmer, "The Strangest and Most Alarming Things in WeWork's IPO Filing," CNBC, August 17, 2019, www.cnbc.com/2019/08/17/wework-ipo-filing-strangest-and-most-alarming-things.html.
10. Britney Nguyen, "The Career Rise, Fall, and Return of Adam Neumann, the Controversial WeWork Cofounder Who Is Back with Another Real-Estate Startup," *Business Insider*, August 17, 2022, www.businessinsider.com/wework-ceo-adam-neumann-bio-life-career-2019-8.
11. Noor Zainab Hussain, "WeWork Shares Jump on Debut After Two-Year Struggle to Go Public," Reuters, October 22, 2021, www.reuters.com/business/wework-shares-jump-debut-after-two-year-struggle-go-public-2021-10-21/.
12. Reuters, "Why Did WeWork Fail, and What Is Next for the Company?" November 8, 2023, www.reuters.com/business/why-wework-failed-what-is-next-2023-11-07/.
13. SEC. "Filing, September 18, 2023," www.sec.gov/ix?doc=/Archives/edgar/data/21076/000120677423001133/clx4242401-8k.htm.
14. Eduardo Medina, "Customers May Struggle to Get Clorox Wipes After a Damaging Cyberattack," *New York Times*, September 19, 2023, www.nytimes.com/2023/09/19/business/clorox-cyberattack-shortage.html.
15. Shannon Thaler, "Clorox Products in Short Supply After Cyberattack Wreaks Havoc on Operations," *New York Post*, September 18, 2023, https://nypost.com/2023/09/18/clorox-products-in-short-supply-after-cyberattack/.

16. Eduardo Medina, "Cybersecurity Issue Forces Systems Shutdown at MGM Hotels and Casinos," *New York Times*, September 11, 2023, www.nytimes.com/2023/09/11/us/cyberattack-mgm-hotel-las-vegas.html.
17. NVIDIA Newsroom, press release, May 22, 2024, https://nvidianews.nvidia.com/news/nvidia-announces-financial-results-for-first-quarter-fiscal-2025.
18. Kif Leswing, "Nvidia Shares Pass $1,000 for First Time on AI-Driven Sales Surge," CNBC, May 22, 2024, www.cnbc.com/2024/05/22/nvidia-nvda-earnings-report-q1-2025-.html; Nasdaq, "NVDA / Historical Quotes," www.nasdaq.com/marketactivity/stocks/nvda/historical?page=3&rows_per_page=10&timeline=m6.
19. Yahoo Finance, "It's Nvidia's Market, and We're All Just Trading in It, Steve Sosnick Says," www.youtube.com/watch?v=44uygIzZjd4.
20. Stephen Gandel, "Moderna Executives Hiked Their Stock Sales After Announcing Positive Vaccine Trials," CBS News, July 21, 2020, www.cbsnews.com/news/moderna-executives-increased-stock-sales-after-coronavirus-vaccine-trial-data/.
21. SEC, "EDGAR Filing, July 14, 2020," www.sec.gov/Archives/edgar/data/1682852/000112760220021495/xslF345X03/form4.xml.
22. Tom Dreisbach, "'Bad Optics' or Something More? Moderna Executives' Stock Sales Raise Concerns," NPR, September 4, 2020, www.npr.org/2020/09/04/908305074/bad-optics-or-something-more-moderna-executives-stock-sales-raise-concerns.

CHAPTER 4

1. Carlyle, "Carlyle Announces Senior Leadership Changes," August 7, 2022, https://carlyle.com/media-room/news-release-archive/carlyle-announces-senior-leadership-changes.
2. New York Stock Exchange, "Carlyle Group Inc. Quote," August 8, 2022, www.nyse.com/quote/XNGS:CG.
3. Maureen Farrell and Peter Eavis, "Revenge of the Founders: A Generational Struggle on Wall Street," *New York Times*, August 29, 2022, www.nytimes.com/2022/08/29/business/carlyle-group-kewsong-lee.html?searchResultPosition=1.
4. Discover, "Discover Financial Services Announces Leadership Transition," press release, August 14, 2023, https://investorrelations.discover.com/newsroom/press-releases/press-release-details/2023/Discover-Financial-Services-Announces-Leadership-Transition/default.aspx.
5. PayPal Newsroom, "PayPal Names Alex Chriss as Next President and CEO," August 14, 2023, https://newsroom.paypal-corp.com/2023-08-14-PayPal-Names-Alex-Chriss-as-Next-President-and-CEO.

6. Netflix, "Shareholder Letter," July 16, 2020, https://s22.q4cdn.com/959853165/files/doc_financials/2020/q2/FINAL-Q2-20-Shareholder-Letter-V3-with-Tables.pdf; Lauren Feiner, "Netflix Shares Fall After Earnings Miss, Weak Subscriber Guidance for Third Quarter," CNBC, July 16, 2020, updated July 17, www.cnbc.com/2020/07/16/netflix-nflx-q2-2020-earnings.html.
7. US Food and Drug Administration, "Vioxx (Rofecoxib) Questions and Answers," September 30, 2004, www.fda.gov/drugs/postmarket-drug-safety-information-patients-and-providers/vioxx-rofecoxib-questions-and-answers.
8. Snigdha Prakash and Vikki Valentine, "Timeline: The Rise and Fall of Vioxx," NPR, November 10, 2007, www.npr.org/2007/11/10/5470430/timeline-the-rise-and-fall-of-vioxx.
9. US Department of Justice, "US Pharmaceutical Company Merck Sharpe & Dohme to Pay Nearly One Billion Dollars over Promotion of Vioxx," November 22, 2011, www.justice.gov/opa/pr/us-pharmaceutical-company-merck-sharp-dohme-pay-nearly-one-billion-dollars-over-promotion.
10. Reuters on CNN, "US Court Rejects J&J Bankruptcy Strategy for Tens of Thousands of Talc Lawsuits," January 30, 2023, www.cnn.com/2023/01/30/business/johnson-and-johnson-talc-bankruptcy/index.html.
11. Jordan Valinsky, "Johnson & Johnson Will Stop Selling Talc-Based Baby Powder around the World in 2023," CNN, August 12, 2022, www.cnn.com/2022/08/12/business/johnson-and-johnson-powder-change/index.html.
12. Johnson to Pay $700 Million to Settle Baby Powder Probe," *Wall Street Journal*, January 23, 2024, www.wsj.com/business/johnson-johnson-to-pay-700-million-to-settle-baby-powder-probe-307c4416.
13. Aimee Donnellan and Robert Cyran, "J&J Breakup About More Than Financial Engineering," Reuters, November 12, 2021, www.reuters.com/breakingviews/jj-breakup-about-more-than-financial-engineering-2021-11-12/.
14. Melissa Repko and Lillian Rizzo, "Bed Bath & Beyond Shares Plummet After Company Warns of Potential Bankruptcy," CNBC, January 5, 2023, www.cnbc.com/2023/01/05/bed-bath-beyond-shares-plummet-as-company-warns-of-deeper-financial-troubles.html.
15. "Bed Bath & Beyond Inc. Announces Strategic Changes to Strengthen Its Financial Positioning, Drive Growth and Better Serve Customers," *Business Insider*, August 31, 2022, https://markets.businessinsider.com/news/stocks/bed-bath-beyond-inc-announces-strategic-changes-to-strengthen-its-financial-positioning-drive-growth-and-better-serve-customers-1031715880?op=1.
16. Cision on PRNewswire, "Bed Bath & Beyond Inc. Provides Business Update," January 5, 2023, https://prnewswire.com/news-releases/bed-bath--beyond-inc-provides-business-update-301714562.html.

17. GlobeNewswire by Notified, "Beyond, Inc., Formerly Overstock.com. Inc., Announces Leadership Transition," November 6, 2023, https://globenewswire.com/news-release/2023/11/06/2774076/33533/en/Beyond-Inc-Formerly-Overstock-com-Inc-Announces-Leadership-Transition.html.

CHAPTER 5

1. Tom Voelk, "Rise of SUVs: Leaving Cars in Their Dust, With No Signs of Slowing," *New York Times*, May 21, 2020, www.nytimes.com/2020/05/21/business/suv-sales-best-sellers.html.
2. Laurence Iliff, "Tesla Easily Passes BMW for the 2022 US Luxury Crown," *Automotive News*, February 16, 2023, www.autonews.com/sales/tesla-easily-passes-bmw-2022-us-luxury-crown.
3. Bank of England, "Ten Years On: Lessons from Northern Rock," September 29, 2017, www.bankofengland.co.uk/-/media/boe/files/speech/2017/ten-years-on-lessons-from-northern-rock.
4. Angela Balakrishnan, "Financial Crisis: Action Taken by Central Banks and Governments," *Guardian*, October 21, 2008, www.theguardian.com/business/2008/oct/13/creditcrunch-marketturmoil1.
5. George C. Nurisso and Edward S. Prescott, "The 1970s Origins of Too Big to Fail," Federal Reserve Bank of Cleveland, October 18, 2017, www.clevelandfed.org/publications/economic-commentary/2017/ec-201717-origins-of-too-big-to-fail#cf-fn-2 .
6. Federal Deposit Insurance Corporation, "The Historic Relationship between Bank Net Interest Margins and Short-Term Interest Rates," *FDIC Quarterly* 15, no. 2 (2021), www.fdic.gov/analysis/quarterly-banking-profile/fdic-quarterly/2021-vol15-2/article1.pdf.
7. Board of Governors of the Federal Reserve System, "Large Bank Capital Requirements," August 2022, www.federalreserve.gov/publications/files/large-bank-capital-requirements-20220804.pdf.
8. Bre Bradham, "Tricida Collapses 94%, Vaxcyte Soars as Drug Trials Diverge," Bloomberg, October 25, 2022, www.bloomberg.com/news/articles/2022-10-24/tricida-collapses-95-vaxcyte-skyrockets-as-drug-trials-diverge?embedded-checkout=true.
9. RTTNews, "Kala Pharmaceuticals Ascends 5% on Getting Fast Track Designation for Its KPI-012," April 12, 2023, www.nasdaq.com/articles/kala-pharmaceuticals-ascends-5-on-getting-fast-track-designation-for-its-kpi-012.
10. Leroy Leo, "FDA Greenlights Amylyx's ALS Drug," Reuters, September 30, 2022, www.reuters.com/business/healthcare-pharmaceuticals/us-fda-approves-amylyx-als-drug-2022-09-29/.

11. Reuters, "Pfizer, BioNTech's Coronavirus Vaccines Get FDA's 'Fast Track' Status," July 13, 2020, www.reuters.com/article/idUSL3N2EK2B8/.
12. Allison Gatlin, "Is Moderna Stock a Sell After Its Sales Guidance Undercuts 2024 Expectations?" *Investor's Business Daily*, November 27, 2023, www.investors.com/news/technology/mrna-stock-buy-now/.
13. George Maybach, "BlackRock Now Owns 10.20% of Kimco Realty," Fintel Data, April 06, 2023, https://fintel.io/news/blackrock-now-owns-1020-of-kimco-realty-kim-118?utm_source=nasdaq.com&utm_medium=referral&utm_campaign=blackrock-now-owns-1020-of-kimco-realty-kim-118.
14. Insurance Information Institute, "Facts + Statistics: US Catastrophes, 2022 Natural Catastrophes," www.iii.org/fact-statistic/facts-statistics-us-catastrophes.
15. Dina Bass, "Microsoft Invests $10 Billion in ChatGPT Maker OpenAI," Bloomberg, January 23, 2023, www.bloomberg.com/news/articles/2023-01-23/microsoft-makes-multibillion-dollar-investment-in-openai?embedded-checkout=true.
16. PwC, "Perspectives from the Global Entertainment and Media Outlook 2023–2027," July 20, 2023, www.pwc.com/id/en/pwc-publications/industries-publications/telecommunications-media-technology/global-entertainment-media-outlook-2023.html.
17. Jessica DiNapoli and Richa Naidu, "Focus: Here's What Twitter Lost in Advertising Revenue in Final Months of 2022," Reuters, January 21, 2023, www.reuters.com/technology/heres-what-twitter-lost-advertising-revenue-final-months-2022-2023-01-19/.
18. Brad Adgate, "Global Ad Revenue for Print Struggles, as Total Ad Revenue Nears $1 Trillion," *Forbes*, March 7, 2023, www.forbes.com/sites/bradadgate/2023/03/07/global-ad-revenue-for-print-struggles-as-total-ad-revenue-nears-1-trillion/?sh=6fc9daa3275a.
19. Netflix, "Netflix to Become New Home of WWE 'Raw' Beginning 2025," January 23, 2024, https://about.netflix.com/en/news/netflix-to-become-new-home-of-wwe-raw-beginning-2025.
20. Broadcast Pro Me, "Media and Entertainment Industry Seeks New Revenue Sources: Salesforce," April 3, 2023, www.broadcastprome.com/news/media-entertainment-industry-seeks-new-revenue-sources-salesforce/.
21. Michelle Chapman, "Home Depot's Same-Store Sales Surge in Final Quarter of 2019," AP News, February 25, 2020, https://apnews.com/article/c9c46e89599aa9d1c18d97122a4e746a.
22. Yimou Lee, "Foxconn Unrest Risks iPhone Shipments, Weighs on Apple Shares," Reuters, November 26, 2022, www.reuters.com/technology/more-than-20000-new-hires-have-left-apple-supplier-foxconns-zhengzhou-plant-2022-11-25/.

23. Carolina Mandl and Ankika Biswas, "Nasdaq Ends Down as Investors Eye Black Friday Sales, China Infections," Reuters, November 26, 2022, www.reuters.com/markets/us/futures-largely-subdued-with-black-friday-sales-focus-2022-11-25/.
24. Melissa Repko and Lauren Thomas, "Online Sales Reach $10.8 Billion on Cyber Monday, the Biggest US e-Commerce Day Ever, Adobe Says," CNBC, December 1, 2020, www.cnbc.com/2020/12/01/holiday-2020-shoppers-spend-10point8-billion-on-cyber-monday.html.
25. Victoria Giardina, "What Time Does Amazon Prime Day 2023 End? Everything You Need to Know to Shop Now," *New York Post*, July 12, 2023, https://nypost.com/article/when-is-amazon-prime-day-2023-what-we-know-deals/.
26. Allison Nicole Smith, "Back-to-School Sales Will See a Boost from Rising Prices," Bloomberg, July 14, 2022, www.bloomberg.com/news/articles/2022-07-14/back-to-school-sales-will-see-a-boost-from-rising-prices#xj4y7vzkg.
27. Melissa Repko, "Back-to-School Delays, Virtual Classes Could Deepen Pain for Some Retailers, and Be Windfall for Others," CNBC, July 30, 2020, www.cnbc.com/2020/07/30/back-to-school-may-deepen-pain-for-some-retailers-be-windfall-for-others.html.

CHAPTER 6

1. David Goldman, "GM is Reinventing Itself: It's Cutting 15% of Its Salaried Workers and Shutting 5 Plants in North America," CNN Business, November 26, 2018, https://edition.cnn.com/2018/11/26/business/gm-oshawa-plant/index.html.
2. Statista, January 26, 2023, www.statista.com/statistics/277430/largest-global-mergers-and-aquisitions-based-on-transaction-volume.
3. "Chapter 2: Vodafone Acquisition of Mannesmann," in *Wealth Creation in the World's Largest Mergers and Acquisitions*, by B. Rajesh Kumar (Berlin: Springer, 2018).
4. Thorsten Schulten, "Vodafone's Hostile Takeover Bid for Mannesmann Highlights Debate on the German Capitalist Model," Eurofound, 1999, www.eurofound.europa.eu/publications/article/1999/vodafones-hostile-takeover-bid-for-mannesmann-highlights-debate-on-the-german-capitalist-model.
5. Schulten.
6. CNNMoney, "Vodafone Sets $138B Bid," https://money.cnn.com/1999/12/23/europe/vodafone.

7. Gautam Naik and Anita Raghavan, "Vodafone, Mannesmann Set Takeover At $180.95 Billion After Long Struggle," *Wall Street Journal*, www.wsj.com /articles/SB949581016407171 70.
8. Amrita Jayakumar, "Men's Wearhouse Finally Buys Jos. A. Bank," *Washington Post*, March 11, 2014, www.washingtonpost.com/business/economy /mens-wearhouse-finally-buys-jos-a-bank/2014/03/11/4143ca88-a93f -11e3-8d62-419db477a0e6_story.html.
9. Svea Herbst-Bayliss, "Sotheby's Ends Fight with Third Point, Loeb Joins Board," Reuters, May 6, 2014, www.reuters.com/article/us-sothebys-third point-idUSBREA440EC20140505.
10. "Merck Withdraws After Bayer Tops Bid for Schering," Reuters, March 25, 2006, www.nytimes.com/2006/03/25/business/merck-withdraws-after-bayer -tops-bid-for-schering.html.
11. Jessica Hall and Lewis Krauskopf, "Pfizer to Buy Wyeth for $68 Billion," Reuters, January 26, 2009, www.reuters.com/article/us-wyeth-pfizer-idUS TRE50M1AQ20090126.
12. Joseph White and Nick Carey, "GM to Slash Jobs and Production, Drawing Trump's Ire," Reuters, November 27, 2018, www.reuters.com/article/us -gm-restructuring-idUSKCN1NV1NB.
13. Ingrid Marson, "Google and NASA Join Forces," ZDNet, September 29, 2005, www.zdnet.com/home-and-office/networking/google-and-nasa-join -forces/.
14. Theresa Howard, "Molson Coors, SABMiller Set Up Joint Venture," ABC News, October 10, 2007, https://abcnews.go.com/Business/story?id=371 0263&page=1.
15. "Elon Musk Buys $2.9bn Stake in Twitter to Become Biggest Shareholder," *Guardian*, April 4, 2022, www.theguardian.com/technology/2022/apr/04 /elon-musk-buys-stake-twitter-share-tesla-spacex.
16. Tom Krisher and Matt O'Brien, "Elon Musk Reaches Agreement to Acquire Twitter for About $44 Billion," Associated Press, April 25, 2022, www .pbs.org/newshour/economy/elon-musk-reaches-agreement-to-acquire -twitter-for-about-44-billion.
17. Rishi Iyengar and Allison Morrow, "Elon Musk Says Twitter Deal Can't Happen Until Bot Account Dispute Is Resolved," May 17, 2022, CNN, https://edition.cnn.com/2022/05/16/tech/elon-musk-twitter-spam-bots -parag/index.html.
18. Jef Feeley and Sarah Frier, "Musk-Twitter Countdown to Close $44 Billion Deal Begins," Bloomberg, October 28, 2022, www.bloomberg.com/news /articles/2022-10-27/elon-musk-faces-countdown-to-44-billion-deadline -to-buy-twitter?embedded-checkout=true.

CHAPTER 7

1. David Mildenberg, "FlyExclusive Starts Trading, Creates Kinston's First Non-Bank Public Company," Business North Carolina, December 28, 2023, https://businessnc.com/flyexclusive-starts-trading-dips-40-on-first-day/.
2. Benjamin Curry, "Stock Buybacks: How Companies Create Value for Shareholders," *Forbes Advisor*, June 14, 2023, www.forbes.com/advisor/investing/stock-buyback/.
3. Annie Palmer, "Amazon Announces 20-for-1 Stock Split, $10 Billion Buyback," CNBC, March 9, 2022, updated August 19, www.cnbc.com/2022/03/09/amazon-announces-20-for-1-stock-split-10-billion-buyback.html.
4. Scott Nations, "*A History of the United States in Five Crashes: Stock Market Meltdowns That Defined a Nation* (New York: William Morrow, 2017), 119, 133–34.
5. Mark Carlson, "A Brief History of the 1987 Stock Market Crash with a Discussion of the Federal Reserve Response," November 2006, updated May 1, 2007, www.federalreserve.gov/pubs/feds/2007/200713/200713pap.pdf.
6. Marc Davis, "How September 11 Affected the US Stock Market," Investopedia, September 11, 2023, www.investopedia.com/financial-edge/0911/how-september-11-affected-the-u.s.-stock-market.aspx.
7. Yi Wen and Iris Arbogast, "How COVID-19 Has Impacted Stock Performance by Industry," Federal Reserve Bank of Saint Louis, March 21, 2021, www.stlouisfed.org/on-the-economy/2021/march/covid19-impacted-stock-performance-industry.
8. US Securities and Exchange Commission, "Trading Halts and Delays," July 23, 2010, www.sec.gov/answers/tradinghalt.htm.
9. New York Stock Exchange, "Market-Wide Circuit Breaker," no date, www.nyse.com/markets/nyse/trading-info.
10. Sabrina Escobar, "Apple Is Borrowing Money to Buy Back Stock; What That May Say About the Bond Market," *Barrons*, August 1, 2022, www.barrons.com/articles/apple-bonds-stock-buybacks-51659361679.
11. Davide Barbuscia and Andrea Shalal, "Moody's Turns Negative on US Credit Rating, Draws Washington Ire," Reuters, November 11, 2023, www.reuters.com/markets/us/moodys-changes-outlook-united-states-ratings-negative-2023-11-10/.
12. Clement Tan, "Moody's Cuts China's Credit Outlook to Negative on Rising Debt Risks," CNBC, December 5, 2023, www.cnbc.com/2023/12/05/moodys-cut-chinas-credit-outlook-to-negative-on-rising-debt-risks.html.
13. Global Times, "Moody's Politically Biased Credit Outlook Cut Won't Affect China's Long-Term Upward Growth Trend: Experts," December 6, 2023, www.globaltimes.cn/page/202312/1303148.shtml.

14. World Government Bonds, "Argentina Credit Rating," www.worldgovernment bonds.com/credit-rating/argentina/.
15. Christine Hauser, "Sunflower Oil Vanishes as Ukraine War Grinds On," *New York Times*, April 30, 2022, www.nytimes.com/2022/04/30/world /europe/cooking-oil-shortage-ukraine.html?searchResultPosition=1.
16. Christian Bogmans, Andrea Pescatori, and Ervin Prifti, "Global Food Prices to Remain Elevated Amid War, Costly Energy, La Nina," International Monetary Fund blog, December 9, 2022, www.imf.org/en/Blogs /Articles/2022/12/09/global-food-prices-to-remain-elevated-amid-war -costly-energy-la-nina.
17. Coryanne Hicks, "Different Types of Cryptocurrencies," March 15, 2023, *Forbes Advisor*, www.forbes.com/advisor/investing/cryptocurrency/different -types-of-cryptocurrencies/.
18. Elizabeth Napolitano and Brian Cheung, "The FTX Collapse, Explained," NBC, November 19, 2022, www.nbcnews.com/tech/crypto/sam-bankman -fried-crypto-ftx-collapse-explained-rcna57582.
19. Kevin Roose, "Is This Crypto's Lehman Moment?" *New York Times*, November 9, 2022, www.nytimes.com/2022/11/09/technology/cryptocurrency -binance-ftx.html.
20. Michael Adams, "Best Crypto Stocks of January 2024," January 5, 2024, *Forbes*, www.forbes.com/advisor/investing/cryptocurrency/best-crypto currency-stocks/.
21. PBS, "Amid Value Drops and Increased Regulation, What's the Future of Cryptocurrency?" March 2, 2023, www.pbs.org/newshour/economy /cryptocurrencies-digital-dollars-and-the-future-of-money.
22. US Securities and Exchange Commission, "Statement on the Approval of Spot Bitcoin Exchange-Traded Products," January 10, 2024, www.sec .gov/newsroom/speeches-statements/gensler-statement-spot-bitcoin -011023.
23. Tom Wilson and Angus Berwick, "Crypto Exchange FTX Saw $6 Bln in Withdrawals in 72 Hours," Reuters, November 9, 2022, www.reuters.com /business/finance/crypto-exchange-ftx-saw-6-bln-withdrawals-72-hours -ceo-message-staff-2022-11-08/.
24. PBS, "Cryptocurrency Exchange Binance Mishandled Funds and Violated Securities Laws, SEC Lawsuit Says," June 5, 2023, www.pbs.org/newshour /economy/cryptocurrency-exchange-binance-mishandled-funds-and -violated-securities-laws-sec-lawsuit-says.
25. Manya Saini and Sinéad Carew, "Crypto Stocks Drop After US SEC Sues Coinbase for Failing to Register," Reuters, June 7, 2023, www.reuters.com /business/finance/crypto-stocks-fall-after-us-sec-sues-coinbase-over -failure-register-2023-06-06/.

CHAPTER 8

1. John Divine, "The Top 10 Largest Private Equity Funds in the World," *US News & World Report*, May 2, 2023, https://money.usnews.com/investing/slideshows/largest-private-equity-firms.
2. Rebecca Baldridge, "What Is Private Equity? What Is a Private Equity Fund?" *Forbes*, updated May 6, 2022, www.forbes.com/advisor/investing/private-equity.
3. National Venture Capital Association, "PitchBook—NVCA Venture Monitor," https://nvca.org/pitchbook-nvca-venture-monitor/.
4. Andreesen Horowitz, "Builders We've Backed," https://a16z.com/portfolio/.
5. Accel, "Noteworthy," portfolio, www.accel.com/noteworthy-categories/portfoliocx.
6. Bessemer Venture Partners, "Our Companies," https://www.bvp.com/companies.
7. Founders Fund, "Portfolio," https://foundersfund.com/portfolio/.
8. Sequoia, "Our Companies," www.sequoiacap.com/our-companies/.
9. Svea Herbst-Bayliss, "Icahn Scores Partial Illumina Win Amid Pressure to Defend Investment Acumen," Reuters, May 25, 2023, www.reuters.com/business/healthcare-pharmaceuticals/icahn-wins-one-board-seat-illumina-2023-05-25/.
10. Federal Trade Commission, "Statement Regarding Illumina's Decision to Divest Grail," December 18, 2023, www.ftc.gov/news-events/news/press-releases/2023/12/statement-regarding-illuminas-decision-divest-grail.
11. Carl Icahn, "Open Letter to Shareholders of Illumina, Inc.," December 18, 2023, https://carlicahn.com/open-letter-to-shareholders-of-illumina-inc-13/.
12. Trian Partners, "Trian Nominates Nelson Peltz for Election to Disney Board," January 11, 2023, https://trianpartners.com/wp-content/uploads/2023/01/Trian-Disney-Launch-Press-Release-01.11.23.pdf.
13. Walt Disney Company, "Mark Parker to Be Named Chairman of the Walt Disney Company," January 11, 2023, https://thewaltdisneycompany.com/mark-parker-to-be-named-chairman-of-the-walt-disney-company/.
14. Trian Partners, "Trian Applauds Recent Initiatives Announced by Disney as a Win for All Shareholders and Concludes Proxy Campaign," February 9, 2023, https://trianpartners.com/wp-content/uploads/2023/02/Trian-Applauds-Recent-Initiatives-Announced-by-Disney-as-a-Win-for-All-Shareholders-and-Concludes-Proxy-Campaign.pdf.
15. Walt Disney Company, "The Walt Disney Company Appoints Morgan Stanley's James P. Gorman and Veteran Media Executive Sir Jeremy Darroch as New Directors," November 29, 2023, https://thewaltdisneycompany

.com/the-walt-disney-company-board-appoints-morgan-stanleys-james-p-gorman-and-veteran-media-executive-sir-jeremy-darroch-as-new-directors/; Trian Partners, "Trian Issues Statement Regarding the Walt Disney Company Board," November 30, 2023, https://trianpartners.com/wp-content/uploads/2023/11/Trian-Issues-Statement-Regarding-The-Walt-Disney-Company-Board.pdf.

16. Walt Disney Company, "Statement from the Walt Disney Company," November 30, 2023, https://thewaltdisneycompany.com/statement-from-the-walt-disney-company-3/.
17. Walt Disney Company, "Statement from the Walt Disney Company," December 14, 2023, https://thewaltdisneycompany.com/statement-from-the-walt-disney-company-5/.
18. Walt Disney Company, "The Walt Disney Company and ValueAct Capital Enter into Information-Sharing Arrangement to Facilitate Strategic Consultation During Company's Transformation," January 3, 2024, https://thewaltdisneycompany.com/the-walt-disney-company-and-valueact-capital-enter-into-information-sharing-arrangement-to-facilitate-strategic-consultation-during-companys-transformation/.
19. Walt Disney Company, "Statement from the Walt Disney Company," January 3, 2024, https://thewaltdisneycompany.com/statement-from-the-walt-disney-company-6/.
20. Walt Disney Company, "Shareholders Vote to Elect Disney's Full Slate of 12 Directors," April 3, 2024, https://thewaltdisneycompany.com/shareholders-vote-to-elect-disneys-full-slate-of-12-directors/.
21. ICE, New York Stock Exchange, www.nyse.com/quote/XNYS:DIS.

CHAPTER 9

1. David Rodeck and Benjamin Curry, "What Is a Recession," *Forbes*, September 26, 2022, www.forbes.com/advisor/in/investing/what-is-a-recession/.
2. Economist Intelligence Unit, "Big Tech: Resilient Despite Macroeconomic Headwinds," August 24, 2022, www.eiu.com/n/big-tech-resilient-despite-macroeconomic-headwinds/.
3. Clement Tan, "The Bank of Japan Just Made a Historic Rate Pivot; Here's What Could Happen Next," March 20, 2024, www.cnbc.com/2024/03/19/boj-bank-of-japan-historic-pivot-interest-rate-hike.html.
4. Sarah Min and Brian Evans, "Dow Pops More Than 200 Points," CNBC, November 3, 2023, www.cnbc.com/2023/11/02/stock-market-today-live-updates.html.

5. Yeo Boon Ping, "A Cool Jobs Report Heats Up Markets," CNBC, November 5, 2023, www.cnbc.com/2023/11/06/stock-markets-a-cool-jobs-report-heats-up-markets.html.
6. Federal Reserve Bank of San Francisco, "Teacher Resources," www.frbsf.org/education/teacher-resources/chair-federal-reserve-economy-simulation-game/.
7. Andrew Michael. "What Inflation Means for Your Investments," *Forbes UK*, March 2023, www.forbes.com/uk/advisor/investing/what-inflation-means-for-your-investments/.
8. Zhang Yukun, "Did China's Youth Jobless Rate Really Hit 46.5%?" *Nikkei Asia*, August 15, 2023, https://asia.nikkei.com/Spotlight/Caixin/Did-China-s-youth-jobless-rate-really-hit-46.5.
9. Andrew Mullen, "China's Economic Recovery Continues to Stutter with Manufacturing Facing 'Downward Spiral' as Demand Weakens," *South China Morning Post*, May 31, 2023, www.scmp.com/economy/economic-indicators/article/3222374/chinas-economic-recovery-continues-stutter-manufacturing-activity-contracts-further-may.
10. Laura He, "China's Economic Recovery Loses Steam as Factory Production Contracts Further," CNN, May 31, 2023, https://edition.cnn.com/2023/05/30/economy/china-pmi-economy-intl-hnk/index.html.
11. JPMorgan, "Debt Ceiling Drama: What You Need to Know," January 20, 2023, www.jpmorgan.com/insights/markets/rates/debt-ceiling-drama-what-you-need-to-know.
12. Menekse Tokyay, "Inflation in Turkey Spikes to Highest Level Under Erdogan," Axios, January 3, 2022, www.axios.com/2022/01/03/inflation-turkey-cpi-36-percent-erdogan.
13. Jeff Cox, "Fed Hikes Interest Rates by 0.75 Percentage Point for Second Consecutive Time to Fight Inflation," July 27, 2022, CNBC, cnbc.com/2022/07/27/fed-decision-july-2022-.html.
14. Jeff Cox, "Powell Warns of Some Pain Ahead as the Fed Fights to Bring Down Inflation," August 26, 2022, CNBC, cnbc.com/2022/08/26/powell-warns-of-some-pain-ahead-as-fed-fights-to-lower-inflation.html.
15. Tanaya Macheel and Carmen Reinicke, "Dow Rallies 400 Points as Powell Hints Fed Could Slow Pace of Rate Hikes, Nasdaq Jumps 4%," July 26, 2022, CNBC, www.cnbc.com/2022/07/26/stock-futures-tick-up-ahead-of-key-fed-decision.html.

CHAPTER 10

1. Matthew DiLallo, "How to Invest in SpaceX in 2023," *Motley Fool*, August 28, 2023, www.fool.com/investing/how-to-invest/stocks/how-to-invest-in-spacex-stock/.

2. Carmen Ang, "How Do Big Tech Giants Make Their Millions?" *Visual Capitalist*, April 25, 2022, www.visualcapitalist.com/how-big-tech-makes-their-billions-2022/.
3. IPOS (Singapore), "Brands, Patents and Company Performance Study: Do Intangible Assets Like Brands and Patents Help Companies Outperform Their Peers? An Analysis of the World's and Singapore's Largest Listed Companies," www.ipos.gov.sg/docs/default-source/resources-library/brands-patents-and-company-performance-study.pdf.
4. Kevin G. Rivette, Henry R. Nothhaft, and David Kline, "Discovering New Value in Intellectual Property," *Harvard Business Review*, January–February 2000, https://hbr.org/2000/01/discovering-new-value-in-intellectual-property.
5. Rebecca Robins, "How a Drug Company Made $114 Billion by Gaming the US Patent System," *New York Times*, January 28, 2023, www.nytimes.com/2023/01/28/business/humira-abbvie-monopoly.html.
6. Peter Loftus and Denise Roland, "By Adding Patents, Drugmaker Keeps Cheaper Humira Copies Out of US," *Wall Street Journal*, October 6, 2018, www.wsj.com/articles/biosimilar-humira-goes-on-sale-in-europe-widening-gap-with-u-s-1539687603.
7. Patrick Wingrove, "Focus: AbbVie's Humira Gets a US Rival, but Costs Could Stay High," Reuters, February 2, 2023, www.reuters.com/business/healthcare-pharmaceuticals/abbvies-humira-gets-us-rival-costs-could-stay-high-2023-01-31/.
8. Patrick Wingrove and Leroy Leo, "AbbVie Posts Weak Sales of Newer Drugs as Humira Faces Fresh Competition, Shares Fall," Reuters, April 27, 2023, www.reuters.com/business/healthcare-pharmaceuticals/abbvie-raises-annual-profit-forecast-humira-demand-holds-steady-2023-04-27/.
9. Counterpoint Research, www.counterpointresearch.com/insights/apple-iphone-market-share-quarter/.
10. Brett Molina, "iPhone 13: Yes, People Still Wait in Line to Get the New iPhone," *USA Today*, September 24, 2021, www.usatoday.com/story/tech/2021/09/24/iphone-13-here-consumers-line-up-get-apples-new-smartphone/5841673001/.
11. Samantha Subin, "What History Shows About Apple's Stock Performance Following a New iPhone Launch," CNBC, September 26, 2022, https://archive.ph/VrTam#selection-1121.1130-1121.1236.
12. Derek Saul, "Apple Beats Quarterly Profit and Sales Estimates—Led by Record Services Revenue," *Forbes*, May 4, 2023, www.forbes.com/sites/dereksaul/2023/05/04/apple-beats-quarterly-profit-sales-estimates-despite-interest-rate-headwinds/?sh=4820a2323637.
13. Martin Baccardax, "Apple Tops $3 Trillion in Value as Tech Extends Market Grip," Street.com, June 30, 2023, www.thestreet.com/investing/stocks/apple-tops-3-trillion-in-value-as-big-tech-extends-market-grip.

14. McKinsey & Company, "Fintechs: A New Paradigm of Growth," October 24, 2023, https://www.mckinsey.com/industries/financial-services/our-insights/fintechs-a-new-paradigm-of-growth#/.
15. Sydney Boyo, "How the Apple iPhone Became One of the Best-Selling Products of All Time," CNBC, January 27, 2024, www.cnbc.com/2024/01/27/how-the-apple-iphone-changed-the-world.html.
16. Verge, "Google Turns 20: How an Internet Search Engine Reshaped the World," September 27, 2018, www.theverge.com/2018/9/5/17823490/google-20th-birthday-anniversary-history-milestones.
17. Jeanine Mancini, "How Early Airbnb Investors Raked in a 499,900% Return on IPO Day from a Simple Idea to Pay the Rent," May 13, 2023, Yahoo! Finance, https://finance.yahoo.com/news/early-airbnb-investors-raked-499-193618823.html.
18. "Airbnb to Compete with Luxury Hotels with New Premium Tier," *South China Morning Post*, June 22, 2017, www.scmp.com/magazines/style/travel-food/article/2099445/airbnb-compete-luxury-hotels-new-premium-tier.
19. Yoolim Lee, "Grab's 70% Tumble Shows the Limits of Singapore's Tech Dream," Bloomberg, October 12, 2023, www.businesstimes.com.sg/startups-tech/startups/grabs-70-tumble-shows-limits-singapores-tech-dream.
20. Sebo Marketing, "A Brief History of Google: Part 1," www.sebomarketing.com/brief-history-google/.
21. Eric Schmidt, "How I Did It: Google's CEO on the Enduring Lessons of a Quirky IPO," *Harvard Business Review*, May 2010, https://hbr.org/2010/05/how-i-did-it-googles-ceo-on-the-enduring-lessons-of-a-quirky-ipo.

CHAPTER 11

1. US Securities and Exchange Commission (SEC), "Investor Bulletin: Trading Suspensions," December 14, 2021, https://investor.gov/introduction-investing/general-resources/news-alerts/alerts-bulletins/investor-bulletins/investor-5.
2. SEC, "How Investigations Work," January 27, 2017, www.sec.gov/enforcement/how-investigations-work.
3. Reuters, "US SEC Threatens to Sue Coinbase Over Some Crypto Products," March 22, 2023, www.reuters.com/legal/coinbase-issued-wells-notice-by-sec-2023-03-22; Paul Grewal (Coinbase), "We Asked the SEC for Reasonable Crypto Rules for Americans; We Got Legal Threats Instead," March 22, 2023, www.coinbase.com/en-gb/blog/we-asked-the-sec-for-reasonable-crypto-rules-for-americans-we-got-legal.
4. SEC, "SEC Charges Wells Fargo Advisors with Anti–Money Laundering Related Violations," May 20, 2022, www.sec.gov/news/press-release/2022-85.

5. SEC, "SEC Charges Former Pfizer Statistician with Insider Trading Ahead of COVID-19 Announcement," June 29, 2023, www.sec.gov/news/press-release/2023-123.
6. Xie Yu, "Explainer: What to Watch Out For as Talks on US-China Audit Deal Drag On," Reuters, August 15, 2022, www.reuters.com/markets/what-watch-out-talks-us-china-audit-deal-drag-2022-08-08/.
7. Jeanny Yu, "China Stocks with US Listings Slump as NYSE Exit Gathers Pace," Bloomberg, August 15, 2022, www.bloomberg.com/news/articles/2022-08-15/china-stocks-with-us-listings-in-focus-as-delisting-gathers-pace?embedded-checkout=true.
8. Criminal Division, US Department of Justice, *United States v. The Boeing Company*, Deferred Prosecution Agreement Court Docket 4:21-CR-005-0 (N.D. Texas), January 2, 2024, www.justice.gov/criminal-fraud/case/united-states-v-boeing-company.
9. Gregory Wallace, Colin McCullough, Evan Perez, and Chris Isidore, "US Justice Department Is Investigating Boeing Over Its Door Plug Blowout," CNN Business, February 29, 2024, https://edition.cnn.com/2024/02/29/business/boeing-justice-department-investigation/index.html.
10. Office of Public Affairs, US Department of Justice, "Electronic Health Records Vendor NextGen Healthcare Inc. to Pay $31 Million to Settle False Claims Act Allegations," July 14, 2023, www.justice.gov/opa/pr/electronic-health-records-vendor-nextgen-healthcare-inc-pay-31-million-settle-false-claims.
11. BBC, "Goldman Sachs to Pay $3bn Over 1MDB Corruption Scandal," October 22, 2020, www.bbc.com/news/business-54597256.
12. Commodity Futures Trading Commission, "Dodd-Frank Act," January 5, 2010, www.cftc.gov/LawRegulation/DoddFrankAct/index.htm.
13. Commodity Futures Trading Commission, "CFTC Orders Three Financial Institutions to Pay Over $50 Million for Swap Reporting Failures and Other Violations," September 29, 2023, www.cftc.gov/PressRoom/PressReleases/8801-23.
14. US Congress, House of Representatives, "HR 3763: Sarbanes-Oxley Act of 2002, Conference Report Filed in House, July 24, 2002," www.Congress.gov/bill/107th-Congress/house-bill/3763.
15. Scott Cohn, "Twenty years After Epic Bankruptcy, Enron Leaves a Complex Legacy," CNBC, December 2, 2021, www.cnbc.com/2021/12/02/twenty-years-after-epic-bankruptcy-enron.
16. US Department of Labor, "Nine Inspections in Four States Find Dollar General Exposed Workers to Obstructed Exits, Fire, Electrical Hazards; Carry $3.4M in New Penalties," OSHA National News Release, May 23, 2023, www.osha.gov/news/newsreleases/national/05232023-0; US Department

of Labor, "Department of Labor Announces Settlement with Dollar General Requiring Corporate-Wide Safety Investments in Stores Nationwide," OSHA National News Release, July 11, 2024, www.osha.gov/news/newsreleases/national/07112024-0.

17. Amy Howe, US Supreme Court blog, "Supreme Court Curtails EPA's Authority to Fight Climate Change," June 30, 2022, www.scotusblog.com/2022/06/supreme-court-curtails-epas-authority-to-fight-climate-change/.
18. Anneken Tappe, "The Economic Consequences of Overturning *Roe v. Wade* Will Be Enormous, Experts Warn," CNN Business, June 24, 2022, www.cnn.com/2022/06/24/economy/economic-impact-roe-wade-overturn/index.html.
19. Leah Rodriquez, "Unpaid Care Work: Everything You Need to Know," Global Citizen, September 13, 2021, www.globalcitizen.org/en/content/womens-unpaid-care-work-everything-to-know.
20. Paul R. La Monica, "Tiny Birth Control Stock Soars Following *Roe v. Wade* Overturn," CNN Business, July 28, 2022, www.cnn.com/2022/07/28/investing/evofem-biosciences-stock-abortion-birth-control/index.html.
21. Eric Rosenbaum, "Worried About Contested Election? Here's What Went Down in Stocks During 2000 Bush-Gore Battle," CNBC, October 26, 2020, www.cnbc.com/2020/10/26/contested-election-what-went-down-in-markets-during-bush-gore-battle.html.
22. Julia Horowitz, "What Is Huawei, and Why the Arrest of Its CFO Matters," CNN Business, December 9, 2018, www.cnn.com/2018/12/06/tech/what-is-huawei/index.html.
23. Krystal Hu, "Shares of These US Suppliers Are Getting Slammed in the Wake of the Huawei Arrest," Yahoo! Finance, December 6, 2018, https://finance.yahoo.com/news/shares-u-s-suppliers-getting-slammed-wake-huawei-arrest-175259398.html.
24. Office of Public Affairs, US Department of Justice, "Huawei CFO Wanzhou Meng Admits to Misleading Global Financial Institution," September 24, 2021, www.justice.gov/opa/pr/huawei-cfo-wanzhou-meng-admits-misleading-global-financial-institution.
25. CBC, "The Meng Wanzhou Huawei Saga: A Timeline," September 24, 2021, updated September 25, www.cbc.ca/news/meng-wanzhou-huawei-kovrig-spavor-1.6188472.

CHAPTER 12

1. Philip Barret and Sophia Chen, "How Stock Markets Respond to Social Unrest," International Monetary Fund blog, May 10, 2021, www.imf.org

/en/Blogs/Articles/2021/05/10/how-stock-markets-respond-to-social -unrest.

2. Nyshka Chandran, "Trump Fires Back at Beijing with Threat of New Tariffs on $200 Billion in Chinese Goods," CNBC, June 18, 2018, www.cnbc .com/2018/06/18/trump-says-he-has-asked-ustr-to-identify-200-billion -in-chinese-goods-for-additional-tariffs-at-10-percent-rate.html.
3. Dominic Rushe, "Stock Markets Roiled as US-China Trade Dispute Escalates," *Guardian*, June 20, 2018, www.theguardian.com/business/2018/jun /19/stock-markets-latest-fall-trump-china-trade-war-tariffs.
4. Yimou Lee and Sarah Wu, "Pelosi Arrives in Taiwan Vowing US Commitment; China Enraged," Reuters, August 3, 2022, www.reuters.com/world /asia-pacific/pelosi-expected-arrive-taiwan-tuesday-sources-say-2022 -08-02/.
5. US China Economic and Security Review Commission, "Chinese Companies Listed on Major US Stock Exchanges," www.uscc.gov/research /chinese-companies-listed-major-us-stock-exchanges.
6. Xie Yu and Selena Li, "US Step to Delist Chinese ADRs Worsen Investment, Listing Outlook," Reuters, March 14, 2022, www.reuters.com/markets/us/us -step-delist-chinese-adrs-worsens-investment-listing-outlook-2022-03-14/.
7. Sarah Zheng, "US to Sell $180 Million Worth of Submarine-Launched Torpedoes to Taiwan," *South China Morning Post,* May 21, 2022, www.scmp .com/news/china/military/article/3085396/us-sell-us180-million-worth -submarine-launched-torpedoes-taiwan.
8. Steven Jiang, "China Raids Global Consulting Firm's Offices on Allegations of National Security Risk," CNN, May 9, 2023, https://edition.cnn.com /videos/business/2023/05/09/exp-china-capvision-raid-steven-jiang-live -050912aseg2-cnni-business.cnn.
9. Patti Domm, "US-China Tensions Could Become a Bigger Headwind for the Stock Market," CNBC, May 22, 2020, www.cnbc.com/2020/05/22/us-china -tensions-could-become-a-bigger-headwind-for-the-stock-market.html.
10. Zhixuan Wang, Yanli Dong, and Ailan Liu, "How Does China's Stock Market React to Supply Chain Disruptions from COVID-19?" Science Direct, July 2022, www.sciencedirect.com/science/article/pii/S1057521922001326 #bb0340.
11. Rintaro Tobita, Iori Kawate, and Takafumi Hotta, "China No Longer Top Exporter to US as Trade Rift Widens," *Nikkei Asia,* July 14, 2023, https:// asia.nikkei.com/Economy/Trade/China-no-longer-top-exporter-to-U.S. -as-trade-rift-widens.
12. Joyce Alves, "Analysis: China Slowdown Prompts Export-Reliant Europe Stocks Rethink," Reuters, July 6, 2023, www.reuters.com/markets/europe

/china-slowdown-prompts-export-reliant-europe-stocks-rethink-2023-07-06/.

13. Joal Ryan, "Supply Chain Issues: 13 Things You May (or May Not) Have Trouble Finding during the 2021 Holiday Season," CBS News, December 2, 2021, www.cbsnews.com/essentials/supply-chain-issues-2021-shortages-out-of-stock-items-christmas-shopping/.
14. Amanda Macias, "Get Ready for a Christmas Tree Shortage, as Supply Chain Issues and Climate Change Team Up," CNBC, November 16, 2021, www.cnbc.com/2021/11/16/christmas-tree-shortage-because-of-supply-chain-issues-climate-change.html.
15. BBC, "Amazon to Pay Billions to Prevent Christmas Shortages," October 29, 2021, www.bbc.com/news/business-59085835.
16. Fred Imbert, "Dow Drops Nearly 3,000 Points, as Coronavirus Collapse Continues; Worst Day Since '87," CNBC, March 15, 2020, www.cnbc.com/2020/03/15/traders-await-futures-open-after-fed-cuts-rates-launches-easing-program.html.
17. Nicole Winfield, "Food Prices Soar to Record Levels on Ukraine War Disruptions," AP News, April 8, 2022, https://apnews.com/article/russia-ukraine-business-health-europe-united-nations-fe2cc912195478f0dd861e6252c8f3b3.
18. Joseph W. Glauber and David Laborde Debcquet, *The Russia–Ukraine Conflict and Global Food Security* (Washington, DC: International Food Policy Research Institute, 2023), 196.
19. Chelsea Ong, "Singapore Imports More Than 90% of Its Food; Here's How It's Dealing with Rising Food Inflation," CNBC, June 20, 2022, www.cnbc.com/2022/06/21/singapore-imports-90percent-of-its-food-how-is-it-coping-with-inflation.html.
20. US Department of Agriculture, Economic Research Service, "Food Security Status of U.S. Households in 2022," www.ers.usda.gov/topics/food-nutrition-assistance/food-security-in-the-u-s/key-statistics-graphics/.
21. Lee Ying Shan, "Global Rice Shortage Is Set to Be the Biggest in 20 Years," CNBC, April 19, 2023, www.cnbc.com/2023/04/19/global-rice-shortage-is-set-to-be-the-largest-in-20-years-heres-why.html.
22. Kristie Pladson, "Investors Cash In on Food Commodities as the Poor Go Hungry," DW, June 2, 2022, www.dw.com/en/investors-cash-in-on-food-commodities-as-the-poor-go-hungry/a-62007084.
23. Peter Goodman, *Davos Man: How the Billionaires Devoured the World* (New York: HarperCollins, 2022).
24. Simon Moore, "Powell's Jackson Hole Speech Outlines What Could Move Rates Higher," *Forbes*, August 25, 2023, www.forbes.com/sites/simonmoore

/2023/08/25/powells-jackson-hole-speech-outlines-what-could-move-rates-higher/?sh=33c7461c602a.

25. Pia Singh and Hakyung Kim, "S&P, Nasdaq Close Higher, Snap 3-Week Losing Streak as Wall Street Shakes Off Rate Hike Fears," CNBC, www.cnbc.com/2023/08/24/stock-futures-are-little-changed-as-investors-await-powells-jackson-hole-speech-live-updates.html.
26. Saumya Roy, "Will Xi and Biden Mend US-China Relations at the APEC Summit?" *Al Jazeera*, November 15, 2023, www.aljazeera.com/economy/2023/11/15/will-xi-and-biden-mend-us-china-relations-at-the-apec-summit.
27. Thomas Black and Dina Bass, "Elon Musk and Jane Fraser Are Just Some of the CEOs Hoping to Woo China's Xi," Bloomberg, November 14, 2023, www.bloomberg.com/news/articles/2023-11-14/musk-citi-s-fraser-among-the-ceos-wooing-china-s-xi-at-apec?srnd=premium&utm_source=newsletter&utm_medium=email&utm_campaign=newsletter_axiosmarkets&stream=business&embedded-checkout=true.
28. "US Invests $280bn in High Tech to Compete with China," BBC News, August 9, 2022, www.bbc.com/news/business-62482141.
29. Mackenzie Hawkins, Ian King, and Cagan Koc, "US Floats Tougher Trade Rules to Rein in China Chip Industry," Bloomberg Law, July 17, 2024, https://news.bloomberglaw.com/tech-and-telecom-law/us-floats-idea-of-tougher-trade-rules-in-chip-crackdown-on-china.
30. Fanny Potkin, "Exclusive: Nvidia Preparing Version of New Flagship AI Chip for Chinese Market," Reuters, July 22, 2024, www.reuters.com/technology/nvidia-preparing-version-new-flaghip-ai-chip-chinese-market-sources-say-2024-07-22/.

CHAPTER 13

1. Yi Wen and Iris Arbogast, "How COVID-19 Has Impacted Stock Performance by Industry," Federal Reserve Bank of Saint Louis, March 21, 2021, www.stlouisfed.org/on-the-economy/2021/march/covid19-impacted-stock-performance-industry.
2. Mike Patton, "How Stocks Reacted During Past Flu Pandemics and Steps You Can Take to Minimize Losses," *Forbes*, February 28, 2020, www.forbes.com/sites/mikepatton/2020/02/28/how-stocks-reacted-during-past-flu-pandemics-and-steps-you-can-take-to-minimize-losses/?sh=713047f1448d.
3. Sven Henrich, "SARS Didn't Sink Markets, but Coronavirus Might," CNN Business Perspectives, February 6, 2020, www.cnn.com/2020/02/06

/perspectives/coronavirus-sars-stock-markets/index.html; Yun Li, "Market Reactions to Past Virus Scares Show Stocks May Have More to Lose," CNBC, January 28, 2020, www.cnbc.com/2020/01/28/market-reactions-to-major-virus-scares-show-stocks-have-more-to-lose.html.

4. Ben Rooney, "The Ebola Stocks: Effect of an Outbreak," CNN Money, October 24, 2014, https://money.cnn.com/2014/10/24/news/ebola-stocks/index.html.
5. Anuz Thapa, "20th Anniversary of 9/11: How the Attacks Impacted the US," TheStreet, September 10, 2021, www.thestreet.com/latest-news/how-9-11-impacted-united-states-economy.
6. CNN Money, "Oil and Gold Prices Spike," September 11, 2001, https://money.cnn.com/2001/09/11/markets/oil/.
7. Clifford Kraus, "Oil Prices Were Going Down Again. Then War Started in the Middle East," *New York Times*, October 9, 2023, www.nytimes.com/2023/10/09/business/israel-gaza-oil-prices.html.
8. Stanley Reed, "Why Are Oil Prices Falling While War Rages in the Middle East?" *New York Times*, November 9, 2023, www.nytimes.com/2023/11/09/business/energy-environment/oil-price-israel-gaza.html.
9. Stanley Reed, "Shipping Costs Soar in Wake of Red Sea Attacks," *New York Times*, January 24, 2024, www.nytimes.com/2024/01/24/business/red-sea-attacks-shipping-costs.html.
10. National Oceanic and Atmospheric Administration, "NOAA Predicts Above-Normal 2024 Atlantic Hurricane Season," May 23, 2024, www.noaa.gov/news-release/noaa-predicts-above-normal-2024-atlantic-hurricane-season.
11. National Oceanic and Atmospheric Administration, "Damaging 2022 Atlantic Hurricane Season Draws to a Close," November 29, 2022, www.noaa.gov/news-release/damaging-2022-atlantic-hurricane-season-draws-to-close.
12. NOAA National Centers for Environmental Information, "Monthly Tropical Cyclones Report for Annual 2023," January 2024, www.ncei.noaa.gov/access/monitoring/monthly-report/tropical-cyclones/202313.
13. United Nations, "UN News Global Perspective Human Stories," July 31, 2021, https://news.un.org/en/story/2021/07/1096642.
14. Li Cohen, "Hurricane Beryl Leaves 'Armageddon-Like' Destruction in Grenada 'Field of Devastation' on Union Island, Caribbean Leaders Say," July 3, 2024, www.cbsnews.com/news/hurricane-beryl-grenada-destruction-communication-system-destroyed/.
15. Intergovernmental Panel on Climate Change (IPCC), Sixth Assessment Report, Working Group II: Impacts, Adaptation, and Vulnerability, "Fact

Sheet: Cities and Settlements by the Sea," 1, November 2022, www.ipcc.ch/report/ar6/wg2/downloads/outreach/IPCC_AR6_WGII_FactSheet_CitiesSettlementsBtS.pdf.

16. Daniel Raimi, Amelia Keys, and Cora Kingdon, "Florida Climate Outlook: Assessing Physical and Economic Impacts through 2040," Resources for the Future, June 30, 2020, www.rff.org/publications/reports/florida-climate-outlook/.
17. IPPC, "Fact Sheet."
18. Ishika Mookerjee and Sheryl Tian Tong Lee, "Stock Investors Watch Four Key COP28 Debates for Market Impact," Bloomberg, December 5, 2023, www.bloomberg.com/news/articles/2023-12-04/stock-investors-think-these-four-cop28-debates-can-move-markets.
19. United Nations, "UN News Global Perspective Human Stories: The Trillion Dollar Climate Finance Challenge (and Opportunity)," June 27, 2021, https://news.un.org/en/story/2021/06/1094762.
20. Christopher Helman and Matt Schifrin, "How Wall Street Banks Will Reap Billions from Tax-Free Renewable Energy Bonds," *Forbes*, December 7, 2022, www.forbes.com/sites/christopherhelman/2022/12/07/big-wall-street-banks-will-reap-billions-from-renewable-energy-bonds/?sh=1027e0ff77a1.
21. Glenn Thrush and Adam Goldman, "China Is Targeting US Infrastructure and Could 'Wreak Chaos,' FBI Says," *New York Times*, January 31, 2024, www.nytimes.com/2024/01/31/us/politics/fbi-director-china-wray-.html.
22. Drew Richardson, "Clorox Shares Slide After Company Says Cyberattack Hit Sales Hard," CNBC, October 5, 2023, www.cnbc.com/2023/10/05/clorox-shares-slide-cyberattack-hit-sales.html.
23. Google DeepMind Technologies, "Welcome to the Gemini Era," no date, https://deepmind.google/technologies/gemini/#capabilities.
24. Jane Callen, "New Small Business Pulse Survey Shows Breadth of COVID-19 Impact on Businesses," US Census Bureau, May 14, 2020, www.census.gov/library/stories/2020/05/new-small-business-pulse-survey-shows-breadth-of-covid-19-impact-on-businesses.html.
25. Brian Sozzi, "Clorox Has Seen 500% Increases in Demand During the COVID-19 Pandemic: CEO," Yahoo! Finance, May 5, 2020, https://finance.yahoo.com/news/clorox-has-seen-500-increases-in-demand-during-the-covid-19-pandemic-ceo-132530052.html.
26. Christie Smythe, "Toilet Paper Prices Are Way Up—Confirming We're Hoarding It (Again) as COVID Cases Jump," September 17, 2021, www.businessofbusiness.com/articles/toilet-paper-prices-are-up-confirming-were-hoarding-it-again-as-covid-cases-jump/.

27. Katharina Buchholz, "Toilet Paper Producers Roll'ing in the Dough," April 2, 2020, Statista, https://www.statista.com/chart/21327/rise-in-revenue-toilet-paper-selected-countries/.
28. Rachael Vasquez, "Kimberly-Clark Hiking Prices on Toilet Paper, Diapers," April 2, 2021, Wisconsin Public Radio, www.wpr.org/economy/kimberly-clark-hiking-prices-toilet-paper-diapers.
29. Nasdaq, "ZM Historical Quotes," www.nasdaq.com/market-activity/stocks/zm/historical?page=95&rows_per_page=10&timeline=y5.
30. Christian Stadler, "Pandemic Winners: The 10 Best-Performing US Companies," *Forbes*, January 18, 2022, www.forbes.com/sites/christianstadler/2022/01/18/pandemic-winners-the-10-best-performing-us-companies/.

CHAPTER 14

1. Felix Salmon, "AI Will Be at the Center of the Next Financial Crisis, SEC Chair Warns," Axios, August 12, 2023, www.axios.com/2023/08/12/artificial-intelligent-stock-market-algorithms.
2. Bob Pisani, "NYSE's Tuesday Trading Glitch Explained," CNBC, January 24, 2023, www.cnbc.com/2023/01/24/nyses-tuesday-trading-glitch-explained-why-some-of-the-trades-may-be-busted.html.
3. Bob Pisani, "NYSE Says Tuesday's Trading Glitch Due to 'Manual Error,'" CNBC, January 25, 2023, www.cnbc.com/2023/01/25/nyse-says-tuesdays-trading-glitch-due-to-manual-error-.html.
4. Jack Shafer, "How AI Is Already Transforming the News Business," *Politico*, February 27, 2024, www.politico.com/news/magazine/2024/02/27/artificial-intelligence-media-00143508.
5. Felix M. Simon, "Artificial Intelligence in the News: How AI Retools, Rationalizes, and Reshapes Journalism and the Public Arena," *Columbia Journalism Review*, February 6, 2024, www.cjr.org/tow_center_reports/artificial-intelligence-in-the-news.php.
6. Hibah Yousuf, "Facebook Trader: Nasdaq 'Blew It,'" CNN Money, May 21, 2012, https://money.cnn.com/2012/05/21/markets/facebook-nasdaq/index.htm?iid=EL.
7. Josh Constine, "Nasdaq's Glitch Cost Facebook Investors About $500M; It Will Pay Out Just $62M; IPO Elsewhere," Techcrunch, March 26, 2013, https://techcrunch.com/2013/03/25/ip-oh-my-gosh-all-that-money-just-disappeared/.
8. Associated Press, "Frequently Asked Questions About Facebook's Initial Public Offering," May 21, 2012, www.businesstoday.in/latest/corporate

/story/frequently-asked-questions-facebook-ipo-mark-zuckerberg-30489-2012-05-21.

9. US Securities and Exchange Commission, "SEC Charges Nasdaq for Failures during Facebook IPO," press release, May 29, 2013, www.sec.gov/news/press-release/2013-2013-95htm.
10. Sarah N. Lynch, "Nasdaq to Pay $10 Million to Settle SEC Charges from Facebook Snafu," May 30, 2013, www.reuters.com/article/us-nasdaq-sec-facebook-idINBRE94S0YQ20130529.
11. Salvador Rodriguez, "Facebook Changes Company Name to Meta," CNBC, October 28, 2021, www.cnbc.com/2021/10/28/facebook-changes-company-name-to-meta.html.

INDEX

ABOUT THE AUTHORS

KAVITA CHANDRAN is a journalism trainer and has worked as a financial journalist for more than twenty years in newsrooms across the United States and Asia. She started her career in New Delhi as a business reporter and news anchor when India was opening up to privatization, and then moved to New York and worked for CNBC, Bloomberg, and Reuters, where she was on speed teams that flashed breaking news to financial traders and clients. She received an MA in journalism from the Indian Institute of Mass Communications in New Delhi, and an MS from Columbia University's Journalism School in New York. She is an accredited journalism trainer with the Thomson Reuters Foundation and the Solutions Journalism Network, and she is also a professor of journalism and communications at Murdoch University in Singapore, where she lives with her family. When she is not training, writing, or grading, she is teaching yoga and meditation.

SALDENE LYTE covered financial and breaking news as an editor for a combined fifteen years on the Headlines desks at Bloomberg News and Dow Jones Newswires, synthesizing and disseminating information about a broad array of industries at a super rapid pace. She began her journalism career as a municipal reporter in Central New Jersey after receiving a BA from Rutgers University and an MS from Columbia University's Journalism School in New York. She transitioned from newspaper reporting to electronic newswires and business journalism—first at Dow Jones, where she wrote augmented summaries of press releases; and then at Bloomberg, composing and sending out headlines in seconds on the fast-paced Headlines/Speed Desk. She is a communications manager and editor at Bank of America. She lives in Princeton, New Jersey, with her family, and she likes to go walking and bird-watching along the Delaware and Raritan Canal towpaths.